457

D1593456

THE WAR IN

1861-65

SOUTHWEST VIRGINIA

by
Gary C. Walker

ISBN-O-9617896-9-7
Copyright 1985 - txu-207-899
Third Edition - Revised
    Printed For:
A & W Enterprise
P.O. Box 8133
Roanoke, Va. 24014
    by
Gurtner Printing Co.
Roanoke, Virginia

*This book is dedicated to Miss
Lelia F. Huddle. Much of her long
and fruitful teaching career was
spent in Southwest Virginia. She
made history come alive for me
and thousands of other students.*

Acknowledgements

A special thanks to those people who shared their time and information so generously for this book: Eddie Dillon, Bill Atkins, Louise Leslie, Melvin Dodson, Lelia Huddle, Cecil Nelson, Ph.D., Joe Compton, William White, Mary Jane Harris, Don Herald, Herbert Surface, S.A. Bell, Roy Hayth, Mary Kegley, James I. Robertson, Ph.D., Alexander McCausland, M.D., Garland Stephens, Marquis G. Witt, David Hahn, and to any person I may have inadvertently overlooked.

Thank you Bettye Lane for the hours you spent proof reading and correcting.

Thank you sons, Chris and Kevin Walker, for your contributions to the art work.

Thank you, beautiful wife, Sue Walker for the many hours you spent correcting and typing.

Table of Contents

— Foreword —

In the mid-seventies I was doing research for another book and needed some information on a battle in Southwest Virginia. I was shocked when I couldn't find any single source. I decided then to do this book.

Although I knew something about the war in Southwest Virginia, I didn't realize until I researched the subject just how critical this area was to the Southern Confederacy. Few historians of national prominence give Southwest Virginia the recognition it deserves.

In the first secession votes, Southwest Virginia elected not to secede from the Union. If Southwest Virginia hadn't left the Union the Confederacy wouldn't have lasted long. Without Southwest Virginia, East Tennessee would have very quickly left the Confederacy. There would have been little salt to preserve Southern food, and little lead for Southern guns. Richmond, the capital, couldn't have held out long.

Not since white man first entered this area has anything so affected the lives of the total population as did those few years when the United States of America was a foreign country. There were many families that were devastated by the war; there were none left untouched. No other war in American history has inflicted as many casualties or caused as much destruction. Approximately one half million killed out of a total population of thirty million.[1]

There are those historians who think it improper to refer to the war as the Civil War, or as the War Between the States, who never refer to the participants as Rebs, or Yanks. I agree, it was neither a Civil War nor a War Between the States, it was a war between the United States of America and the Confederate States of America.

I used material by those who participated, witnessed, and wrote about the war shortly after it occurred. Regardless of the geographical location they referred to the war as a rebellion, and a civil war. The term "War Between the States" didn't become popular until after the turn of the century.

The history of the Confederate Department of Southwest Virginia is told from the viewpoint of the average person living in that department. I used their material and chose to try to reflect their ideas and concepts in their words without passing judgment on them over a hundred years later.

I tried to consider the view point of the writer of each piece of source material. No two witnesses or participants would give the same account of a battle. Many times they had a vested interest in presenting the material. It was to their benefit to present themselves, or their ideas, in the best possible light.

The generals that participated are a good example. All generals want to appear winners, even if they lose. When they won they wanted their superiors to believe it is because of their skill and courage against overwhelming odds; when they lost they wanted their superiors to believe it was because of overwhelming odds not their lack of skill and courage. Losing generals don't stay in command long. It reached a climax at one of the battles of Saltville where the opposing generals both claimed victory.

Much of the material written about the war is opinionated, biased, and erroneous. It is sometimes difficult to distill the truth. There are many stories and legends about the war. Some seem to grow from some true event, others seem to grow out of thin air.

Anytime I made a statement that is likely true, but for which I have no absolute proof, I used words or phrases such as "It appears, probably, assumed, etc."

Because no state or section of any state exist in a vacuum, but affects and is affected by events occurring outside its border, I have placed Southwest Virginia in the major events that did occur. By showing how the events that did occur in Southwest Virginia were a result of events elsewhere, and by showing how events elsewhere were a result of events in Southwest Virginia, it gives the reader a more complete picture.

I dealt in more general terms with events, international, national, and state wide. I dealt in much detail with events occurring locally.

I have presented the material in a time sequence. This caused a major problem in writing the book. It is difficult writing about several events that are occurring at different places in the same time frame. I hope I have added to the readers understanding and not promoted confusion.

It has been my pleasure to research, organize, write, and rewrite the manuscript for this book. I sincerely hope that it adds to your knowledge of the war and to more fully appreciate what many of your ancestors experienced.

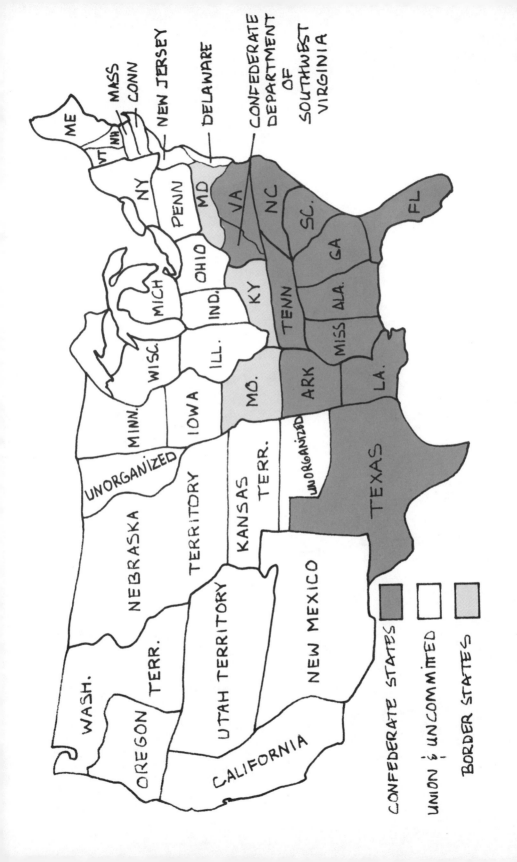

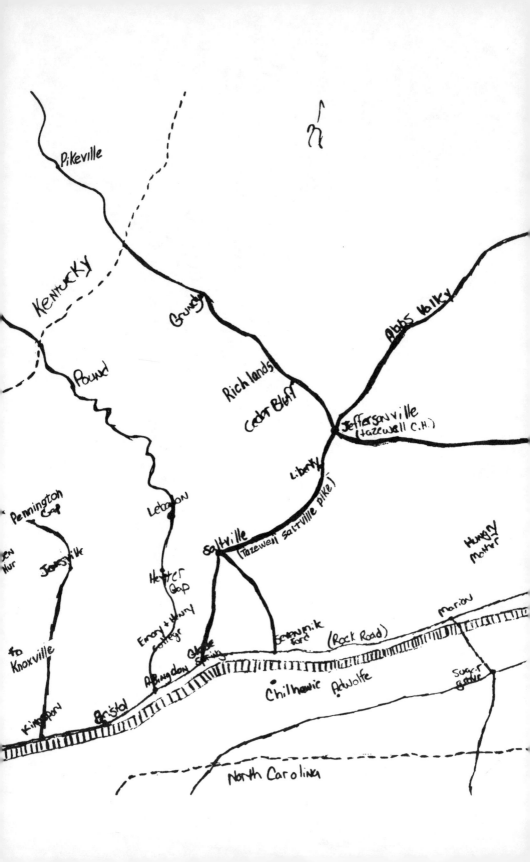

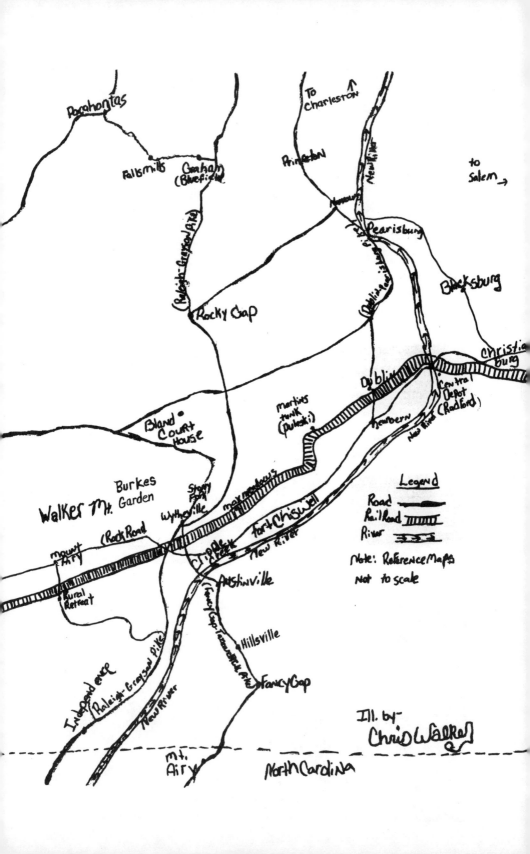

Chapter I

Before the War

The war in Southwest Virginia did not occupy the front page of large newspapers during the war. It has been virtually overlooked since. The large battles and campaigns that determined the fate of the Union and Confederacy were fought elsewhere.

Men from Southwest Virginia spilled their blood on all the major battlefields of the war. They fought with Lee, Beauregard, Johnston, and Hood. Although usually overlooked, the counties they came from and the battles in those counties were very important to the outcome of the war.

To more fully appreciate and understand the events of the early 1860's, one must leave our century, our way of life, our way of thinking. There is no electricity, no cars, no refrigeration, no modern plumbing, no plastic, no telephone, no oil furnace, etc. When a person traveled he walked, rode a horse, or traveled on the train, which had just come to this section of the country. Mom cooked on the only source of heat in the house, the fireplace. When nature called one went to the shack out back. Most men made their living farming. There was little formal schooling provided for the children of working class people. Mother usually provided what education she could. The family Bible may be the only reader the child had. The upper class had private tutors for their children.

If one's family were wealthy there may be a slave or two around the house. Female slaves were most popular to help the wife around the house. They were often regarded as status symbols. Most farms were small so it wasn't economical to have slaves. The larger spreads may have had a slave or two, but most farms were devoid of slaves. There were a few notable exceptions where much slave labor was used.

By the 1840's farmers were demanding and getting action from the state legislature. A series of roads were being built throughout Southwest Virginia to facilitate the movement of crops from farm to market. The largest cash crop was wheat, and the demand for wheat was increasing, especially in the big cities along the Atlantic Coast.

Regular scheduled stage service went into effect on most of these state roads. The roads, although an improvement, were still primitive by today's standards.

They were narrow, sometimes so narrow that two wagons could not pass. They were bumpy, and had water washed ruts in them.

Some of the roads that directly affected the war were completed in the 1850's. The Fancy Gap to Tazewell Courthouse Turnpike was completed in 1852. It roughly predated the following routes. From the North Carolina line it went to Hillsville and to Wytheville via Route 52. The road then cut to the west toward Ceres and wound through Burkes Garden. Then toward Clearfork where it followed Route 61 to Tazewell Courthouse. The town of Tazewell was then called Jeffersonville and the court house was a new structure.

Around 1858 the Tazewell - Saltville Turnpike was completed. It ran from Tazewell through the Cove area of Tazewell County over Clinch and Little Brushy Mountains, then via Poor Valley to Saltville.

Also in the 1850's a road west was built from Buchanan County to Seven Mile Ford. Another road came from Raleigh County across Mercer via Princeton, over the mountains of Bland through Wytheville and on into Grayson County. It was known by several names according to the geographical location, as the Wythe-Grayson-Raleigh Turnpike. In Raleigh they called it the Raleigh-Grayson Turnpike.

By far the biggest and most ambitious road built in Southwest Virginia was the "Rock" road. It was so called because the road base was formed of crushed rocks. It proved a smooth and enduring surface which allowed for faster, easier travel. The Rock Road ran east and west over the same general path as route 11 now covers. The road was the most traveled, as it led to the markets for farm produce and provided a link with western migration in this country.

From the 1840's to the end of this century could be described as the "age of the railroad." These iron bands tied the country together. They changed the peoples' concept of time and distance. Now large numbers of people and great amounts of freight could be moved to long distances in a short period of time. Trains could run 30 mph with "perfect safety."[1]

Trains also changed economic bonds between sections of the country. No longer did mid-western farmers depend on the Mississippi River to move their grain to New Orleans and then to the cities of the East Coast. Now the trains moved the grain directly to New England. The economic bond between the mid-west section and the South was greatly reduced. When the war came the mid-west was more closely tied to the North both economically and philosophically. Railroads had a large effect not only on the conduct of the war, but helped determine which sections would be in opposition.

The railroad came to Southwest Virginia in the 1850's. It brought prosperity and prestige to the towns along its line. As the Virginia-Tennessee Railroad (now the Norfolk Southern) built west, it by-passed other towns. Newbern was the county seat of Pulaski County but railroad interest changed that. There was no town of Rural Retreat until the railroad, then Mt. Airy on the Rock Road was by-passed and it started to die. The railroad was in Dublin by 1855 and passed through Wytheville in December 1858, on its way to Bristol and Knoxville. A rail link was established between Bristol and Knoxville in 1856.

Along with the railroad came the telegraph. The dots and dashes flew at the speed of light. Major news happenings could be published the next day in local newspapers. People read the news when it was news.

The telegraph would be used in the coming war to direct coordinated campaigns in far-flung parts of the country. Central commanders could direct the war effort more effectively, bring manpower and fire-power to bear on the enemy at the weakest point.

By the 1860's the U.S. of America was a house divided. Most people identified more with their state or section of the country than they did with the Union. New England was rapidly becoming a manufacturing power. With her industrial base and commercial fleet, she was now challenging the European countries supremacy. Her population was growing with immigrants that worked her factories and mines. With this increase in population and wealth, she was becoming predominate in national politics. Laws and tariffs were passed that were designed to protect her industry and force the rest of the country to buy her goods.

Not only was New England becoming the leader in politics, she also took it upon herself to be the conscience of the country. The main subject that she preached was the evils of slavery. Only after Harriet Beecher Stowe's book *Uncle Tom's Cabin* did the movement gain its impact. (The fact that the North was anti-slavery did not mean that she was pro-equality between the races).

The mid-west farmer was no slave owner, but didn't seem to be too concerned over slavery in the South. They were more concerned about land development and selling their crops to the cities on the coast, mostly in New England. The tariff did not effect them much because of the cost of transportation. Imported goods from Europe cost about the same as those manufactured in New England by the time they reached this section of the country.

By the 1850's the South felt like she was the whipping boy for the North. Her political power was decreasing. The North was trying to prevent any more slave holding states from joining the Union. The South felt the North would eventually be able to legislate the end of slavery, and slavery was the economic foundation of the South.

The South resented the anti-slavery preaching of the abolitionist. Slave owners used the Bible to support their point of view. They believed the North should get its house in order before preaching to others. Southerners pointed to the fact of starvation wages paid to the factory workers, that children were chained to machines and forced to work 10 to 12 hours a day. The fact that children labored in dark, dangerous mines and couldn't run and play in the fresh air, was constantly thrown back at the North.

"It had long been an article of planter faith that the civilizing influence of slavery had transformed savages into happy beings who, under white supervision fulfilled the role to which God, in His infinite wisdom, has assigned them."[2] The South didn't view slavery as evil, but as God ordained.

The slave owner had a whole list of rationales to justify the enslavement of the Negro. Their rationales were diverse and often contradictory. For example, one school of thought believed that slavery was a means to save the Negro's soul. While another school held that Negroes had no soul, therefore they were sub-human and should be enslaved.

Although slavery was an emotional issue, it was not the only cause of the war. The economy, the culture, the philosophy, the lack of communication and inter-marriage between the South and North, the divergence of views for the future of the country, the separate life-styles all contributed to the break up of the country.

Southerners no longer felt that their goals could be achieved when so unequally tied to the Union.

When the war started, the South was already behind. The North had an industrial base, and they had control of the sea lanes. Not only did the North have almost twice the amount of railroad track, but they had more population to build an army from, plus access to immigrants from overseas.

The estimated population of the U.S. in 1860 was between 29,922,537[3] and 31,443,321.[4] The Northern population was approximately 22 million. During the war an additional 4 million people entered Union ports. The South had a population of approximately 9 million, of which 3,953,760[5] were slaves. There were approximately 488,070 free Negroes in the U.S., most of whom lived in the South. The North had approximately 1,556,678[7] men in the armed services during the war, while the South could field only 600,000 to 900,000 (estimates vary widely because of incomplete records).

In 1859, a year before the presidential election, an event occurred that clarified and polarized the nation. John Brown and a handful of supporters took over the U.S. arsenal at Harper's Ferry, Virginia. John Brown wanted to start a massive slave revolt. Col. Robert E. Lee restored order and retook the arsenal.

There was much concern in the South that John Brown wouldn't get "what he deserved." There was much concern in the North that he would. Rumors were rampant that abolitionist would free him and that he might continue to try to incite a slave rebellion.

Many counties sent military units to insure that Northern abolitionist would not interfer. A small company was sent from Wythe County. It was headed by Joseph Kent and William Terry.

The deep suspicions and hatred that came to the surface because of this incident couldn't be quieted before the election.

Many communities throughout the South were so fearful that a slave revolt might occur, that they formed a local patrol unit. On December 17, 1859 one such group was formed to patrol Wytheville and a one mile radius. They were instructed to aid in catching runaway slaves and"...to take any person so found in any unlawful assembly."[8]

It was a divided, fearful, suspicious country on the eve of the 1860 presidential election.

The country was divided and so were the political parties. Southern Democrates could not accept Stephen Douglas and his lack of enthusiasm for Southern values (slavery). The Southern Democrates bolted and nominated John C. Breckinridge of Kentucky.

John Bell headed a new party the "Constitutional," while Abraham Lincoln headed the Republican party.

During an earlier campaign, Lincoln and Douglas held a series of debates. During these debates Lincoln adopted a hard line anti-slavery stance, which confirmed Southern suspicions that if Lincoln got in, slavery was going out. During the debates Lincoln made it clear that he opposed slavery but that he felt that the Negro was, and always would be, inferior to the white man.

When the election was over and the speeches ceased, the ballots were counted. Lincoln had 1,857,601, Douglas had 1,291,574, Breckinridge had 850,082 and Bell had 646,124. Lincoln was 930,170 short of a majority, but he carried the New England states with their big electoral vote.[9]

Breckinridge took the South except for Virginia, Maryland, and his home state of Kentucky. They went for Bell.

Douglas, who had the second highest popular vote total, only received 12 electoral votes (less than any other candidate).

Lincoln won big in the electoral college and received 180 votes. He was elected and the South started to secede, the Union was splitting.

In his inaugural address in March 1861, Lincoln tried to back off his hard line anti-South rhetoric that got him elected. He said "I have no purpose, directly or indirectly to interfere with the institution of slavery..."[10] Although he tried, he could not placate the South and restore the Union.

The cry was "Southern Independence" and until that mouth was silenced there would be no Union.

In the solid and deep South, states like South Carolina and Georgia voted themselves out of the Union. There was no doubt that they had the right to withdraw from the Union they had voted to join less than a hundred years before.

The border states like Missouri, Kentucky, Maryland, and Delaware with divided loyalties and divided populations were having a much harder time making up their minds. When Southern forces fired on Fort Sumter, South Carolina on April 12, 1861, they knew time was running out.

South Carolina had been trying to buy the little fort in Charleston's harbor since the end of January, but the U.S. government would not consider it. Its military importance was not as great as its political statement to South Carolina and the states who seceded. The federal government did not recognize the sovereignty of the state that was no longer in the Union. Foreign military forces were now on South Carolina soil and refused to move. There was no other course open to the sovereign state but to expel the foreigners and repossess their land.

The legislature of the noncommitted states met formally and informally, or at least attempted to do so, to formulate a state policy. The federal government was able to successfully interfere with the state legislatures of Missouri, Kentucky, and arrest pro-secessionist legislators in Maryland. These men were jailed for months without being charged. Maryland's full legislature was never allowed to consider the secession question.

In Virginia, meetings considered the question but no clear mandate could be formed. The central and eastern part of the state were more closely tied to the deep South and pushed for secession. The western part of Virginia was more closely tied to the Union and opposed secession. Southwest Virginia was not bound either north or south, but was more local and isolationist in its outlook. Southwest Virginia sided against secessionist forces because it wanted no part of the coming war.

On April 15 the die was cast, President Lincoln declared the secessionist states to be in a state of rebellion and called on each state to send 75,000 armed men to force them back into the Union. Meetings were again held in Richmond. The delegates from Southwest Virginia now moved to the front of the secessionist parade. It was inconceivable that Virginians would fight their Southern brothers for exercising their constitutional right to withdraw from the Union.

William Ballard Preston, of Montgomery County now became a leader. He helped in the committee that drew up the articles of secession.

The western part of the state voted against the resolutions, with the exception of delegates from the Beckley area and maybe from Mercer County. There is a debate to this day if Mercer County was for or against secession and whether it should be in Virginia or West Virginia. Their votes not only determined whether Virginia would be for or against the South, but also determined the boundary of a new state that would be formed.

On April 17, 1861, the delegates voted to accept a resolution "to repeal the ratification of the Constitution of the United States by the state of Virginia."[11] Virginia was on her way to secession and joining her Southern sister states. Virginia was the 8th state to secede. The separation from the Union was such a monumental step that it was submitted to the state's voters to make the final decision. On June 25, the vote was made public. 128,884 Virginians were for secession and only 32,134 opposed. Some slave owners voted against secession, some small farm owners voted for secession.

George Robertson who lived during this time summed up the Southern sentiment about this vote when he wrote "...Rebel, who was not a rebel, but a patriot. He was fighting for the Constitution of the United States of America, which guaranteed to every state in the Union the right to withdraw from the Union."[12]

"The speeches, elections, drum rolls, and cannon fire were announcing a new birth into the world family of nations. The Confederacy was born. The origins and goals of the new nation are debated to this day. What is fact is that the free people of ...Southern states in free elections, freely decided to withdraw from a Union they had freely joined in the third quarter of the 1700's."[13]

Boundary lines were being drawn that set section against section and state against state. Maybe the war would have been less tragic if everyone north of the Mason-Dixon line was a Unionist and everybody south of the line was a Confederate; but love and loyalty knew no boundaries. Family was set against family, cousin fought cousin, father against son, brother against brother, neighbor now hated neighbor. This was especially true in the border states. In the counties of Southwest Virginia and the counties that became West Virginia, there was much divided loyalty, and much hatred that didn't exist before.

Chapter II

Components and Strategy

In the early stages of the war the South's grand strategy was simply defensive. There was a number of reasons for this policy. Politically it was wise for public opinion domestically, in the North, and in Europe. The Southern government wanted to show itself in the most favorable light and the North in the worst.

For those in border states it was shown that the North was the aggressor, wanting war and invading the South. This helped raise sympathy and volunteers for the "Cause" (Southern Independence).

The effect was to be the same on Northern public. The North was sending their sons to fight a people that only wanted peace. As the war dragged on, as the casualty list lengthened, and the South was still holding on, apparently strong, the policy seemed to be working well. Before the end of the war there was a large peace movement in the Union.

Internationally the South was desperately needing formal recognition. With recognition would come arms and financial credit. The Southern role of a small, peaceful country under attack by a superior aggressor, played well to the upper classes in both England and France. It also helped with the bad image that the South had with the English middle and lower classes. *Uncle Tom's Cabin* had a large impact and most of these classes associated the Southern cause with slavery.

At the first of the war most Southern planters believed "King Cotton" would rule diplomatic recognition from England. They believed that England would intervene with recognition to break the sea blockade to secure Southern cotton. Without Southern cotton, it was believed, English factories would close and the economy would be badly affected, so that the lack of cotton would bring recognition for the South.

The grand strategy of the North was proposed by Chief-of-Staff, Winfield Scott. The old man's plan was rejected because it was too slow. After a year or so of war, after Scott had been replaced, his grand strategy was adopted. According to the plan the South was to be blockaded, cut in two via the Mississippi, and the capital taken.

Northern activities in Southwest Virginia were designed primarily to accomplish the last objective. Southwest Virginia was recognized as the chief supplier of salt and lead to Gen. Lee and his Army of Northern Virginia that defended the capital. Southwest Virginia also supplied food for Lee. It was the South's only communication and transportation link to Knoxville and East Tennessee.

Battle strategy for Southwest Virginia was dictated by the topography of the area. The topography of the region precluded an army of occupation. The narrow valleys and poor road conditions would have made it almost impossible to supply a sizeable army. A relatively small Southern force could cut supply lines at will and starve a large army into submission. Attacks on this section of Virginia would have to be accomplished by relatively small, fast moving units. Long sieges and occupations were simply not worth the cost of trying. The weather too would fight with the South. Snow could make roads impassable for weeks at a time. A heavy rain could turn small streams into difficult water hazards and make creeks unfordable.

As previously mentioned, this was a railroad war. The destruction of the Virginia-Tennessee Railroad was one of the three major goals the North wanted to accomplish. The railroad moved the vital supplies of lead, salt and food. It also was used to transport troops to meet Union attacks from Chattanooga to Richmond. It was also used when Southern feet trod on Northern soil. Total destruction of a railroad by a small, fast moving force is an impossibility. Depots and bridges were major targets along the route. Two bridges received particular attention. "Long Bridge" at Radford (known as Central Depot before the war) over New River and the "High Bridge" west of Wytheville over Reed Creek. These afforded opportunities to disable the railroad for weeks or months.

Iron works with names like Cedar Run, Barren Springs, Eagle, Raven Cliff, and others were scattered from Bristol eastward throughout Southwest Virginia. They produced iron for the cause. The railroad demanded large amounts of iron for the rail that no longer came from Northern mills. Iron was used to produce cannon and cannon shot. The Speedwell furnace also produced iron for many of the kettles used at the huge saltworks at Saltville. Despite all efforts the South was constantly short of iron and this contributed to the poor condition of Southern railroads. Foundries were sprinkled throughout the area. They were secondary targets of Northern attack. Wytheville Foundry made building material, farm equipment, and those all important iron rails. Perhaps the largest and most diversified foundry in the area was Barrett's Foundry. It was located one mile south of Wytheville and used a dam on Reed Creek to provide power for the machine shop. The foundry has a grist mill, wool carding plant, a plaster grinding machine, and did all kinds of casting. When the war came, the foundry produced small cannons and cannon balls. The skilled workmen repaired rifles and re-made some of the over 100,000 flintlock type rifles the South captured from Federal arsenals at the beginning of the war.

The old flintlocks were smooth bore and spark ignited. The foundry cut the rifling into the barrel and replaced the flints with percussion cap nipples. The foundry was one of the few places in the entire South that produced percussion caps. This foundry was one place that Northern forces wanted to visit.

Wagons were used to allow the army to operate away from their supply base. Without wagons a military unit would be greatly limited in range of operation or be forced to forage as it went. Foraging not only generates ill will from the populous, but it also would slow the unit and contribute to disunity in command. Ambulances were necessary to transport the wounded and dead. Without a saddle the horse would not be a very effective weapon of war. The McWane factory in Wytheville produced wagons, ambulances, and saddles. (Confederate contracts were supervised through the Quarter Master Department from Richmond). Northern generals also wanted to tour this factory.

The second major goal the North wanted to accomplish in Southwest Virginia was the destruction of the lead mines at Austinville in Wythe County, the only such mines in the Confederacy. Without the lead from these mines Southern independence would have been "stillborn" because it could not defend itself. The mines produced approximately "60,000 pounds"[1] of lead for Southern barrels each month.

Production schedules were often interrupted due to snow and an inflexible draft policy. Before the end of the war slaves were employed at the mines. This is when they fell under the Nitrate and Mining Bureau Division of the Ordinance Department of Richmond.

Napoleon noted that an army marches on its stomach. Before the plains states were developed and transportation (railroads) were built, Pennsylvania and Virginia were the "bread baskets" of the nation. As noted the Southwest Virginia area was not only providing for its needs, but was also marketing its surplus by the 1840's. This section was not a major supplier of food like the Tidewater sections of Virginia and North Carolina, or the area around Atlanta, Georgia, but still of some importance.

Some estimated food production figures were available for some counties in Southwest Virginia in 1840.

County	Wheat	Rye	Corn	Oats	Potatoes	
Russell	59	8	294	142	21	
Tazewell	34	13	150	126	16	
Lee	37	7	446	103	23	
Scott	40	2	294	112	14	(1,000 Bushels)[2]

As noted, most farms were small family farms. The war came and the men left to fight. Production began to decline in 1861 and declined at an accelerating rate throughout the war. Not only was labor reduced, areas under cultivation decreased. Armies are organizations of destruction; as they battle through the country much more than the other army is destroyed. As the tide of battle turned against the South and Northern armies occupied Southern soil, less and less food producing areas were available.

While the men were off earning glory on the battlefield, the women at home were earning no glory working the fields. Not enough can be said of these women who tried to fill the man's role, whether wife of the large plantation owner or of the sod buster. They moved to a new endeavor when they assumed responsibility for managing the land. They supervised and/or labored on the farm. They produced the food. They kept the house. They sent letters of encouragement to their loved ones far away. They made the clothing. They gently rocked the cradle while defending the homestead from robbers, deserters, and bushwhackers.

The slave was Southern property and a source of production. After the first year or so of the war, the North began to recognize and appreciate the role of the slave. Slaves labored in coal mines, lead mines, in foundries, salt works, on railroads, in ordnance factories, as well as in agriculture.

As Northern armies invaded and tried to destroy the Confederacy, one of their objectives was the disruption and destruction of slavery. They attempted to remove the slave from his master by offering him freedom or by force if necessary. As the war lengthened, there was another reason Northern armies wanted young male slaves. Today's slave was tomorrow's colored soldier, and one less Northern white youth would be drafted.

Because of the small number of slaves that one owner had in the Southwest Virginia area, there was a personal bond between owner and slave. Slaves often intervened heroically to attempt to protect the master and missus or their property. When the Union forces approached, slaves took the livestock to the mountain and hid with them until the danger passed. Many of the slaves who were captured later escaped and returned to their owner. Many slaves, of course, left willingly.

William Pendleton in his History of Tazewell County noted: "Nothing more worthy of commendation transpired during the war than the faithful service performed by the slave in Tazewell County, in proportion to their condition and opportunity, they did as excellent service as the gallant men who fought for the Confederacy."

The third major objective of Northern attack was the saltworks at Saltville. They had been producing salt for the Southwest Virginia and some of East Tennessee area since about 1788. When the war came, normal trade routes were stopped and the amount of salt available to the South was reduced. Northern armies made every attempt to destroy Southern saltworks.

In the days before refrigeration salt was all important. No other agent was available to preserve meat on a large scale. Without salt the Southern armies would starve.

In 1819 improvements were made to the saltworks so that it produced 1,000 bushels a day. At its peak production in 1864 over 2,000 slaves were used, and "hundreds of wagons lined the roads for miles."[3] Salt production increased dramatically as the Southern sources of salt decreased. There was over 300,000 bushels produced in 1863. Many states of the Confederacy built their own furnaces for boiling the brine to salt. Salt which cost 65¢ a sack at the first of the war, rose to over $20.00[4].

The Commissary General in the Bureau of Subsistence kept his eye on Saltville. The bureau was responsible for feeding and clothing the army. Saltville was vital to their effort.

Despite all their efforts the South wasn't able to feed her armies properly. Much desertion and disease was related to this fact.

One of the objectives of the North was more political than military or economic in nature. It was the destruction of the Southern press. Newspapers made no pretense of objectivity. They too, waged war. They threw their verbal barrage with emotion, fury, and some truth. When Northern generals read captured Southern newspapers they were infuriated. When a Northern army came to a community that had a newspaper, it always stopped to visit the office.

The Crimean War in Europe preceded the rebellion in the United States. Many a West Point graduate studied that war. Some went to Europe as military observers. The lessons they learned influenced the conduct of the Civil War.

The South was a new nation. It had to organize a new government and fighting force. Naturally, the organizers drew on previous experience and modified it to suit their needs and objectives. Most of the civil and military administration was similar to the Northern counterpart. Civil employees of the U.S. were invited to stay in their position and continue working for the C.S.A. The only immediate change was the name of their employer. Very few employees declined the new government offer.

The military had to be built from scratch. Military districts or departments were drawn assigning responsibilities for each geographic area of the Confederacy. This section was called the Department of Southwest Virginia, or Department of Southwest Virginia and East Tennessee. The name varied as the department's responsibilities increased.

The largest military unit assigned to the Department of Southwest Virginia was the brigade. It was headed by a brigadier general and was supposed to average 8,700 officers and men. Southern brigades were known by the commanders or ex-commanders name, for example Floyd's Brigade. Northern brigades used numbers as identification.

A brigade consisted of two or more regiments. They were commanded by a colonel and were projected to be 1,850 men.

A regiment had ten companies. Each company had a captain, a first lieutenant, a second lieutenant, four sergeants, some corporals, and majors, maybe even a musician or two. The Southern soldiers selected their own lower ranked officers by vote.

There were four parts of army organization. They were the infantry, cavalry, artillery, and engineers.

Rebel units were almost never up to the fully authorized strength. Even in the early days when enthusiasm was high and recruits plentiful, most units were so desperately needed at the front that they shipped out before fully manned. The four D's combined to continually reduce the units strength. (Death, disability, disease, and desertion). Southern policy favored creating new brigades (instead) of recruiting to maintain the older ones. By war's end some brigades consisted of less than 100 men.

At the beginning of the war not only did whites across the South volunteer for "the cause", but in some cities where there was a large free Negro population, many companies formed. President Davis politely rejected their offer to do combat for the South. As one general put it "if Negroes made good soldiers then our whole concept of slavery is subject to question."[5]

To increase military power and control local slave populations, on May 14, 1862, the General Assembly of Virginia authorized the creation of the home guards.

The act provided that the home guards must not operate outside the state. It was not to stay on duty more than 30 days at a time. They furnished their own guns. The state would furnish food and ammunition. Not every county had a home guard unit "listed" and very few had a muster roll recorded at Richmond. The home guard commander knew his fellow citizen soldiers and did not inform the central government of each person's name.

As the war dragged on, casualties increased and recruits decreased, both sides resorted to the draft. The draft was more unpopular in the North than in the South. In the North an estimated 160,000[6] men fled to Canada or the far west. "Draft officials were killed and maimed and anti-draft riots broke out in scores of cities and towns."[7]

Shortly after President Lincoln issued his "Emanicipation Proclamation" on January 1, 1863, he also ruled that "all" Negroes were to be drafted. Kentucky used Negroes to "fill their quota of soldiers and thus avoid the application of the draft."[8]

Not only were "all" Negroes drafted and only some whites, but Negroes received seven dollars less pay each month than the white soldiers. Of the estimated 180,000 Negroes in the Northern army less than 100 ever rose above the rank of private.

The Northern whites could find a substitute to take his place or pay the U.S. government $300 in cash.

In the South a substitute had to be found, which led many a soldier to complain that it was a "rich man's war, a poor man's fight."[9]

In Southwest Virginia the draft decreased labor and production in the economy, particularly in agriculture, which continued to decline. The rigid draft regulations made no distinction between the uneducated laborers and the high skilled engineers. If drafted, both most go or a substitute found. Production efficiency on the railroad, in the lead mines, and at the saltworks suffered greatly because of the draft.

The War Between the States, like all wars, boiled down to the soldier and his weapon. The standard weapon of the cavalry was the Sharps Breech loading rifle. It was 54 caliber"...just what a skirmish line needed for effective work."[10] It used a single round that was placed in the chamber that closed via a lever, a percussion cap (usually simply called a cap) was used to detonate the gun powder. It was shorter than standard infantry weapons (more suitable for use on horseback), and could fire somewhat more rapidly. Few cavalry units in the South and none in Southwest Virginia could be fully equipped with these.

Cavalry was used "...when the enemy exposed a weapon, or when disorder appears in his ranks."[11] Before the war a march of 30 miles a day was considered good for a cavalry unit; 50 miles for a forced march.

In Europe the cavalry fought strictly from horseback with the gun and a saber. One lesson the Americans learned from the Crimean War was the cavalry, at times, was more effective dismounted. Southern cavalry also preferred pistols to swords.

An American hybrid was the mounted infantry unit. The soldier and equipment were strictly infantry. The horse was only a means to deliver the soldier to battle rapidly and less tired.

Re-creation of Union mounted troops.

The infantry soldier with his 58 caliber Enfield or Springfield was taught "A good infantry can always sustain itself against the charges of cavalry."[12]

The rifle in the hands of a sharpshooter was deadly as far as a half mile. It's "effective range, that is, the range at which massed infantry fire would hit often enough to be adequately damaging"[13] was approximately 200 to 300 yards.

The single shot 58 caliber rifle weighing 14 lbs. and costing approximately $20.00, also used a percussion cap to detonate the gun powder. One of the few factories to manufacture caps was Barrett's at Wytheville.

Toward the end of the war the North introduced the Spencer Repeating carbine. It used a cartridge with a self contained detonater. The bullets were fed into the chamber via a lever mechanism. The rifle could be fired 7 times before reloading. The Southerners would say you can load it up on Sunday and shoot it all week.

A Southern artillery battery usually consisted of 4 or 5 cannons. Cannons were usually referred to as "guns." Only field artillery was used in Southwest Virginia. Most of it was "6 pound or pounder" bronze cannon. Called 6 pounder because of the weight of the projectile. The barrel weighed approximately 880 lbs and was mounted on a cassion, which was horse drawn. There were some 12 pound cannon and some 12 pound howitzers used in Southwest Virginia.

The artillery man could chose from a variety of projectiles. Solid shot was a general purpose projectile. It was used on most occasions but was more effective on thick-walled buildings and fortifications than any other projectile.

The crash of musketry. Re-creation of massed Union infantry firing on Reb position. Note company flag.

Hollow shot or shell contained gun powder that exploded on impact or by a timed fuse. The exploding projectiles were sometimes referred to by the soldiers as bombs or grenades. The cast iron shells were particularly effective on thin wall buildings and defense earthworks.

Case or canister was the dread of the infantry or cavalry. Sometimes referred to as grapeshot it was a tin canister filled with round musket ball. It has a devastating "shot gun" effect on massed infantry or cavalry.

The range of the 6 pounder was approximately 800 yards. The 12 pound cannon shot about 1,000 yards, while the 12 pound howitzer shot approximately 500 yards. The effective range of canister projectiles was 300 to 500 yards.[14]

Because the South was basically agricultural most of the soldiers were farm boys. They were healthy, robust, and used to the outdoor life. They were good horsemen. They were poorly educated, few could read or write, but they quoted and mis-quoted the Bible. They knew God was on their side.

Most were honest, "a gentlemen's word was his bond," but some bent the truth. Many recruits who were under the age of 18 (the age of enlistment at the beginning of the war) wrote the number "18" on a piece of paper and placed it in their shoes. They told the enlistment officer "I am over 18."[15]

Their military discipline was often lacking. They may disobey the very officers they elected. Often, the officer was only one of the boys from their own county. Maybe the only reason he got elected was because he could read the orders and write the reports.

Re-creation: pre-1863 Confederate artillery battery.

The Southern soldier had heard about the political and economic reason for the war, and how a new, better government was good for him. He listened to the ideals but fought because his state's native soil had been invaded by those damn Yankees. His state, his land, his women were threatened and he would fight hard, fight to the death to protect them.

The Southern soldier was a gambler. He used cards and dice although he believed these to be evil in nature. Before the battle, cards and dice were discarded. No soldier wanted these to accompany his dead body back home. Chess was also a very popular game during the war.

A privates pay was $11 a month, which seemed like a lot at the beginning of the war to a farm boy that rarely had cash money.

The war department guide lines called for each soldier to receive 8 ounces of pork or bacon, 1 lb. of salt or fresh beef, 24 ounces of flour or cornmeal, and 8 quarts of beans or peas per 100 rations.[16] These guide lines were rarely and inconsistently met at the first, but never met toward the end of the war.

The soldier that guarded Southwest Virginia was luckier in some ways than their counterparts in Lee's Army of Northern Virginia. Southwest Virginia soldiers were bivouacked in semi-permanent locations. They could and did build shelters or cabins to protect themselves against the elements. A tent was the main home of most of Lee's men. Because of the almost permanent location a soldier could accumulate some measure of personal comfort items. He did not have to carry all his private possessions in a "haver sack" across his shoulder.

At the first there were almost enough blankets, uniforms, clothing, and shoes. The Southern soldier was no fool, he knew the North had better supplies, but he believed this was going to be a short, glorious, victorious war. A battle or two and the North would know that the South was determined to stay out of the Union and they would go home and leave the South in peace.

Before the Northern armies could invade the South, the Southern army was invaded by rats, fleas, ticks, lice and other insects. Very little was known about sanitation and communicable disease. Measles, mumps, dysentery caused the first casualties of the war. Disease would debilitate and kill more Southern soldiers than Union bullets.

The sides were chosen, the strategies determined, the generals moved their green armies into place, all was in readiness for the most glorious, and horrible war that has ever occurred in American history.

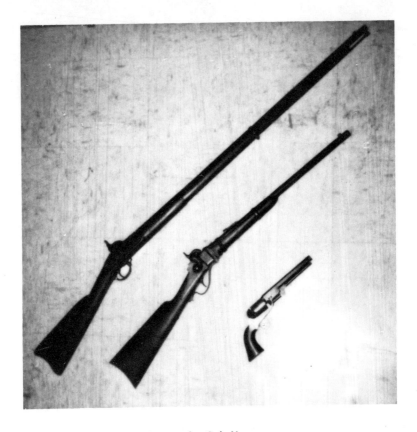

Springfield long rifle, a Sharps carbine and a Colt Navy.
(Courtesy of The Museum of the Confederacy, Richmond, Virginia)

Chapter III

1861

The year 1861 was a year of great excitement. The excitement was so thick in the air, one could feel it, and it continued the full year. Perhaps it was the most exciting year since the revolution.

A new president was elected in 1860. Now the eyes of the nation turned toward the deep South. What would those states do? Would they really secede? Would no compromises be reached? What then? War? The leader of the deep South states was South Carolina. The nation held its breath and watched events there. South Carolina had formally announced that it would secede on 12/20/60.

People throughout Southwest Virginia tried to keep abreast of the events. Newspaper sales were up. The newspaper, of course, got their news from the telegraph wires that followed the railroad west.

At many locations throughout Southwest Virginia the local milita began having their Saturday drills. This was highly unusual because they only drilled from spring to fall and then only irregularly. Now their training began to take on some sense of purpose and urgency. Would there, could there, be a war? If so, they had to be ready. Even though they didn't know on whose side they would fight.

Some of the units that were formed or started training included: Washington Mounted Riflemen — Col. James F. Preston; Glade Spring Rifles — Cap. Carson; Washington Independents — Cap. James White; Goodson Rifle Guards — Cap. John Terdy; Smyth Blues — Cap. A.G. Pendleton; Floyd Blues — Cap. David Dunn; Wythe Grays — Major Joseph Kent; Cap. Frank Kelly's Co. from Burkes Garden; Co. B - 48th Va. Regiment — Cap. Milton White; Co. 1 - 48th Va. Regiment, Cap. James Campbell; Co. H - 48th Va. Regiment - D.A.P. Campbell; Co. H - 37th Va. Regiment — Cap. Robert Grant. Even Bland County which came into being at 12:01 A.M. on January 1, 1861, formed a company, Bland Rangers.

James Alexander Walker began training at Newbern in Pulaski County. He was later to assume command of "Stonewall" Jackson's Brigade when Jackson died. This same Walker, while a cadet at V.M.I., had challenged professor Jackson to a duel to the death. Fortunately for the South, the duel never took place.

The news and rumors flew thick and fast. The deep South states began to line up to march the road to secession. Ears hung on every dispatch from Charleston and Washington. South Carolina was starting to exert her sovereignty. The state flag was being hoisted over Federal buildings. In Washington, President James Buchanan tried to control and cool the situation. He tried to do nothing that would damage the situation before the new president was inaugurated.

Increasingly the people of Southwest Virginia began to hear of a fort somewhere in a bay near Charleston, S.C. This fort, Fort Sumter, was becoming a focal point for the nation. The new nation of the Confederacy, led by Jefferson Davis, considered this fort an intolerable infringement by a foreign power, the U.S. of America. President Lincoln had been in office over a month. Negotiations to buy the fort were making no progress; something had to be done.

Something was done. A fuse on a Southern cannon was lit on the night of April 12, 1861. The blast split the Union. Before the split was closed by force of arms, untold millions in property would be destroyed, thousands of souls sent to their final reward, millions of lives changed, mountains could be made of the bodies, and rivers from the blood of men who tried to build a nation, and men who tore it down.

Events moved rapidly. President Lincoln called for volunteers on April fifteenth. On April seventeenth, with support from the delegates from Southwest Virginia, Va. seceded from the Union. Virginia was out of the Union, and everyone knew she would be in the front line if war did come. Virginia needed her men and militia units and her people responded.

Re-creation: Camp life early in war.

Many units enlisted the day Virginia seceded, like the Wythe Grays of Wythe County. At every major town along the railroad, camps sprang up. The camps were staging areas. Here men and supplies were organized to be moved East by rail. Most of the earlier units to leave this section went to Richmond. As they assembled in Richmond they met other companies from this area. Like the Montgomery Invincibles, Montgomery Highlanders, Smyth Blues, Grayson Dare Devils, etc. They lost their names. Instead of being the Grayson Dare Devils, they became numbers, like Co. H 4th Va. Regiment 1st Brigade. From Richmond they were relocated to the more Northern parts of Virginia along likely approaches from Washington.

Across the South recruiting stations were set up at every crossroads. Typical of these was the one at Musser's Mill on Blacklick in Wythe County. A rally was held in the field above the mill. Isaac Kender, Jack and Frank Musser were the leaders, waving the flag, playing the drum and fife. After some firey speeches they led the group to the mill where the new recruits signed up.

The women throughout the South were very enthusiastic. They urged their men to join the army. Many a commitment was made between the belle and her beau. Long goodbyes were said, the trains smoked and puffed as they moved the men east.

The college of Emory and Henry was almost without students. Some former students now drilled on the college green in their new uniforms. The new course they were studying was war. Some students went North to study. One professor, William E. Peters, quit to join the South. The campus was now under the command of Cap. William E. "Grumble" Jones.

William Edmondon "Grumble" Jones.

Everyone knew that if war really did come it would be a short glorious affair, that these green mountain boys were the new revolutionary heroes. Very few could resist this call to arms and glory.

Shortly after Virginia joined the Confederacy on May sixth, the capitol was moved to Richmond.

Many people, both North and South, could be skeptical or hopeful that war would not come. South Carolina had been out of the Union since December and only small fighting incidences had occurred. Maybe all the military buildup was just posturing before negotiations would find a way to placate the South and bring her back into the Union. After all, the U.S. Post Office was still delivering letters as usual. It was all parties, music, and marching, nothing was really happening.

Even when the dissatisfied delegates from the western part of Virginia met in Wheeling on June 17, to start forming a new state, not much importance was attached to it.

Nothing much had really happened since Fort Sumter; informal negotiations were not moving forward. Everyone knew, both North and South, that time was running out for Lincoln. He would either have to let the South go in peace or take concrete action. It was put-up or shut-up time.

Lincoln put-up. He ordered the Northern army to invade Virginia. The military objective was a small railroad junction called Manassas.

Troops from Southwest Virginia were there to meet the Yanks for the first time when the cry went up "...There stands Jackson like a stone wall, let's rally behind the Virginians". Part of the Virginians they rallied behind were from Southwest Virginia. The South called the battle Manassas because they received news via a telegraph from that place. The North called it Bull Run, after a small stream there. At Bull Run, the Yanks ran. Everyone was sure that the war was over, and Southern independence was a fact, but the soldiers did not come home.

The trains still left Southwest Virginia with their human cargo. The trains returning brought the dead, dying, and disabled. Now Southwest Virginia was learning more about the glorious battle at that previously unknown junction. This was only a trickle of the flood to come.

Among those returning was Col. Preston. He was going back to his home at Abingdon, home to die.

On August 10, Lincoln ordered his Postmaster General, Montgomery Blair, to stop all post traffic with the Confederacy. The postal system began to deteriorate. There were no Southern stamps and little Southern money. Postal rates increased during the war, but service fell.[1]

On August 20, news came from the dissatisfied delegates at Wheeling in the far northern panhandle of the state, they had decided to call their new state "Kanawha." Not much was made of the news.

Very few people in Southwest Virginia even noticed or gave much importance to the loss of a salt mine in Missouri. Union forces pushed the small Southern forces and destroyed the works. Few knew how important this first step would be to the outcome of the war.

The Confederate Government began to let contracts by autumn. Barrett's Foundry began to produce small cannon and cannon ball. They also reworked some of the flintlocks captured from Federal arsenals.

Only at harvest time did people notice that there were fewer laborers. The farm boys were now warriors. Those left, labored hard to bring in the crops. As winter approached loneliness was being felt on the home front.

At Cheat Mountain (West) Virginia on September 14, Robert E. Lee was badly beaten. Most of the North's more seasoned troops were from Ohio. The new government at Wheeling was now a power to be taken seriously.

Court records show that not all was orderly in the camps along the railroad. The camp at Abingdon was experiencing considerable troubles. Some of its would be soldiers became jailbirds before they could become soldiers.

On November 10, Gen. Jacob Dolson Cox (North) attacked Gen. John Buchanan Floyd, Virginian and ex-Secretary of War under Buchanan, at Gauley Ferry, (West) Virginia. He pushed Floyd back and burned the courthouse in Boone. The South was just learning to lose and the taste of defeat was bitter after the sweetness on Manassas.

Refugees, deserters, and cowards were words that began to work their way into the conversations on Southwest Virginia. No longer could the South count on complete control of their West Virginia portion of Virginia. Although the South maintained a presence, it was not in full control. West Virginia was the most important wool producing section east of the Mississippi. Few Southerners were aware of this fact as the year closed.

People in Southwest Virginia were disappointed that Maryland, Kentucky, and Missouri could not or would not leave the Union and join them. They were also disappointed because of the temporary loss of part of West Virginia but knew that it would stay with Virginia when victory came and the North finally recognized Southern Independence.

As Christmas approached many local boys returned from the far away front. There were parties and happiness. The belles were whirled about the dance floor by their Johnnies in gray wool uniforms. A magical kingdom of beauty and Southern chivalry existed, if only for a moment. The servants attended the master and all was in its proper order. Toasts were made to the cause, and to the glory of battle.

Some neighbors and former friends were not at the party. They were Northern sympathizers, and friction was developing in the community.

This friction and the minor losses of 1861 were dismissed. There was a feeling of confidence and satisfaction. A new nation existed. They had won a big important battle and the North had not seriously attacked the east since then. King Cotton was still on his throne and the new revolution expected only victory and glory in the new year.

The ineffective sea blockade was of no particular concern in Southwest Virginia. Thoughts of the dead and wounded were crowded from the mind by happiness, excitement, and lasting glory. On to Southern independence, hopefully in peace but by war if necessary!

Chapter IV

1862

The bells chimed in 1862 on a gleeful and enthusiastic note. Surely this year would be the year of Southern independence. This would surely be the last year of the glorious war!

In Southwest Virginia the presence of the Confederate government and military was clearly evident. Dublin township in Pulaski County was selected as military headquarters for Southwest Virginia. From here troops were directed via telegraph and messenger. The railroad transported supplies and men as needed to different areas of the command.

Major Gen. William Wing Loring commanded approximately 10,000 troops scattered throughout Southwest Virginia. They were divided into four brigades.

The first brigade was commanded by Brig. Gen. John Echols and was located primarily in Monroe and Greenbriar County. Echol's troops were the 22nd Va. Infantry, 45th Va. Regiment, 23rd and 26th Va. Battalion, and one battery of artillery, Chapman's.

John Echols.

The fourth brigade was commanded by Col. John McCausland. He had the largest number of units if not troops. McCausland commanded the 36th, 60th Regiments and Bryn's Battery. Also in the area was Gen. Albert Gallatin Jenkins and his cavalry units. Jenkin's force included the 8th, 14th, 17th, 19th Regiments — 34th, 36th, 37th battalions, plus some unattached troops, including Triggs 54th, 2 companies of partisan rangers (guerillas) and Otey's Battery. McCausland was headquartered at Princeton.

Located at Narrows at the most likely invasion route from the North was the 3rd Brigade under Gen. Gabriel Calvin Wharton. His command consisted of 15th, 50th Regiment, 30th Battalion Va. Infantry, and Stamp's Battery.

While the 1st, 3rd, and 4th brigades guarded the most likely invasion route into Southwest Virginia, the 2nd brigade was headquartered near the far west end of the command at Saltville. It was felt that a permanent guard was needed at this important site.

John McCausland.

Brig. Gen. John Stuart Williams commanded the 63rd, 64th Regiment, 45th Battalion, and the 21st Va. Cavalry, Lowry's Battery and some partisan rangers.[1]

Union Gen. Jacob Dolson Cox started a slow push against Loring. Cox's eye was on Dublin and the railroad when he started this first major push into Southwest Virginia. On January 15, he was in Logan County where he burned the courthouse. He was in no great rush as he planned his next move toward Mercer County.

John Stuart Williams

Both sides sent scouting parties to probe the defenses of the others. Most scouting parties had at least a member or two that were native to the area to be reconnoitered. These local boys knew who was pro-Southern or Northern. They knew whose sons or husbands were fighting in each army. When they came to an area they always stopped at a sympathizers farm and asked if the enemy was near. These sympathizers provided a great deal of accurate information on troop movement and intentions. They provided relatively safe shelter for man and beast as the scouts moved in and out of unfriendly territory.

Before the party left the area it might make a call on opposition sympathizers. They might harass the sympathizers, steal or destroy some property, maybe leave some false information that would be transmitted to the enemy.

Soon Southerners began to refer to their sympathizers in occupied or contested areas as "patriots for the cause," while at the same time they called Northern sympathizers "tories"[2] an allusion to the 1776 Revolution.

Although no major battles were occurring in the area commanded by the Army of Northern Virginia, it was not all peace in the ranks. Honor and prestige were still high and treasured values in the Southern officers corps. It is not possible to accurately say what did occur in the 4th Regiment of Virginia Infantry, but there was trouble in the ranks. Perhaps Joseph Kent, who led the Wythe Grays into service, was passed over for leadership.

Kent was promoted from Major to Lieutenant Colonel on January 31, but that wasn't enough. One of his former subordinates now commanded the unit he organized. He said in his letter to the governor dated February 3rd "...I herewith,..., return you the proffered commission of Lt. Colonel...which has this moment reached me..."[3] Officers had more privileges than the enlisted man. The colonel for a moment, packed his belongings and headed for Wythe County.

He later used the excuse of poor health to justify his resignation. This may have been true, but in his letter of resignation he never mentioned health.

He told the governor ..."sufficient reasons for this stop (resigning commission) are doubtfully too well known to you to render any at this time."[4] The army had lost an officer but the county had gained their military leader.

The year was still young when people in Southwest Virginia began hearing about a place called Fort Donelson somewhere in upper west Tennessee. Some men from Southwest Virginia were there and the news was not good. People found out that the Confederacy had been out-maneuvered and surrendered on February 16. Now the upper part of the Mississippi River was open to Northern invasion.

After this battle, stories and rumors were heard of willful mistreatment of Southern prisoners. Maybe they were just rumors. Maybe most Northern commanders were gentlemen. After all weren't Northern generals returning run away slaves to their rightful masters?

By the middle of March, people in Southwest Virginia began hearing of a strange naval battle near Norfolk between two ironclad warships, the USS Monitor and CSA Merrimac. Both fought but neither won. The illegal blockade of the South was now being taken more seriously. Some shortages of goods were being blamed on the blockade.

Little had been heard from Gen. Cox since January, but as the sap began to move so did the general.

In Southwest Virginia the war seemed far away. The trains rolled daily with their cargoes of salt, lead, food and men. Business was good as the sun started swelling the first blossoms of spring.

Some Kentucky troops began to move into Southwest Virginia to fill the void that was created by the units sent to Richmond a year ago. General Humphrey Marshall moved to Tazewell County, and set up headquarters on the farm of William E. Perry. Under Marshall was another Kentucky Colonel, A.J. May and his 5th Kentucky cavalry. There was also another small band of Kentucky cavalry under Col. Bradley.

Humphrey Marshall.

Cox was moving. He organized his assault force into two infantry brigades. The first was under the command of Col. Eliakin Parker Scammon. It consisted of the 12th, 23rd, 30th Ohio Regiments and McMullins Battery. The 2nd was under Col. A. Moor. He commanded the 28th, 34th, 37th Ohio, Simmonds Battery, plus the 2nd Va. Cavalry (W.Va.) under Col. Boler and Smith's Ohio Cavalry. (Some units in West Virginia that were organized before secession kept their Virginia designation even though they were in the Union Department of W.Va.).

Cox had a supply train of over 250 wagons for his force.

Jacob Dolson Cox.

On April 30 the advance forces of Cox occupied the house of Henry Clark near Camp Creek above Princeton. On the morning of May 1, the Rebs opened the skirmish. The South was winning until Col. Scammon sent the 23rd Ohio forward. It was commanded by a future president, Rutherford B. Hayes, William McKinley, another future president, also was there.

When Hayes arrived the Southern forces withdrew toward Princeton. The South had taken 8 casualties all wounded while inflicting 20 casualties on the North, one dead, 19 wounded. Southern forces lost one man killed on Camp Creek as they moved to Princeton.[5]

The decision was made to abandon Princeton to the enemy. The Bland Rangers, under Cap. William Harman, were ordered to form a skirmish line to cover the retreat.

Confederate Col. Jenifer ordered Princeton burned; he said to protect the supply train falling back to Rocky Gap. It is to be remembered that these are green troops and inexperienced officers. This is the first battle most have seen. Jenifer's order would seem irrational to the veterans of 1864.

William McKinley.

When the forces of Cox occupied Princeton they helped put out some of the fires the Rebs set. They also set others. They burned the courthouse. Before the North was driven back almost half of Princeton lay in ashes; even churches were burned.

From military Headquarters orders were sent and troops began to assemble to oppose Cox. At Wytheville Col. Jenifer stopped running. He combined with Wharton's command and the 51st Virginia Infantry.

At Tazewell Courthouse, Gen. Marshall began to move toward Princeton. He had the 5th Kentucky, the 29th Virginia, and a small battalion of Virginia Infantry under Major Dunn, a battalion of Kentucky Cavalry under Col. Bradley and artillery under Cap. Jeffins.

At Dublin the largest force assembled under Brig. Gen. Henry Heth. It consisted of the 22nd, 36th, 45th Virginia Infantry, the 8th Virginia Cavalry (dismounted) and three battery of artillery. Chapman's, Otey's, and Vauter's.

Both generals, Cox and Heth, were cautious and deliberately slow. Cox was aware that Southern troops were being massed against him. After he had consolidated his position at Princeton, he organized his troops and started toward Pearisburg. Of course, his final goal was Dublin and the railroad.

It took five days for the advance column of Cox's army to reach Pearisburg. Major Comby reported he had taken Pearisburg by surprise on the 6th. He burned no dwelling. He did, however, capture several Rebs. Included in the catch was one Major, one Lt. Col. and 15 to 20 privates.[6]

Col. Hayes and the 23rd Ohio joined Comby in Pearisburg on the 7th.

Cox moved with the main army to East River 11 miles South of Princeton by the 10th.

On the 10th Heth brought his army to bear on the advance of the Union column at Pearisburg. Col. Hayes fought the 23rd Ohio forward but Heth and his artillery were too much. The North began retreating from Pearisburg suffering 2 killed and several wounded, including Hayes himself. The South's losses, 2 killed and 4 wounded. these would be considered insignificant later in the war, but they were very important to each green army.

When Cox heard of Hayes defeat and retreat, he began to make plans to withdraw north. He started moving back to Princeton.

Each army moved cautiously. Cox cautious back. Heth cautious forward. The troops from the Tazewell and Wytheville areas began to move in on Cox.

At 10:00 A.M. on May 17 the battle of Pigeon Roost Hill occurred very near Princeton. Southern Major Peter J. Otey and his men found themselves between two Northern units. Otey was aware the Yanks were there, but they had not detected his presence. Otey formed his men in 2 lines so as to defend both sides.

Col. VonBlessing (Union) was moving his command to rejoin the main body. His men had captured a Reb medical supply wagon. Much to the Yanks delight, this wagon was full of whiskey. All of a sudden most of VonBlessing's command was sick and decided to doctor themselves with the captured whiskey. Some over medicated.

VonBlessing and his men were very close to Otey's line of defense before they knew it. The Southern boys let fly with a volley or two and VonBlessing's men fell back in disorder. Otey ordered his command to charge and VonBlessing went into full retreat. Some of the Yanks threw their guns down and ran for their lives.

The North lost 18 killed, 56 wounded, and 14 prisoners taken. The South only lost 1 killed, and 9 wounded.

Cox moved north out of Princeton. Loring took command. He was just as cautious as Cox and didn't chase the Yanks vigorously and try to win a complete victory.

It was none the less a victory. Both green armies were tested in battle. A few were killed, a few wounded. Lessons were learned. Southwest Virginia was safe. The Union forces were regrouping near present day Charleston on the Kanawha River.

By May a formal contract was let for Emory and Henry College. The school received $2,500 a year from the Confederacy. The institution also sold food to the army. The buildings were used as a hospital and barracks. New recruits marched about the campus, Professor Buchanan left school to help the South mine saltpeter for gun powder more efficiently.

Also the elegant spa in Montgomery County, White Sulphur Spring, was converted into a hospital. The hospital was used mostly to treat small pox victims. Brave Roman Catholic nuns from Richmond tended the sick. Many of them and probably hundreds of soldiers were buried there.

As the year 1862 continued, more and more families in Southwest Virginia were learning the true meaning of "not knowing". A loved one was "missing in action" or "taken prisoner". The uncertainty and worry was almost unbearable. It was almost as bad as reading "killed in action".

Families both North and South did not want their loved ones buried in an unmarked, uncared-for grave. They especially didn't want their family member to rest eternally on enemy soil. Families took the train and sometimes wagons and brought the dead home to bury.

Often the soldiers were given a military funeral. The flag ("The soldiers loved their flag and fought to the bitter end for it's honor")[7] was dropped low, only inches above the street. Then came a military band. Following the band, the coffin, on a caisson pulled by horses. Then came family and mourners. There was a rifle company that fired a volley over the grave of a fallen comrade. The service was repeated thousands of times; only the names, faces, and places changed.

In June the Yanks were beating at the door of Richmond and men from Southwest Virginia stood in their way. The fighting was so bad that Joseph E. Johnston, the Southern general in charge, was severely wounded and had to be removed from the field. President Davis picked a relatively unknown general to replace him in the middle of a very crucial battle. Gen. Robert E. Lee was to command the Army of Northern Virginia. The man who was to be the South's greatest general was now center stage. The cost was high but the Federals were pushed back and the capital saved.

Lee recognized the importance of the lead and salt from Southwest Virginia.

As the number of captured Rebs grew, more and more was heard about Yankee atrocities on the prisoners and to civilians also. Much was said about Yanks burning houses, barns, and running livestock off or slaughtering them.

On August 4, the North made it official and started the draft. It was beginning to look more and more like Lincoln wasn't going to let the South go, and that the short, glorious war may take longer than anyone expected.

In August people in Southwest Virginia heard about a raid by Col. Hayes and the 23rd Ohio on the Mercer Saltworks. The works were on New River not far upstream from Hinton. There was no doubt what this successful raid meant to Southwest Virginia. More pressure on the saltworks at Saltville and on Southern food supply and transportation.

During the months since the victory at Princeton, the main Reb army under Loring had been cautiously pushing Northern forces back. At Fayette, Va. (W.Va.) the 34th and 37th Ohio combined to whip Loring. He retired south and was relieved of command. General Echols took over temporarily. Soon Maj. Gen. Samuel Jones took command of the Department of Southwest Virginia.

Gen. Humphrey Marshall had retired from command after the battle of Princeton. Marshall didn't do well at all against Cox and now Loring was out for the same reason.

By the fall each side was beginning to realize that this fight, for or against, Southern independence was going to be a long one. Southerners knew the North had to have more men and financial backing. Financial backing for the South would come with foreign recognition (diplomatic recognition from France or Britain).

Recruits for the cause would be found by the thousands in the border states that didn't secede like Maryland, Missouri, Kentucky (or so it was thought).

Soldiers from Southwest Virginia in Lee's army sang "Maryland, my Maryland. Virginia has come to claim thee," as they crossed the Potomac. No one in Southwest Virginia had heard of South Mountain or Antietam until the two greatest armies in the Western Hemisphere met there. Not many Maryland men

William Wing Loring.

joined Lee but many Virginia men were permanently laid to rest under Maryland's soil. Antietam was the South's largest single loss to this point in the war. September 17, was a black day for the Confederacy.

On September 27, a small cavalry battle was fought on the Kanawha near Charleston. A Colonel, John Toland, attacked and drove back the Confederate cavalry under Jenkins. Few people of Southwest Virginia even knew Toland's name but in less than a year it would be a household word.

Not until the first of October did the people of Southwest Virginia hear about another Federal attack on a saltworks. This time they destroyed a work at Bluffton, South Carolina. The pressure on the South's salt supply increased.

Union forces in Kentucky were too strong and the provisional Confederate Government was forced out of the state. On October 31, the Provisional Government of Kentucky was moved to Abingdon, Virginia.

Harvest times and the crops were not as bountiful. Spot shortages were occurring in the soldier's diet. The amount and quality of the food was decreasing but still it was almost adequate.

People were learning the meaning of a new term, bushwhacker. The more civilized definition was an enemy guerilla soldier. The more common usage was an enemy, maybe a deserter, that robbed, raped, and murdered innocent civilians.

By this time the money supply was very mixed. In a normal day's transaction a merchant may see over five different species of money. The economy was based on gold. Gold coins circulated as well as paper money backed by gold. Both the U.S. and Confederacy issued paper which was redeemable by gold. Many local banks issued their own money. Soldiers used the slang expression 'shin plaster" when referring to local currency.

In the Confederacy coins were very scarce. As a result people began to use uncanceled postage stamps as substitutes for small change. Before the end of the war even the substitutes were scarce.

By late 1862 civilians and soldiers were starting to experience some shortages of coffee. The blockades' effect were beginning to be felt.

The war was no longer young. The enemy was now referred to by a variety of names. They could be called Northerners, Federals, Unionist, Billy Yank, Billy, Yankee, Damn Yankee, Blue Belly, or Blue Coats (an allusion to the Red Coats of the 1776 Revolution). The Southern soldiers also had acquired a few different names: Rebels, Reb, Secessionist, Johnny (Reb), Confederates, and Gray Backs.

On November 15, there was a brisk skirmish near Fayette (West) Virginia. The Union Gen. Samuel Davis Sturgis pushed the South back. After this the quiet winter prevailed along the lines in Southwest Virginia.

Since major attacks were not anticipated during the winter, the larger armies could be disbursed somewhat. Troops were relocated to areas where food and shelter were plentiful. In Tazewell County "Camp Georgia" was built. It was so named because of the 3 or 4 companies of Georgia artillery wintered there. They built cabins on the land of Sam Perry.

Some cavalry units sent part of their horses to North Carolina for the winter. Fodder was more plentiful there.

Although most fronts were relatively quiet toward the end of the year, Lincoln tried to end the war before the year ended. "On to Richmond" was the Northern battle cry and by mid-December Gen. Ambrose Burnside had captured Fredericksburg. One more push and the way to Richmond was open.

Lee and his army were on the heights above the town. Before Burnside was forced to withdraw, over 20,000 Yankees lay casualties on the slope. Another major victory for the South and Lee's stature continued to grow.

Few soldiers from Southwest Virginia would be home by Christmas. They were on the heights above Fredericksburg or chasing Burnside's demoralized Army of the Potomac back north.

It was now the second Christmas of the war. The short, glorious war was not over. The bright, crisp uniforms of last Christmas were showing their age and usage. Civilians were becoming well accustomed to the medical term "amputee" when they saw the young farm boy with one arm or saw him hobble about on two crutches and one leg.

There was a sense of bewilderment and confusion settling on the South. They believed in 1861, if they showed the North they were willing to fight for independence that they would be allowed to leave the Union. They believed that Britain and France would rush to recognize and help the new Confederate Government. It was a French tradition. The English wanted to dominate world shipping so they would be happy to see the U.S. weakened. They wanted revenge for the revolt of '76, it was believed, and would help the South. If for no other reason Britain would help because she needed Southern cotton and would allow no interruption of its supply to her mills.

Nothing was happening the way it should. Now Lincoln was drafting soldiers, the short war may be a little longer than anyone wanted or expected.

Very few in the South believed the North would win. They had faith that their robust Southern gentlemen and farm boys could win. A Southerner could beat four Yankees.

Still Southerners shook their heads. How long would Northern mothers send their sons to die fighting against a people that only wanted to be free and live in peace? How long before the foreign super powers would intervene to help the Confederacy? Both events would occur they thought. But when?

The soldiers had an expression "try our metal." It was a challenge to the enemy to attack and see just how strong the Southern line was. The civilians of the South also began to adopt that phrase as the year 1862 closed.

Chapter V

1863

The sound of the church bells that welcomed the new year had hardly left the ears of the people of Southwest Virginia when they began hearing about Lincoln's latest outrage.

Why, that Yankee president had the gall to free slaves in the Confederacy. He called it Emancipation Proclamation, the South called it hypocritical and irrelevant. He freed the slaves in states that were not part of his country and not under his control. He was careful to emphasize that there would be no change in slave laws in border states like Kentucky, Missouri, Maryland and Delaware. He didn't want to upset the population there if he could help it.

Southern newspapers branded the proclamation, propaganda for foreign consumption. By making the Confederacy appear to be a villain that enslaved men and making the U.S. appear to be the champion of the oppressed, it would make it more difficult for the Confederacy to gain political recognition and financing from Europe.

If there was anyone left in the South that thought there could still be any reconciliation with the North, this proclamation convinced them otherwise. It was a fight to total victory or total defeat, there could be no compromise.

Coupled with his proclamation, Lincoln issued new guide lines for the draft. In the past some white boys had been drafted to fill state quotas if there weren't sufficient volunteers. To reduce the draft's negative political effects, now all Negro boys of military age were subject to the draft. So states filled their requirements with volunteers, then Negro draftees, and only then with white draftees.

No longer would runaway or captured male slaves be returned to their master. They were all potential soldiers. As Northern armies invaded, they took as many male slaves north with them as they could. A slave today was a soldier against the South tomorrow. Of course, the Negroes were assigned to all Negro units commanded by white officers. There was much discrimination against the Negro soldier. As one writer put it "Northern soldiers,...., were almost as bitterly hostile as Southerners to Negro troops".[1]

The Southern army used slave labor. The governor of Virginia asked Washington County to send 120 slaves to work on the defenses at Richmond. Similar calls were made to other counties.

Maybe that is what happened to Issac Leftwich's slave. Issac had been ordered to send his slave to work on the defenses around Richmond. Of course, Issac was reimbursed by the government when Issac's "Boy ran off". When the government didn't pay him promptly for his lost property, Issac sued in Wythe County Court on May 11, for $2,200[2]. Did Issac's slave go North and become a soldier?

Gen. Sam Jones commanded the department. He planned an attack on the Dept. of West Virginia near Charleston on the Kanawha. It would be a three-pronged attack. Jenkins would move the cavalry through Tazewell County and then head north through McDowell County as if the target were in Ohio.

McCausland moved toward Lewisburg. Part of his command, the 26th Va. Battalion under Edger, was defeated near Lewisburg on May 26. The 2nd West Virginia Cavalry under Col. William Powell was there to greet them. It wasn't a major battle but it was enough for Jones. The attack on Camp Piatt on the Kanawha was called off.

Not until the late spring did the Army of the Potomac make another attempt to take Richmond and end the war. Lee ordered "Stonewall" Jackson to bring his army from the Valley of Virginia. Two of the greatest military minds the South possessed made their plans to stop the invading enemy.

At Chancellorsville the South won a great victory. At Chancellorsville the South suffered a great loss. Lee and Jackson smashed the Army of the Potomac and sent it scurrying north to the protection of Washington, a great victory. Stonewall Jackson, while doing some night reconnaissance was mistaken for a Yank by his own men. He fell, mortally wounded, a great loss.

Lee had to find someone to command "Stonewall's" old brigade. He knew where to look. He looked to a son from Southwest Virginia, Col. James Alexander Walker, who mustered in from Pulaski County. Walker had done a superior job at Fredericksburg. He held a collapsing line, which prevented a Union victory. Later he led the attack that broke the Union lines and gave the South the great victory. He was promoted from Early's command to Brigadier General of the Stonewall Brigade.

This event, Jackson's death, that took place far away from Southwest Virginia was to have a profound and direct effect on Southwest Virginia and the whole Confederacy in the coming July. July was the darkest month the new nation had known.

While the Yanks were moving north out of Virginia, other Yanks were closing in on the small railroad town of Vicksburg, Mississippi. Ever since Fort Donelson the Union had been trying to cut the South in two via the Mississippi. They moved south from Tennessee and north from New Orleans. The only finger hold the South still held on the Mississippi was Vicksburg. By late April Generals Grant and Sherman had cut the railroad and laid siege to the town. Efforts to break the siege failed. The town was constantly being bombarded: food and ammo were running low.

There was no hope for the town and the Confederate commander knew it. Yes, he could hold out a little longer, but that only meant more death and suffering for nothing. He believed that surrendering on the 4th of July might produce more lenient terms for his men and the town. On the 87th birthday of the U.S., Gen. John Clifford Pemberton gave the U.S. a birthday gift, Vicksburg.

The North was jubilant and the South mourned. The Confederate Dept. of the Trans-Mississippi (Texas, Arkansas and the territories) was now almost another country. The South was split. This closing of the Mississippi affected a factory at Wytheville directly. Barrett's foundry produced percussion caps for Southern rifles which used mercury oxide in their manufacturing process. Mercury used to come from Mexico.

There was no rail left to Mexico. There was little mercury to be had in the Confederacy. Production would suffer and supplies of caps would be scarce by late 1864.

With Vicksburg gone the small amounts of wool the Confederacy was receiving from Texas was gone. Without West Virginia and Texas, wool was very limited.

While Grant and Sherman were tightening the noose around Vicksburg in mid June, Lee was pushing his army over the Potomac heading north. He had seriously defeated the Northern army at Fredericksburg and Chancellorsville. Lincoln was desperately searching for a new general, now was the time to strike the demoralized army.

A victory on Northern soil would help the growing peace movement in the U.S. It may also help in getting the desperately needed foreign recognition. It may help relieve pressure on Vicksburg if Union forces had to be sent to Washington. It would be nice to gather Northern crops from the fertile valleys of Pennsylvania and Maryland into Southern storehouses.

Lee's army was poised so it could strike Washington, Harrisburg, or Baltimore. The Union had to do something. The new Union, Gen. George Gordon Meade, force-marched his army from Northern Virginia. Advanced units of both armies clashed at Gettysburg, Pennsylvania, when Southern men came to town looking for shoes.

J.E.B. Stuart was cut off from Lee so Lee did not have accurate information on his enemy's strength or position. It was hot and dry and the carnage was horrible those three days at the first of July. When Lee withdrew, he had taken over 20,000 casualties (dead and wounded) in what was the largest battle ever fought in the Western Hemisphere. Many boys from Southwest Virginia did not retreat from Gettysburg.

Lee was retreating south; those all important fords on the Potomac must be protected. If Lee was cut off north of the river the entire Army of Northern Virginia might be lost. On July 7, the Secretary of War at Richmond ordered Sam Jones at Dublin, to move most of his command toward Staunton to cover Lee's retreat.

Gen. Benjamin Franklin Kelley commanding the Dept. of West Virginia (Union) was ordered into action. For one brief moment in history Kelley held the entire course of the war in his hand and he was found wanting.

Benjamin Franklin Kelley.

If Kelley would assemble his forces and march rapidly he would be between Lee and the fords. His small force would be annihilated, but a couple days delay and the Army of the Potomac would overtake Lee. Kelley would not be battling for victory, or land, or to inflict casualties, but for time. He knew it and the whole Union command knew it.

Kelley was the kind of man that only wanted to fight if he was 100 percent sure of victory with few casualties. He delayed. Finally Secretary of War for the Union, Edwin Stanton, personally intervened and sent a stinging telegram to Kelley. He concluded "...It will be a matter of deep regret if, by tardy movement, you let the chance escape. There should be no rest, night or day. Why are you still at Clarksburg"?[3]

"The old woman" as some Rebs called Kelley because of his lack of desire to fight, didn't interpose to delay Lee. Lee was now over the Potomac, but the Army of the Potomac was still in pursuit. Lee was not completely out of danger.

When Kelley telegraphed that he had avoided a close encounter with Reb cavalry and been involved in a "Brisk Skirmish", Meade probably felt like attacking Kelley after the Hell he went through at Gettysburg. To vindicate himself, Kelley also mentioned that he had ordered the attack into Southwest Virginia.

The attack on Southwest Virginia had been in the planning stage for months. The plan and men were ready but until now it was believed that the Confederate forces were too strong to attempt such a deep penetration of enemy territory.

Yankee intelligence was good. They knew a great deal about the Reb forces and their moves in the area. Newspapers, both North and South, printed any news about troop movements gathered. The North knew that troops were being rushed from Southwest Virginia to cover Lee. They knew their time to strike had come.

The success of the raid depended in a large measure on the officer picked to lead it, Col. John Toland, a West Pointer, and on a scout who's name is lost in history. The scout had intimate knowledge on Southwest Virginia. He had undoubtedly traveled much there before the war, perhaps he had lived there and moved north to join the Union army. Although his name is hidden, it is known that he was with Co. A 2nd West Virginia Cavalry.

Of the three major military targets to attack (the saltworks, the lead mines, or the railroad) the saltworks were chosen. The attack began with a diversionary move against Fayettville. The diversionary move would at least "freeze" Reb forces in position to prevent reinforcements at Saltville. If the Yanks were lucky then forces would be withdrawn from Saltville and sent to the other side of the command to fight the fake attack by Gen. Eliakin Scammon, and increase the odds that the real attack on Saltville would succeed.

Re-creation of Union mounted troops on the move.

Eliakin P. Scammon.

On July 9, Col. John McCausland (the "Old Gobbler", he graduated from V.M.I. first in his class and with no demerits) was operating near Fayettville and requested reinforcements from Gen. Sam Jones, head of the Dept. of Southwest Virginia at Dublin, because of a big build-up of Northern forces in his area. Jones told him he had none to send because his forces were moving up the Valley of Virginia to cover Lee. Jones then telegraphed the Secretary of War and asked that his troops be returned to Southwest Virginia to meet this threat. The President, Jefferson Davis, personally telegraphed Jones to move what troops he could to help Lee. There would be no major recall of troops to protect Southwest Virginia.

By the 15th McCausland was in retreat. His dispatch to headquarters said the North had turned both his flanks, that he was now at Flat Top Mountain and falling back on Princeton. It would appear that the Northern attack was following the same route as Gen. Cox's attack of the year before. Were the Federals heading to Dublin and the Long Bridge on New River? That's what the Yanks were hoping the Confederates would think.

On the same day McCausland was falling back on Princeton, Gen. William L. Jackson sent word that he had information that there might be a "raid" on Southwest Virginia. This shows how good Southern intelligence was.

Jackson was called "Mudwall" Jackson by his men. He was a cousin of the martyred Stonewall Jackson and had served on his staff early in the war. To eliminate the confusion between the two, Gen. William Jackson became "Mudwall".

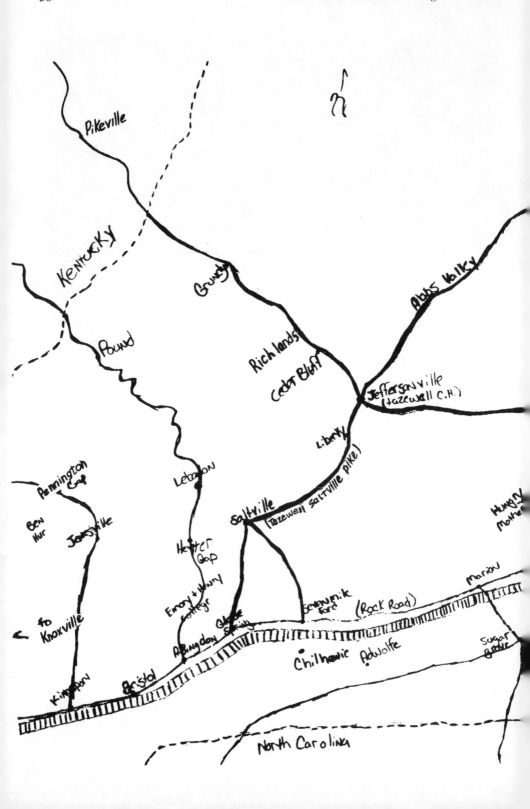

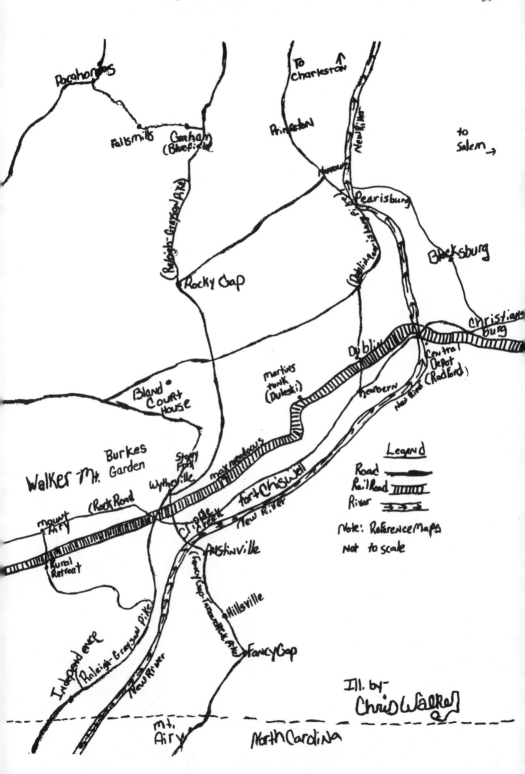

Pocahontas

To Charleston

Falls mills

Graham (Bluefield)

Princeton

to Salem →

(Raleigh-Grayson Pike)

Pearisburg

Blacksburg

Rocky Gap

(Dublin Pike)

christians burg

Dublin

Central Depot (Radford)

martins tank (Pulaski)

newbern

New River

Bland Court House

Burkes Garden

Stony Fork

max meadows

Walker Mt.

Wytheville

fort Chiswell

(Rock Road)

mount Airy

reed creek

New River

Austinville

Rural Retreat

Legend

Road ——
Rail Road ▯▯▯▯
River ⇉⇉

Note: Reference Maps Not to scale

Hillsville

(Fancy Gap Taswell Pike)

Independence

(Raleigh-Grayson Pike)

New River

Fancy Gap

Ill. by Chris Walker

mt. Airy

North Carolina

The raid into Southwest Virginia began on July 13 at 4:00 P.M. from Camp Piatt in the Kanawha Valley near Charleston. Col. John T. Toland was in over all command. Col. W.H. Powell was 2nd in command. He was in charge of the seven companies of the 2nd West Virginia Volunteer Cavalry of 367 men. Third in command was Lt. Col. Freeman E. Franklin. He was in charge of the 34th regiment, Ohio Mounted Infantry, 505 men strong.[4]

On the 16th, at Coal Creek, the men drew 4 days rations and three for the horses, then they continued to Wyoming County Court House. They were now deep into enemy territory and heading deeper; time was critical. If they were to successively attack and destroy Saltville, it must be done quickly before the Confederates could prepare the defenses and get reinforcements. Minutes were precious.

Col. Toland and his subordinates did an outstanding job of rapidly advancing the column and keeping it tight. The dust must have been oppressive at the end of the column but no straggling was permitted. Stragglers would slow the column and be easy prey this deep in enemy territory.

On the 17th, Friday, the head of the Union column was near Tug Mountain. Here Toland "ascertained that a small force of enemy were stationed in Abb's Valley"[5]. The word "ascertained" meant what a Northern sympathizer living in the area wanted them to know. Undoubtedly Toland knew the location and number of troops the South had when he sent 3 Companies of West Virginia Cavalry under Col. Powell forward. This was a proper use of cavalry, a quick strike against a small enemy force.

Abb's Valley is a narrow, fertile area between Pocahontas and Tazewell. This valley was an extremely important mountain pass which is why Reb troops were stationed here permanently. The purpose of the troops was not to hold the valley but as an early warning outpost.

There were 36 men under the command of Maj. Joel E. Stalling who were supposed to watch for the enemy's approach and send messengers if they sighted same. On the morning of the 17th they had no idea a Northern force was near, but the North knew they were there.

Powell charged with such speed that no effective defense could be made. They caught the Rebs completely off guard. It doesn't appear from reports that a single shot was fired in defense. Powell's force did well, they bagged 20 fresh horses, many stands of "goods, arms, and considerable supplies of quarter master and commissary stores".[6] The buildings and stores that could not be carried, were burned. Thirty five of the thirty six Rebs were captured. The prisoners were moved to the rear of the column and the march continued its advance toward Tazewell.

The one mounted Reb continued on in Toland's thoughts.

Meanwhile, by the afternoon of the 17th, party invitations were being sent out in Wytheville. It was to be a formal affair, on the 20th. The "Committee of Invitation" was composed of Maj. R.L. Poor, Cap. J.H. Gibboney, Mr. E.T. Osborne, Lt. James Bellay and Mr. W.R. Cooper. The printed form also listed the "Committee of Arrangements" as Maj. R. McMohon, Cap. Thomas S. Morgan, Lt. W.L. McQuire, Mr. Miner L. Pope, Mr. F.O. Anderson and Mr. Humphroy S. Castlemen.[7] This was the excitement in this sleepy town of 1,800[8] people in mid July 1863.

As the sun set the Federals were establishing camp on the farm of Charles Taylor in Abb's Valley 5½ miles from Jeffersonville or 6 miles from Tazewell Court House.

Toland held a council of war with his subordinates that night. The column had moved 40 miles deeper into enemy county that day and had bagged 35 of the 36 Rebs. That one had spoiled their plans because Toland believed he had alerted Confederate forces. To attack Saltville would be futile and suicidal. Cavalry attacks against fortified positions backed by artillery had proven totally ineffective in the Crimean War.

A new target was chosen for the raid, the Virginia-Tennessee Railroad. The destruction of the High Bridge at Wytheville would break the line for weeks. There was also a possibility of attacking the lead mines only 7 miles from Wytheville at Austinville. Wytheville should be an easy but important target. There were no permanent troops stationed here. Gen. Scammon should be holding McCausland near Princeton, Gen. Williams and Preston were surely consolidating their forces at Saltville; Wytheville should be wide open.

Time was the greatest enemy. Wytheville lay 45 miles away. If the Confederates learned of the intentions in time they could move troops to Wytheville. It was decided that the column would leave camp at 3:00 the next morning. That meant the men must be up by 2:00. Very little rest for the men after a long day.

Purely by accident Gen. John S. Williams, 2nd Brig. Commander, was making an inspection of his outposts. He recalled that about 11:00 P.M. on the 17th he was at Liberty Hill (about seven miles from Tazewell on the road to Saltville) when he received word of the Federal forces in Abb's Valley. According to this report there were 1300 men heading his way.

He immediately sent couriers to alert his forces and call for a consolidation at Liberty Hill. General Preston in Abingdon was asked to move. Couriers were sent to "hunt up"⁹ Preston's cavalry. Col. W.E. Peters and his green troops on the Holston, near Saltville, were ordered to move toward Liberty Hill. A message was sent to Abingdon to telegraph Headquarters at Dublin and inform Jones of the Yankee raid.

Williams had only recently been assigned to the area. His assignment was only "temporary" or so he believed. Williams had been a Brigade Commander but was "relieved of command."¹⁰ His new brigade had a few men, mostly Kentucky soldiers of the 10th Kentucky Cavalry. Gen. Williams was to recruit from the border counties of West Virginia and Kentucky to fill out his brigade.

Gen. William Preston at Abingdon was responsible for the defenses of Saltville at this time.

Around midnight of the 17th Maj. Andrew Jackson May, commander of the 10th Kentucky Cavalry camped in Bowen's Cove in Tazewell County, received his messenger from Williams. They broke camp and started toward Liberty Hill in the darkness. They were undermanned because a part of the force was sent to Pike County, Kentucky on a scouting mission on the 15th.

Williams also sent scouts out that night to locate and track the Federal forces.

At 3:00 A.M. the Northern force started moving toward Tazewell. The Reb scouts raced toward Williams with the news.

Near dawn on the 18th, Maj. May and Maj. John D. Morris combined forces of about 250 men and reached Williams at Liberty Hill. Williams informed them that scouts had reported the Union force moving toward Tazewell and was sure that the North was going after Saltville. With this in mind May was to move forward "and check them at advantageous positions, and gradually fall back until they met Peter's dismounted men"[11] (coming from the Holston).

May moved up the valley to a position near Tazewell. Here he had the men dismount and form a skirmish line across the valley floor. All to do now was wait for the enemy to come to him.

From General Headquarters and at Dublin, Jones was sending telegraph messages. Despite the personal appeal from Jefferson Davis, Jones was calling some of his troops home. He directed the mayor of Lynchburg to send his troops back at once.

By dawn Toland's men had burned Lain's Mill and Kiah Harman's house, and were starting out of Tazewell. The head of the column was at the house of Cap. William E. Perry (CSA). Samuel Graham, John Hambrick, Tom Richie Perry, and the man who would later write the History of Tazewell County, William C. Pendleton, had spent the night at the house. Pendleton recalled, "Suddenly two Northern cavalrymen rode onto the porch and picked up our guns; the house was then completely surrounded by troopers".[12]

John Hambrick did some quick thinking and jumped in bed pretending to be sick. Samuel Graham "assumed the role of his physician".[13] When the Yanks came in they believed their story and did not bother the two men. Pendleton was now a Union prisoner and was forced outside.

Pendleton, who was sixteen at the time, along with Perry age nineteen, were placed with about 20 prisoners both young and old in the barn lot.

Pendleton saw the Yanks steal about 8 or 10 horses from the farm. They couldn't get his horse because it jumped the fence. They left two horses that were worn out.

While there the Federals discovered some old Kentucky rifles that had been stored in the granary since 1862. They broke the guns, added wood, and set fire to them. Some of the guns were loaded. The heat from the fire started them discharging. The crackle of the musketry caused the Yanks to scatter. In the confusion, Pendleton simply walked away from his guard and went back into the house. The Northern column left without him and moved up the road toward Burkes Garden.

The scouts that Williams had sent to track the Union column were racing with the news that the Yanks had changed direction and were heading to Wytheville via the Tazewell Court House - Fancy Gap Pike.

It was probably near 6:00 A.M. when May and the 10th Kentucky received the news that their battle plans and waiting had been in vain. The Yanks were not coming their way. May held his position and passed the information on to Williams at Liberty Hill.

From Libery Hill, Williams sent a messenger toward the railroad and telegraph at full speed. Jones must be informed immediately if Wytheville was to be saved. Williams also sent a messenger to May ordering him to follow the Union and "harass them",[14] and send a courier back each hour to keep the general informed.

Re-creation: Confederate scout or courier.

Sam Jones.

Williams ordered Peters back to his camp on the Holston. This was done to protect the saltworks if the Yanks decided to move on them through Rich Valley.

A courier was sent to McCausland at Princeton by Williams informing him of the enemy's movement toward Wytheville.

About 9:00 May started after the Federals. At 10:00 he was passing through Tazewell leading his column carrying a "Pennant or small flag."[15] Toland had approximately 4 hours lead but May's command was smaller and could move faster.

It was still early A.M. in Burkes Garden when "they came through here like a streak of lightening".[16] The Federals burned Claypool's Mill, D. Harold Perry's store and house and "everything Dr. Carnahan had in the world".[17] The Yanks stole between 20 and 30 horses in the Garden (fresh mounts were badly needed). Because of their haste Toland couldn't do much damage in the area, but the citizens believed that he would be back their way. They feared the destruction they believed was coming when the Yanks retreated North through their village.

If the Yanks could strike them now, would they come back in the fall and "destroy all the grain"?[18]

Some citizens of the Garden apparently fired on the Union column but inflicted no casualties. Third in command, Col. Freeman Franklin wrote later "a company of bushwhackers,...very soon dispersed"[19] by the command.

When May rode through several hours later, some citizens noted that some of his horses were "give out".[20]

The Yanks were heading over steep and winding mountain roads and up Big Walker Mountain. They didn't know May was pursuing them, but the common soldier knew that the deeper they went into enemy territory the less likely he was to come back. The men had to be somewhat nervous as they pressed toward Wytheville.

As Toland led his column he no doubt had the chief scout from Cap. Millard's 2nd West Virginia near him. The two conferred on the details of the battle plan for Wytheville. The scout's knowledge of the area was vital to the plans success.

It was probably after 12:00 when Jones at Dublin received the telegraph message from Williams informing him that the Yanks had changed direction. They were not going to Saltville but to Wytheville. There was no organized fighting force at Wytheville, (only a supply depot. Jones sent a telegraph to Maj. Williams Gibboney, Assistant Quarter Master and party planner on the "Committee of Invitation").

Jones informed Gibboney of the movement of the "1300" Yanks from Abb's Valley and the capture of Maj. J.E. Stalling's Company. Jones stated despite the fact there were no troops at Wytheville "...but if the citizens will turn out as they should do, they could check so small a force as the enemy has in the mountain passes leading from Tazewell Court House to Wytheville".[21]

Jones also sent a telegraph to William Preston at Abingdon ordering him to move his command to Wytheville.

At 1:30 P.M. on the 18th Jones ordered Maj. T.M. Bowyer, Chief of Ordnance there at Military Headquarters in Dublin to assemble a force and move to Wytheville. Bowyer took command of two companies that were at Dublin, plus he enlisted civilian employees at Headquarters and any local citizen he could find. He had 130 men, soldiers and civilians and two pieces of field artillery plus extra arms and ammunition.

The mail train was commandeered. The passengers were ordered to leave and Bowyer's command entrained at 3:00 P.M., but the train departure was delayed because there was a freight train moving east toward Dublin. It had to pass before Bowyer could move to Wytheville. This delay was critical.

Meanwhile at Wytheville as the news that the Yanks were coming spread, so did confusion, dismay, and panic. The citizens of the town started looking for their military leader, "Colonel for a day", Joseph Kent. Kent had led the locals in the Brown crisis (when they traveled to Harper's Ferry to see that no abolitionist interferred with the hanging) and had led them off the war. After Manassas he resigned and returned home. He resigned the day he received his commission as Colonel. Kent was found working his farm 3½ miles east of Wytheville.

Kent went straight to the courthouse, which was located on Main Street near the present Post Office, and had the bell rung to assemble the citizens.

Some considerable amount of time passed as Kent tried to organize the panicked citizens. The first concrete step Kent took was sending volunteers toward Walkers Mountain as scouts. The rest of the volunteers were told to return home and get their weapons and reassemble as soon as possible. At the time of the battle there were about 40 citizen volunteers, mostly old men and young boys. Many were poorly armed with small pistols and flintlocks.

By late afternoon of the 18th the Federals had crossed Big Walker Mountain and were halted at the bottom of the mountain along a cold mountain creek called Stony Fork. Here Toland started the plans for the attack.

Cap. Millard, the chief scout, and two companies of the 2nd West Virginia were detached from the main column. Theirs was the most important part of the attack. They were to burn the high railroad bridge over Reed Creek west of Wytheville. They were sent over the Black Lick Road, (Rt. 680) toward the railroad station at Rural Retreat. Their job was to destroy the depot, the telegraph, and track. This would stop communications west of Wytheville and prevent the South from moving troops to oppose Toland and the main column at Wytheville. Then they were to proceed toward the town and destroy the high bridge before rejoining the main column.

Toland had the prisoners (around 75) placed under guard. The prisoners would only be a nuisance when they attacked Wytheville. The prisoners and their guard were to be picked up when the column left Wytheville. Cap. Cutler, Company C, 34th Ohio, was in charge of the guard.

The Federals received information "that the enemy's force was small, not exceeding 300",[22] at Wytheville. The source of the information is not known. Maybe a Union sympathizer or foolish citizen or a captured scout that Kent had sent out.

It was 5:10 P.M. when Bowyer and the reserves arrived at Wytheville from Dublin. The field artillery was taken off the train but no horses or harnesses were readily available, so a search was begun. Bowyers also began distributing the extra rifles to the citizens which he had brought with him.

Bowyer found Wytheville to be "in a great state of alarm, and confusion."[23] Because of the confusion there was "a considerable delay"[24] in distributing the rifles and in looking for horses and harnesses. Apparently Kent, who had been trying to organize the volunteers since sometime after 1:00, hadn't accomplished a great deal with the civilians. Bowyer later recalled that Lt. Col. Abraham Umbarger and Maj. Joseph Kent helped him distribute the weapons.

Before the means to move the field artillery was found, Lt. C. L. Minor with one of the reserve companies from Dublin, informed Bowyer and Kent that the enemy was reported about a mile from town. There was no time to continue looking for horses and harnesses. Cap. Oliver, who commanded the gun crews, was ordered to find the horses and harnesses and to follow toward town as soon as possible. Meanwhile the reserves and volunteers moved toward town from the railroad station at about 5:30.

As Kent and Bowyer moved toward town from the railroad station south of the town, the enemy was approaching town from the north. There was a thinly manned skirmish line established across the road coming from Big Walker Mountain. The little battle line controlled the ridge of the hill. It is not clear if Kent had directed some of the citizens to station themselves at that line or if they had taken that action on their own.

As Toland's column approached up the slight grade the Yanks "discovered"[25] the Reb line. They probably discovered the line when the excited volunteer soldiers started firing at a distance too great to have any effect on the Federal column.

The column halted momentarily and Toland ordered Powell to charge with the 1st and 2nd West Virginia Cavalry. Because Powell couldn't see the Reb's position and had no idea of their strength, he suggested to Toland that the 34th Ohio Infantry be dismounted and moved forward. (This would have been the correct strategy for the situation). Toland, a West Pointer, rejected Powell's suggestion. He ordered Powell to charge "in unnecessary language."[26] Toland was going to battle, not a church social.

Powell ordered his West Virginia troops forward. That was all it took for the citizen volunteers. The lightly held skirmish line was quickly abandoned without a fight. The panicked volunteers ran down Tazewell Street going south toward town.

As the panicked citizens were streaming into town, Kent and Bowyer were near the courthouse on Main Street starting up Tazewell Street. Realizing the enemy was almost upon them, Bowyer suggested to Kent that they retreat to the depot. Bowyer wanted to make the most of the field of artillery. Kent had battle experience, knew the volunteers, and knew the lay of the town. If the enemy struck before the command could be deployed at the depot, then there was no chance to stop the enemy.

Kent rejected Bowyer's suggestion. Kent told Bowyer to send his men into the houses along Tazewell Street. Kent's citizen volunteers did move into the houses but most of Bowyer's command stayed with him at the lower end of Tazewell Street near the courthouse.

Tazewell Street was lined with houses on both sides. There were high stake fences around the houses that fronted on the road. The property owners had erected them to keep live stock and pigs, which roamed the streets, off their property. Those staked fences which kept the livestock out were to create a deadly hazard for the approaching Union column.

Powell with his West Virginia Cavalry (1st and 2nd) was glad to see the Reb skirmish line evaporate. Cap. Gilmore of the 1st West Virginia was at the head of the column as it galloped toward the town. There was no enemy resistance in sight, and no major resistance expected, as the column moved down Tazewell Street.

The West Virginia Cavalry was surprised at the volleys of fire that poured on them so suddenly from the windows and doorways of the houses. The staked fence kept them confined to the street, easy targets for the men firing from their protected positions.

Even though he was taking casualties, Gilmore did not halt his command but pressed forward toward Main Street.

The dash for Wytheville was checked about two blocks north of Main Street when Kent ordered a volley fired. The bodies of horses and men blocked the fenced road. Col. Powell was wounded from a pistol ball in the back. Maj. Hoffman's horse was shot from under him and the major was stunned from the fall.

The West Virginia Cavalry was blocked in front and hemmed in on the sides. The soldiers panicked. Col. Franklin reported "I regret to state that the second West Virginia Cavalry did not behave so well, but were thrown into considerable confusion, many of them dismounted and leaving their horses, while they sought their own safety".[27]

Toland, with the 34th Ohio, was following the progress of the West Virginia Cavalry. He had heard the shooting at the head of the column. When the charge halted, he galloped forward to assess the damage and take personal command. He saw Powell, Hoffman, and the others writhing in pain among the dead and wounded horses. He was aware of the incoming fire as he rode through the smoke. Some trooper yelled that he should take cover.

He was reported to have said words to the effect that the bullet that would kill him hadn't been made yet. He was wrong. No sooner had he stopped speaking than he was shot in the heart and died instantly. He lay corpse on the dirt road in front of the present grade school. Cap. Delaney was dead and Guseman severely wounded. Some said Bob Bailey, a teenager, shot Toland. Others say it was another teenager named Andrew Parish. Still others said it was an unidentified woman.

Within minutes the Union had lost their first and second in command. The 2nd West Virginia was panicked and scattered. The 2nd never did reform into a regiment during the action at Wytheville but some captains led their companies gallantly.

Bowyer didn't throw his command forward toward the stalled Union column. He believed that the North would be victorious because of their numerical advantage. He still believed the only way to balance the power was with the artillery. He ordered his men to withdraw toward the railroad depot, double quick! Lt. Bozang's and Lt. Alley Alexander's companies were to form a line to slow the enemy so the others could retreat.

Bowyer had no way of knowing that Oliver had found horses and harnesses and was moving the guns toward downtown.

Franklin didn't know that Toland was dead and Powell was wounded, or that he was in command when he started the 34th into action. The 34th was a mounted infantry command, not a cavalry unit. They dismounted and flanked both sides of the road. They were not sitting ducks like the cavalry, bunched in the center of the street. As they moved forward with their superior manpower and fire power, Reb resistance on Tazewell Street began to crumble rapidly, but as the Union forces approached Main Street, Reb resistance increased. Kent was headquartered at the courthouse with local forces posted in "public and private buildings on Main Street",[28] plus Bozang and Alexander of Bowyers command had formed a skirmish line to delay the enemy.

At this time Oliver came dashing toward Main Street with the two pieces of artillery. Lt. Bozang recognized that the artillery was heading straight into the enemy's hands, unprotected. He moved his men quickly to try and provide protection.

Oliver moved as quickly as possible to unhitch and load the guns.

Gilmore, who's company had been stalled on Tazewell Street where Powell was wounded and Toland killed, saw the Reb artillery moving forward. Gilmore's company with a detachment of the 34th, charged Bozang's forming line and the artillery. Bozang and his command was "conspicuously brave", but the Union charge was too much too fast. His line crumbled before it was completely formed. Oliver did get one cannon in service and fired[29] into the head of the attacking column at only 30 yards distance. (The noise of the cannon made the team of horses with the second gun bolt. They turned the cannon over as they ran.)

Even the cannon shot did not slow Gilmore's men. They broke through Bozang's line and killed Oliver and two of the gunners. The rest of the gun crew fled for their lives. The artillery Bowyer was hoping to use on the Yanks was in their hands.

Bozang was wounded and cut off from the rest of Bowyer's command. Gilmore blocked their retreat and they were greatly outnumbered; further resistance was futile. Lt. Bozang surrendered his command.

Bowyer now ordered his remaining soldiers to join the locals in the buildings along Main Street. Many buildings were locked as his men sought position.

The two commanders, Maj. Kent and Maj. Bowyer, were probably not at the same location on Main Street but both knew the facts. They had a force of less than 200 men combined and almost half were untrained civilians. The Yanks had 1300 men (or so they believed). The Yanks had captured the artillery. They controlled the north end of town. They were taking control of the streets and more blue bellies were coming down Tazewell Street all the time. Houses and buildings that offered resistance were being burned. The only conclusion that could be reached was Wytheville was lost. To fight further would only increase casualties and not change events. They must retreat now before the Union completely controlled the streets where the only option would be surrender or die!

Because the soldiers and civilian soldiers were separated into different buildings there would be no organized retreat. The order to retreat must have been shouted from one building or house to the next.

Kent's order was to get away with all possible speed. Each man was responsible for his own safety.

Bowyer ordered his men "to quit the town as best they could and rally at the water-tank"[30] (railroad).

Because the Federals had lost their leaders and were disorganized, they were in no position to effectively intercept the fleeing Rebs. Probably before they knew it the sound of musketry had died down and they were in possession of the town. There was confusion in the streets as Reb soldiers and civilians fled the town. The civilian soldiers left their guns, (be it one of the rifles Bowyer brought or the old flintlock squirrel rifle) and ran down the street. The Yanks had trouble identifying their enemy now that he no longer carried a gun.

Many of the local soldiers and citizens found refuge in buildings on the old fair ground just outside of town. Other citizens, unable or unwilling to leave their homes, took refuge in the cellar. Other citizens simply fled in terror into the woods where they would spend the night with no shelter.

When Bowyer reached the water tank at the railroad and started to assemble his command, he was greatly angered. He wasn't so much upset that the battle was lost, that 3 of his men were dead, 4 or 5 wounded, and 25 captured, but because the train had left without him. The conductor had decided to back the train to Dublin to avoid the possibility that the Union would capture it. Bowyer wrote later "...the conductor, for some reason which has never been explained to me, moved off with his train, thereby compelling the command to make their way back to Dublin on foot."[31]

It was now approaching 7:00 E.S.T. The battle of Wytheville had lasted about 45 minutes.

During the same general time frame that the battle of Wytheville was occurring, two other important events were occurring in the Dept. of Southwest Virginia.

Re-creation: rest after the battle.

At Princeton the courier sent by Williams in Tazewell County to McCausland had arrived. As McCausland read the dispatch, his mind was racing. Williams had informed him of the Union raid and that the raiders were apparently heading for Wytheville. McCausland immediately realized that Scammon's push on him had been a diversion to hold him in place and the raid was the North's real objective. Without orders, McCausland sent a dispatch to Jones in Dublin informing him of his troops movements. A considerable portion of McCausland's command were being pulled out of Princeton and then divided. Part of his troops, including infantry, artillery and cavalry, were being sent to the narrows on New River where Wolf Creek empties in, and part were being sent to Rocky Gap. Rocky Gap was a crossing point in Bland County for the road that ran east from Saltville to Princeton (Tazewell - Princeton Pike) and the Raleigh - Grayson Pike that ran north and south.

It was McCausland's intention to seal these two likely escape routes which were in his area of operation. Part of the contingent sent to Rocky Gap was the Bland Rangers. McCausland felt their intimate knowledge of the country might be very useful.

In Tazewell County, Williams had been trying to gather additional troops to follow the Yanks. The troops from Russell County and Saltville that Williams had ordered forward had fallen back instead. They were following orders Gen. Preston had given before Williams was assigned to the Saltville area. J.B. Holladay, with 400 men, had fallen back to protect Lebanon in Russell County. Col. Hodge was heading for Saltville with 600 men. Col. Crittenden was at Hyter Gap with 200 more men. Williams again sent couriers to Preston and his commanders asking them to join with him at Liberty.

May was pushing his men to catch the Yanks. Over the steep, curved road that winds over Burkes Garden Mountain south of the Garden, he rode. The timber and undergrowth were very thick, and vision was very limited, only a matter of feet.

His column emerged into the farm valley near Ceres and turned east for a short distance and then followed the road which the Yanks had taken toward Wytheville over Big Walker Mountain. This road was also winding, steep, and vision limited.

Because May was chasing the Yanks with all possible speed and because of the limited vision, it is likely that May didn't know the Union was there before his column struck their position.

At approximately the same time that the head of the Union column was approaching Wytheville, the head of May's column was approaching Stony Fork.

At Stony Fork, Cap. Cutler's Company C. 34th Ohio had been resting while watching their prisoners. They probably only had seconds warning that anything was wrong when they heard the horses of May's men approaching. It was too little time to form a defense line and to cover the prisoners.

May's men didn't know they had caught the blue bellies they had been chasing all day until they saw them and heard their guns firing. There was no organization on either side. As the Rebs rode into the Union position they fired at the Yanks. The Yanks returned the fire as best they could while seeking cover. The prisoners, no doubt, yelled to their fellow countrymen not to shoot them as they too dove for cover.

May's men kept pouring into the Union position. Their number and fire power overcame the Northern resistance. Within minutes the whole action was over. As the smoke cleared, two or three Yanks lay dying, and about eight were captured.[32] There was no mention made of Yanks escaping into the undergrowth or of Reb casualties.

May probably detailed a small number of his men to guard the Federal prisoners and organize the freed Southern prisoners. Most of the prisoners were from Cap. Joel Stalling's Company which the Yanks had captured in Abb's Valley the day before. There were some civilians and slaves.

May continued toward Wytheville with Cap. A.J. Harris's company in the lead. At approximately 3 miles from Wytheville they came upon the rear of the Union column, probably the 34th Ohio.

The Yanks quickly turned and formed a line. May knew that he had struck the main body of the Union. What could his small column do against so many Yanks? To fight on this open, relatively flat land would be suicidal.

The Yank line charged. The only logical course was retreat as fast as possible to the mountain at Stony Fork Creek. A few shots were exchanged but there was apparently no casualties taken on either side.

Harris' command of about 40 men which was in front was cut off from May as he withdrew. They were in real danger of being surrounded and captured so Harris moved his men off the road through the farm fields and headed toward the mountains as fast as the horses would move.

The Union soldiers didn't press the attack on Harris with much vigor. Their goal was Wytheville and they had no orders to press the fleeing Rebs. The Rebs ran and the Union troopers continued toward Wytheville.

May would not and could not contest the Yanks for the possession of Wytheville and as darkness approached the Union was taking complete control. Bowyer's command had been drawn off to the water tank at the railroad and was starting back to Dublin on foot. Kent's command of citizen soldiers was evaporating. Some were seeking shelter in the cellars, some disposing of their guns and were running from town before the Federals captured them. Some joined the civilians at the buildings on the fair grounds. Some tried to reorganize at Kent's residence until they too were told to disperse. Only occasionally was there gun fire in the town.

Only now did Franklin realize that he was in command. Toland was dead, and Powell was "mortally wounded".[33] Franklin was not psychologically prepared to take on the responsibility of first in command.

The Federals seemed to operate on orders of their immediate superior or on their own. After the town was secured, the Union dead and wounded were removed from the dirt streets. A makeshift first aid station was apparently set up under the bridge that used to cross the town branch on Main Street. Powell was brought there.

Already men acting on their own had entered the stores to loot what they could carry, and destroy what they could not.

E.W. Clark, the Union acting Adjutant General, gave orders that the "Court House and private and public buildings immediately adjacent", were to be burned.

These were the buildings where Kent and his locals were stationed and "from which the Reb fire had been the hottest".[34]

One of the buildings Clark wanted burned was the Crockett Hotel. One story states, in it was the body of Clayton E. Cooke. He was one of the three "citizens" killed by the Yanks. He was firing on the Union with a squirrel gun and had turned to reload when struck by a minie-ball.

The other story states that Cooke was an old man who met his end outside of the hotel. Apparently Cooke was deaf and didn't hear the order to surrender. Neither did he hear the shot that killed him.

Pat Helligan was a stubborn Irishman who was killed in the doorway of his home. He refused to surrender because he was neither Confederate or Yank, but an Irishman. The soldiers were not there to debate international politics. He wouldn't surrender, so they shot and killed him.

An old man by the name of Wilkes Carico was killed on North Street near the intersection of Tazewell Street.

George wasn't considered a "citizen". George was the "faithful slave of Ephraim McGavock".[35] He was trying to help master escape when he was shot. George died but McGavock didn't escape.

Franklin did send a detail to destroy the railroad "left"[36] (east) of town. They reported back that they had destroyed one short bridge and one culvert. They were tired and wanted to rest or loot and believed they could pull a fast one on their new leader. (The Southern report said the track was repaired in one hour's time). As the detail was damaging the railroad, it passed directly under the telegraph lines and did not cut them. Reb communications were never broken.

Franklin felt the railroad was cut to the east by his men and to the west by Millard's company which included the "only reliable guide".[37] Millard had been detached by Toland to cut the railroad before the battle. The South couldn't move troops directly into Wytheville via the rail, Franklin thought.

It was dark when Franklin was informed that Cutler's Company with the prisoners at Stony Fork had been overrun by "300 Rebel Cavalry".[38] Cutler was missing.

Franklin was alarmed that an enemy force was at his rear. He tried to call a council of war to organize his force and make a decision as to their next move. When he called the roll, he found his command structure was greatly destroyed or was missing. From the 34th Ohio, Millard and the guide were still detached. Franklin needed the guide to help make a decision on what route to follow when the command left Wytheville. Also from the 34th Lt. Hayes was wounded and Cap. Cutler was missing.

The 1st West Virginia Cavalry had Captain Delaney killed, 1st Lt. Guseman and 2nd Lt. Livingston severely wounded. The 2nd West Virginia had Powell "mortally"[39] wounded and 1st Lt. Barber slightly wounded. They were of no help.

Franklin decided the best thing he could do with his command was to try to preserve it. The South was undoubtedly sending troops against them from the east and the west along the railroad. There was an enemy force of 300 in his rear. Time only increased the danger. He would have to start his retreat now if they were going to succeed in returning north.

The prisoners which had been taken from the town were assembled in one place under guard. The two captured six-pound cannon were made ready. Franklin was making preparations to move as soon as Millard and the guide arrived.

The Union soldiers were incensed that they had been fired upon from buildings both public and private. They felt that somehow the South had cheated using the structures for protection instead of meeting them on a field of battle. Not only had the soldiers shot at them but "...citizens, and even some of the women fired from private dwelling houses, taking deliberate aim".[40]

The soldiers felt no guilt nor did they consider it a war crime to burn buildings and houses. **They filled their Blue Bellys with Reb food and their haversacks and** saddle bags with loot as they destroyed and burned.

Fire destroyed or damaged the railroad depot, a Confederate Storehouse on Main Street, the Courthouse, a hotel, the Cumberland Presbyterian Church, and eight to ten private residences. Cap. William Gibboney's house and David St. Clair's printing press were singled out for destruction before the raiders came to town. This shows the Federals had intimate knowledge of Southwest Virginia. It was a common practice for the Union to burn the homes of Southern officers when they invaded. Gibboney's house was looted before it was burned. Cap. William H. Fortescue stole a dictionary. After the war he returned it to Gibboney. David St. Clair's printing press was targeted because it was considered almost a military target. St. Clair printed most of the money that was issued by banks throughout Southwest Virginia. Not only was his press damaged but his house also. Rumor has it that he relocated his business to Tazewell after the raid.

If it wasn't for the women, children, and slaves who had been hiding in the cellar during the battle, more houses would have been burned. For example, Mrs. Haller was hiding in the basement when she heard the Federal soldiers break into her house (now the Rock House Museum). She arrived in time to see them set fire to the beds. The soldier told her he had orders to set the house on fire, but he didn't stay and watch them burn. He lit the bed and left. Mrs. Haller, with the help of slaves, threw the mattress and burning materials out of the window. The floor in one room still bears the scorch marks of that night. A hotel on Main Street (maybe Kincannon) and the Morrison house were saved by Daniel Sheffey, slave of the Morrison's.

The rumor flew among the citizens that the Yanks said they would finish the job of burning the town if they came back. Franklin reported "the main part of the town was fired and reduced to ashes".[41] (Somewhat of an overstatement).

It was probably after 9 P.M. when Millard's company arrived in Wytheville with their cock and bull story. They were probably less sad than any of the other Yanks to find the confusion and change in command. Apparently Franklin swallowed the story hook, line, and sinker. They told him that they hadn't burned the depot at "Mount Airy" (Mount Airy was the closest settlement to Rural Retreat Depot). They couldn't because it was defended by "300 Rebels".[42] (There were no troops stationed at Rural Retreat, if there had been they would have been sent to Wytheville). They couldn't attack the depot so they went to their next objective and main thrust of the entire raid, the high bridge over Reed Creek. Boy, were they ever going to destroy it; but they couldn't! Wouldn't you know it, those Rebs had it "strongly garrisoned".[43]

What had Millard's boys in blue been doing all afternoon? The objectives were wide open to attack. The mission's highest goal hung on their shoulders and they failed; the mission failed. Could the "one reliable guide" have gotten lost? Could the troops have overrun a Reb moonshine operation and tried to destroy it? (Making whiskey was common among the mountain people). Could the boys in blue have decided to catch a few winks of rest before they completed their mission and sleep all afternoon? No answer was found.

Franklin must have slapped his head in frustration. The railroad west was open. The enemy could move troops into position at will. Any thoughts of waiting to retreat were pushed aside. They must move and move now.

By 12:00 the troops loaded with loot began to move out of Wytheville via the road which they attacked from (Tazewell Street). The Yanks had 86 prisoners with them, about 60 were local citizens and the remainder were soldiers and citizens Bowyer had brought from Dublin. Some of the citizens were elderly and walked slowly. The two captured field pieces and every horse the Yanks could steal went with them.

But the Yanks did leave something. They left the town in flames. They left debris in the streets and smashed merchandise in the stores. They left the citizens terrorized. They left their dead (probably 9). They left the wounded (6 to 8) who couldn't travel. An assistant surgeon and 2 other attendants were also left.

The moon must have been bright and the sky unclouded as they slowly withdrew from Wytheville toward Big Walker Mountain. Franklin was sure the Reb force of "300" (May's men) were blocking their retreat. He no doubt conferred with the guide. He must keep moving and bypass the enemy. A plan was agreed upon. The force would leave the road at the top of Walker Mountain and follow a bridle path through the mountain to Bland and then to the Tazewell-Princeton Pike to the Raleigh-Grayson Pike heading north at Rocky Gap.

The slow moving prisoners were no longer an asset; they must go. At the top of the mountain they were paroled. (The parole said they would not fight against the U.S. again. On their promise and signature or mark, they were released). The prisoners started down the mountain toward Wytheville.

There were no roads for the artillery. The teams of horses were removed and the gun was pushed into a ditch. The Yanks said they were "destroyed", the Rebs said they were "recovered".

As a bright moon shone in a cloudless sky on the night of July 18 or early morning of the 19th, this was the situation in the Dept. of Southwest Virginia. The defense perimeter around Princeton was contracting as McCausland was sending troops to Narrows and Rocky Gap. Williams was at Liberty Hill waiting for troops from Preston's command to join May. May was retreating from Big Walker Mountain in the direction of Burkes Garden with the freed Reb soldiers and citizens. It was his intention to fall back on the Burkes Garden area and establish a strong defensive line in the mountain near the Garden. He was going to greet the Yanks as they returned by their invasion route. Harris of May's command, who had been cut off, was now regrouped and following the road back to Burkes Garden.

The troops Jones ordered to leave Abingdon to aid Wytheville were at Abingdon. Either Gen. Preston was absent or he chose to guard the saltworks until he knew the danger was past. Bowyer was walking back to Dublin with his command, minus 25 or 30 who were killed, wounded, or captured. Bowyer was angry at the train conductor because he had to walk.

The conductor and his train were safe in Dublin waiting for the all clear before he proceeded with his run.

In Dublin, Jones was gathering troops and preparing to leave in the morning to fight at Wytheville.

In Wytheville the flames still burned. The citizens had been terrified. They were anxious about loved ones and property. Some hid in cellars. Some hid at the fair ground. Some hid in the woods. Some lay dead in the streets.

Other citizens of Wytheville and those captured from Dublin, were making their way down the mountain to Wytheville, parole in hand. They were the only ones with something to be happy about.

As the Yanks left the road (Tazewell-Fancy Gap Pike) and turned right, down Walker Mountain on a hog back called Rams Horn, they were a motley crew. They were tired (both man and beast had been on the go for almost 3 days without rest and had traveled 60 miles in 24 hours and fought a major battle) dirty, stinking (there was no time to bath and these were the days before deodorant), and scared (their leader was new, they were deep in enemy territory, the retreat path blocked, and the enemy closing in on them).

At or near dawn, McCausland had completed his troop movements. The escape routes at Narrows and Rocky Gap were sealed. The men were improving their defensive line or resting. McCausland no doubt, sent couriers to May at Burkes Garden informing him of his location and asking, "Where are the Yanks"?

At Burkes Garden, May had picked a sight to do battle with the retiring Yanks. Using the mountain and undergrowth they knew could stop the Union column dead. The men were breakfasting on freshly slaughtered beef, they had been joined by locals who provided food. Harris would soon join them.

No doubt May sent couriers to McCausland informing him of his location and asking "Where are the Yanks"?

Williams was still at Liberty Hill waiting.

As the sun's beams chased the darkness from the hills and valleys the frightened citizens of Wytheville began to adventure toward town. They came in groups, or singly, moving cautiously. The fires of the night were gone. The shouting was gone. Were the Yanks gone?

The citizens were unprepared for the scene that greeted them as they ventured back into their once quiet, sleepy town. The roads were covered with litter. Store merchandise, burnt material, wrecked wagons, and an occasional body were seen in the roads. Smoke still rose from some of the buildings and houses, but no Yanks were seen.

When the wounded Federals and those that stayed to care for them were spotted, the fear and terror of some of the citizens turned to rage. They wanted to kill those damn Yankees for what they had done to their town.

Apparently the women of the town intervened to stop a massacre. They pleaded with the men not to harm the Federals. They hid some of the wounded from the people. Powell, the highest ranking Union soldier, became the focal point of the people's anger. Mrs. Spiller, Mrs. Morrison, and Mrs. Kincannon hid him in the Kincannon Hotel.

It is not known exactly when on Sunday the 19th, Jones arrived from Dublin with his troops. The train halted about one-half mile east of the depot because of the damaged tracks. He soon restored order, took possession of the wounded, and organized a burial detail. The Union officers were buried in the Catholic Cemetery. (Now East End Cemetery).

As Jones surveyed Wytheville and learned more about the fighting he later wrote about the raid "...it failed chiefly,..., because the leaders were killed..."[44]

Jones sent a telegraph back to Dublin stating "...the enemy was roughly handled at Wytheville...they commenced leaving last night, and retreated toward Tazewell Court House".[45]

C.S. Stringfellow, the Adjutant-in-Chief at Dublin, sent a telegraph to Lynchburg informing them that their troops were not needed. They could be used to help Gen. Lee.

By this time the paroled prisoners were starting to filter back into town. Many families were relieved to be reunited. Many prisoners were exhausted.

After Jones learned that they were prisoners only briefly, he declared their paroles to be of no effect. The former prisoners could fight and would be expected to fight, if the Yanks came this way again.

Sometime early on the morning of Sunday July 19, Preston at Abingdon concluded that the saltworks were indeed safe from attack. He sent word to his sub-cavalry commanders: Holladay with 400 men at Lebanon, Hodge at Saltville with 600 men, and Crittenden at Hyster Gap with 200 men to join Williams at Liberty Hill. 1,200 men were moving in for the kill on the fleeing Union column. The South was preparing to attack the Yankees, if they could only find them.

Near dawn the bleary-eyed Yanks were picking their way out of the forest of Walker Mountain and were in the valley that leads to Bland Court House. Very weary and sleepy, this command was in no shape for a head on fight, but that was where they were heading. They were moving down the valley toward Rocky Gap. At Rocky Gap McCausland was anxious to meet them.

With infantry, artillery, and cavalry it would be no contest against the exhausted Yanks. The blue column would be meat for McCausland's grinder.

The Yanks pushed forward. At William Stower's farm they stopped for a brief rest. They no doubt stole food and horses. To rest and feed their mounts they turned their horses loose in his wheat field. What the horses didn't consume, they trampled.

The rest was over and they moved east, ever nearer McCausland's line. At Charles Grayson's place they found out they were riding into a trap, whether Charles or someone else told them is not known. Maybe a loyal Reb happened to let it slip or maybe a Union sympathizer deliberately warned them. Whatever the reason, the great victory the South would have won at Rocky Gap never happened.

Franklin reversed the column and headed west. West toward Liberty Hill where Williams had ordered the troops to consolidate. Franklin knew he had to avoid detection and confrontation with Reb units, so he asked directions from local citizens as he moved west so he could avoid the main road (Saltville-Princeton Pike).

The Yanks went through a gap of Brushy Mountain over what was then called "Laurel Road,"[46] and down Laurel Creek to Frank Suiter's place. There in Hunting Camp Valley they stole Suiter's horses.

From the valley they followed a bridle path over Round Mountain to Wolf Creek, at Isaac Stower's farm.

While the Union column was backtracking and moving west to avoid McCausland at Rocky Gap, McCausland received word that his plans to greet the Yanks were in vain; the guests were not coming.

McCausland knew that his infantry and artillery would move too slowly to overtake the Union cavalry. He detached the small amount of cavalry he had with him (the 8th Virginia Cavalry under Cap. H. Bowen with less than 50 troopers) and sent them after the Federals. Even though the Yanks had several hours head start, because the Rebs stayed on the main road, they were catching up fast.

In the same time frame word reached May that the Yanks weren't retreating from Wytheville toward him on the Tazewell Court House-Fancy Gap Pike. Perhaps a scout was sent from Gen. Jones at Wytheville with the word.

May broke up the defense line he had established and wanted to move his men east toward the general direction of the enemy as fast as possible. To do this he left the main road at Burkes Garden and proceeded down the Wolf Creek Valley.

Neither of the three parties knew for certain where the others were. McCausland's cavalry, under Cap. Bowen, was moving west over the Saltville-Princeton Pike. William's cavalry, under May, was moving east down Wolf Creek. The Yanks moving west through the mountains were on Wolf Creek.

The Union won the race off Wolf Creek to Crab-Tree Gap to cross Rich Mountain. May sighted the rear of the Union column as it headed over the mountain. At this point Bowen arrived. He placed his command under May, and they pursued the Union. May also sent a courier to Williams still at Liberty Hill that the enemy had been sighted and the direction in which they were moving.

The Yanks may not have known that the Rebs were that close to them as they came down Rich Mountain and turned east on Clearfork road. (Rumor has it that a local citizen, perhaps named Burris, was guiding the Union. He may have been sent to Richmond and executed later. No official documents were found to support this theory). There is a branch called Cove Creek that flows into Clearfork Creek at Henry Dill's place. It flows off of East River Mountain to the north. The road that follows Cove Creek to the top of the mountain was the Federals' escape route.

As the rear of the column left Clearfork and started up Cove Creek road, May struck; "several"[47] Yanks were killed and some captured. A few horses were taken, no mention of Confederate loses.

The Yanks raced as fast as they could over East River Mountain via George Gap. They then descended near Graham (now Bluefield, Va.). Because the Yanks could steal fresh horses, they could out distance May over Stony Ridge and into

Brown's Meadow near Falls Mills. It was dark and every fiber of their bodies demanded rest. In the last approximately 42 hours they had ridden almost 100 miles, fought a battle, skirmish, had no sleep and little rest.

At Liberty Hill, Williams got the dispatch from May. It was 4:30 in the evening that the first troops from Preston's command began to arrive. Holladay arrived with 150 men, not the 400 Williams thought he had at Lebanon. Their horses were "very much jaded".[48]

Soon Williams learned that Hodge with 600 troopers wasn't coming. Apparently Preston changed his mind and repositioned them between Saltville and Glade Spring. To Preston the Saltworks were paramount.

Williams decided not to push after the Yankees until after dawn. Holladay's horses and men needed the rest.

It was apparent that the Yanks were heading toward Abb's Valley going north. Williams would pursue them in that direction through Tazewell Courthouse. He sent a courier to May so that they could both be at or near Abb's Valley by sun up.

May must have gotten under way at early dawn (1 hour before sunrise). He probably felt that Williams may have been strengthened during the night by additional troops from Preston. If he, May, could slow the Union column, perhaps Williams moving north through Abb's Valley, could catch and crush the Blue Bellys.

It was "day break"[49] on Monday, July 20th, when May struck the Union column. Some of the Northerners may still have been asleep, others were preparing to burn Falls Mills (the mill from which the place derives its name). They didn't finish sleeping or burning..

The Union formed a rear guard to fend off May. This allowed the column to advance to Abb's Valley.

The Yanks, of course, didn't know that Williams was moving toward them up the valley from Tazewell. With the rear guard holding May at bay, Franklin ordered that cattle and horses be gathered and moved north.

The Federals had gathered "several hundred beef cattle", when Williams attacked. The Yanks fled leaving the cattle, "and a number of the stolen Negroes".[50]

Franklin apparently placed the West Virginia Cavalry in the rear and the 34th Ohio mounted infantry in front, and made a speedy retreat. Williams pressed the rear of the column as they withdrew. Apparently there was much shooting but few casualties as each side moved up Abb's Valley.

Franklin later wrote "the paths along which we passed presented obstacles almost impassable, being filled with fallen timber and winding over rocky steeps". He had a plan and it was perfect terrain. Company F. of the 34th was dismounted and "placed in ambush".[51]

William's men, in hot pursuit, were "met by a galling fire...emptying fifteen saddles at one volley".

Williams confirms that "I had 3 men killed". The pursuit stopped. Williams concluding "That I would lose more men than the Yankees, I gave up the chase".[52]

The Federals moved unmolested north. All was quiet in the Dept. of Southwest Virginia by the late afternoon of the 20th.

Re-creation of Union cavalry returning to camp.

It was several days later that Franklin and his remaining command could finally rest back at Camp Piatt on the Kanawha near Charleston. When Franklin made his report several days later a few stragglers were still coming into the camp. He knew that 17 of his men were captured for sure, but there were still 25 unaccounted for.

One of those 25 stopped at Jonathan Hendrickson's home near Graham (Bluefield). He demanded and received a meal from the women folk of the house. Mattie, Jonathan's young daughter, helped serve the enemy soldier. "When he arose from the table he was looking into the muzzle of his own carbine, which was pointed at the Yankee by Miss Mattie Hendrickson. She politely told him he was her prisoner; and she held him as such until a squad of Confederates came along and took him in charge".[53]

Franklin recorded that the Union lost 11 dead, including two officers, 32 wounded, including 5 officers; 17 prisoners, including 1 officer, and 25 missing. He had to leave over 300 horses because they were completely broken down. The Yanks had managed to steal enough so that most of the men rode back to camp.

It was clear that the raid had failed. Of the three major targets, the saltworks, the lead mines, and the Virginia Tennessee Railroad, only the railroad was damaged, and it took the Rebs about an hour to repair it.

There was no single source that gave the loses for the Southern forces. A close guess came from the Wythe County Court House. Reb loses were approximately 14 killed, 31 wounded, and 7 prisoners.

Sometime after the fighting at Wytheville, the Union Cap. William H. Fortescue wrote "...and though I was afterwards on many hotly contested fields, I was never upon any that was more so than Wytheville".[54]

On the Confederate side Dr. Bagby of Richmond later described the Battle of Wytheville "as the bravest fight of the war".[55]

One of the Union dead should have been Col. William Powell. Both Union and Confederate surgeons agreed, he was "mortally wounded". Powell didn't follow his doctor's advice but improved under the care of a Wythe lady, Mrs. Spiller. Although his health was improving, he was still in danger. Jones from Dublin sent a telegraph to the War Department. He didn't want Powell exchanged for a Confederate prisoner in the north because he believed Powell was directly responsible for the burning of Austin Handey's house (a Confederate sympathizer) and barn near Lewisburg, West Virginia on January 10, 1863. Jones also stated that a prisoner had told him "...that this Col. Powell had given orders to burn Wytheville..." Jones concluded, "His conduct, as I understand it, was in violation of the laws of this state and the rules and useages of civilized warfare. (Therefore) ...he should be held to answer for his crime".[56]

He was transported to Richmond, first to a hospital and then to Libby Prison. He was placed in solitary confinement on charges of "robbery and murder".[57] Here he lingered not knowing his future.

The ladies of the area also nursed Southern soldiers in their homes until they could return to duty.

It is not known when Mrs. Toland received three of the most horrible words a government can write to a citizen. The War Department informed her that her husband was "killed in action".[58]

Mrs. Toland felt like most people North and South, that the very idea of their loved one being buried on enemy soil was repugnant. She and another officer's widow were escorted by Union troops (perhaps from the 34th Ohio) under a flag of truce. The empty wagons, the troops, and the ladies moved south out of West Virginia over some of the same roads the raiders had followed a few days before.

Mrs. Toland must have been touched and her burden lifted by the greetings she got from the Southern women as she made her tearful journey.

The same women whom her husband had terrorized a few days before were opening their hearts and homes to her. It seemed that the bond between women both North and South was greater than the hatred and fury of the war. The Southern women knew of Mrs. Toland's loneliness and pain. Rumor has it that she spent the night at Compton's house in Bland as she traveled to Wytheville.

The bodies of the Union dead were removed from the Catholic Cemetery and the empty wagons filled. Mrs. Toland again spent the night at the Compton's as she returned. Her husband's body may have spent the night in the parlor.

Toland and the last of the Union raiders left the Department of Southwest Virginia in pine boxes, under a flag of truce.

Part Two

The smoke and battle between the North and South had just cleared when a battle of words started between the commanders of the troops in the Department of Southwest Virginia.

McCausland filed his report from Princeton. In it he states "I am sure that some one is to blame for the escape of the enemy, I am also of the opinion that the cavalry that was in Tazewell, under Gen. Williams and Col. May (promoted from Major), was sufficient to have captured the enemy, *If it had been properly managed*...again, if Gen. Williams had moved with the celerity that the occasion required, and attacked the enemy in force, instead of skirmishing with his rear, he would have defeated them,...."[59]

To say the least Williams was upset because McCausland's report was so offending. He seems to call McCausland ignorant when he wrote "..., McCausland does me great injustice,... (he) knew nothing...and was not prepared to judge whether I was to blame or not". Although Williams was upset at McCausland he was livid toward Gen. Jones because Jones had sent McCausland's report to the War Department "without comment". Williams discovered that his report had not been forwarded to Richmond.

Williams wrote "Now, why McCausland's report about an affair with which he had but little, if anything; to do, but which reflected unjustly and injuriously upon me, should have been deemed by you (Jones) worthy of a place in the archives of the country, and my report on one of the most important military operations which had transpired in your whole department, and which was a complete vindication of myself and command from the unjust reports circulated by your personal staff, should have been lost among waste paper, and no effort made to retain a copy until the call of Congress, I will not undertake to decide".[60]

The state of affairs between Williams and Jones and his staff were a great deal less than desirable.

As a result of the raid the people knew that the war wasn't only at Richmond, Gettysburg, or far off Vicksburg, but that the war was also in Southwest Virginia. Their mountain communities were also open to attack. Most towns in Southwest Virginia began to take advantage of the Home Guard Act passed by the state of

Virginia in 1862. The citizen soldiers at Wytheville were among the first to sign up. No longer would the Yanks find the towns unorganized and defenseless. There would be a home guard to meet them. The home guard, of course, was mostly composed of those too young or too old to fight, but soldiers home on leave, those convalescing, and those partially disabled were expected to join the ranks in time of emergency.

State law didn't require that home guard units send a formal muster roll to Richmond. Very few home guard units did send in records, none from Southwest Virginia.

The local military commander (example the Department of Southwest Virginia - Gen. Jones) would encourage the formation of the home guard to increase strength in his area. He would also keep records on the strength of each unit.

On the national scene President Lincoln decided to follow the great Union victories of Vicksburg and Gettysburg with a political offense also. This would have an effect on events in Southwest Virginia the following year.

At the first of the war the North didn't protest Southern action toward colored soldiers. When the colored were captured often the Negro was returned to slavery, either for his master if the Negro could be identified, or to labor for the government or railroad.

Sometime during a battle colored troops might try to surrender. On occasions the white flag would not be recognized by the Southern troops who would adopt a "no quarter"[61] policy (kill them all) and the North had not protested.

By the middle of 1863 each side held a different view of the Negro soldier. To the North, he was a soldier regardless of background, and should be treated as such. (Even though the North treated them as inferiors, i.e. pay and leadership).

In the South they were viewed as mostly runaway or captured slaves. They were sent South to fight and kill their masters and owners. They were traitors to the master and the nation. They deserved only what was due a traitor, death. Being returned to slavery was an undeserved kindness.

These different views of the colored soldier made them a constant problem for both sides throughout the war.

Lincoln used this issue for his political advantage. On July 30, he announced that Reb prisoners would be put at "hard labor"[62] as punishment for the treatment of Union colored troops.

This played well to Northern abolitionist and in Europe where the South was desperately trying for formal recognition. Lincoln wanted the people of Europe to associate the Confederacy with cruel slavery, and not as a people wanting to throw off the heavy yoke of a government they opposed.

Lincoln wanted to reduce the power of the Northern peace movement (Copperheads). He was also worried about a pro-Southern armed rebellion that recently occurred in Ohio. He hoped this policy would help reduce domestic opposition to the war.

Lincoln's Secretary of War, Stanton, was delighted with the policy of punishment of the Rebs. He started with hard labor but went beyond. Reb prison camps became even more crowded and less sanitary. Torture was common. A policy deliberately denying the prisoner food and clothing was adopted.

While it was true that Northern prisoners in the South also received less than adequate food and clothing, it is to be remembered that the South could not adequately provide food and clothing to its army in the field. Could the South be expected to do more for the captured enemy than for her own army? Shouldn't the North provide better for the Southern prisoners when Blue Bellys seldom went hungry and often quail eggs and oysters were served at the officers mess?

The statistics reinforce the punishment policy. There were, during the war, approximately 270,000 Northern prisoners in the South and 220,000 Southern prisoners in the North. The South had approximately 50,000 more prisoners confined than did the North, but the total death and death rate were much lower in Southern prisons. Approximately 26,436 Southern soldiers died in Northern prison camps, while 22,576 Northern soldiers died in Southern camps. 3,860 more Rebs died, even though there were less Rebels in prison in the North.[63]

One source states the death rate for Northern soldiers in Southern prison camps was high, 9%, but the death rate for Southern soldiers in Northern prisons was an even higher 12%.[64]

There were many families in Southwest Virginia whose husband or son was listed as captured or missing. The figures were growing each day. When the people heard stories of the conditions of the prison camps, and the torture, they were in mental anguish for their loved ones.

J.B. West, one of Gen. John Morgan's men, was captured in Ohio in July, 1863. He later wrote about the prison camp and torture. He said there was little food and disease was rampant. In the winter prisoners were ordered to strip and were sent to sit in the snow. "Pointing for corn" was a favorite game the guards would play with Southern prisoners. The men were forced to remain stiff legged and bend over and touch the ground until they fainted.

It cost $5.00 to bribe a guard to escape. Some prisoners caught escaping were "Suspended by the thumbs...they (the prisoners) remained as dumb as oysters, although suspended until the balls of the thumbs absolutely burst open".[65]

Prisoners sometimes had to ride "John Morgan's Mule" (named in dishonor of Gen. Morgan whom the North feared and hated). It was a 2x4 20 feet long with the 2 inch side up. The soldiers were forced to ride.[66]

Ernest Holen Wart (Union) is one of the few persons qualified to address the issue from a personal basis. Early in the war he was captured and imprisoned. Later he was exchanged and spent the remainder of the war as a guard in a Northern prison camp. He recalled... (Southern guard's food) "not much better than our own (while he was a prisoner). Their treatment in prison was...good".[67] Even though being a prisoner was bad; it was worse in the North in his opinion.

In August Gen. John Floyd was back in Abingdon. He had been at the Confederate disaster of Fort Donelson. President Davis was upset because he and part of the other Virginians escaped and the Mississippi troops were made Federal prisoners.

Without court martial proceedings. Davis removed Floyd from command. Floyd did receive a commission as general from the state of Virginia but his health was gone.

He was in Abingdon for his appointment with death, which he kept on August 26, 1863.

John Floyd.

In the Department of Southwest Virginia. Jones was getting nervous about his job. Perhaps in part because of the bad relation with Williams, but he didn't mention this in his telegraph to the War Department on August 13. He said that citizens and soldiers were circulating petitions to get him replaced by Gen. John Echols. He couldn't understand why "...unless it be that I have undertaken no expedition of any magnitude against the enemy". He went on to say that he had been "...cursed with intrigued political plotters".[68] He had reason to worry about his job.

The next military action to occur in Southwest Virginia started from Cincinnati, Ohio. Captain Wilson and his 25 to 30 men were promised promotions if they succeeded in reaching and damaging the Virginia-Tennessee line. They were a small group and hoped to move undetected to their target. Once they entered the Department they quit traveling by day and marched by night. They used a compass to keep their bearing in the dark. To say the least it is difficult to move in a straight line direction over mountains, streams, and through thickets.

They moved undetected along the Sandy River to Tazewell County. While they were resting during the day near Horse Pen, Charles Taylor discovered them and they drew a bead on him with their rifles.

It was still a gentlemen's war in some respects. Taylor was released unharmed after he had taken an oath not to tell of their presence.

Patsy Hall was also captured and released on her oath. The old woman forgot her oath quickly and James Sheffey of Marion called out the home guard.

The guard moved toward the Hungry Mother section where the Yanks had been spotted. Cap. Joseph Thomas was leading the troops at 1:00 A.M. when they saw the Yanks cross the road and disappear into the woods. Because Thomas had been hurt the day before by falling from his horse he was unable to pursue the raiders on foot. He turned the command over to Lt. James McDonald.

McDonald followed the Yanks down the south of the mountain to a stream about one-third of a mile.

Here the Yanks were "Roasting green corn..." on an open fire.

Jonathan Olinger, who was over age 60, spotted the Yanks first and fired on them.

There was an exchange of gunfire in the darkness. John Atwell of the home guard was wounded in the thigh, as the raiders scattered. Before day break the guard had 14 prisoners.

Two of the Yanks that scattered met up with Stephen Groseclose who was home on leave. They gave themselves up to him saying, "We tried to surrender to the home guard, but the damn fools kept on firing so we broke and ran and we are mighty glad to find a Confederate soldier to whom we can surrender."[69]

The remainder of the raiding party apparently escaped. The South did capture two Union compasses and no damage was done to the railroad.

Louise Leslie, in her history of Tazewell, mentions the "Battle of Ward's Cove",[70] but gives no dates or details; only that the enemy was heading for Saltville when encountered.

Although Southwest Virginia had no major military action before the year ended, Jones made some use of the home guard. For example, on August 24, Giles Cooke, Assistant - Adjutant - General from Dublin, alerted the guard in Southwest Virginia. To Major Kent at Wytheville, he telegraphed that the enemy was last heard from yesterday at Warm Springs. He believed the Federals "...will make a raid on some point on the railroad...most probably New River bridge...there is no telling when Wytheville will be threatened from Prestonsburg or from another point on your front. This information is given that you may be ready for any move they make".

Jones must have felt he needed the guard because later that same day Maj. Kent received another wire, "Have your guns and ammo. issued to your command immediately. The enemy's cavalry 1,200 strong are reported advancing on New River bridge. Hold your command in readiness to move at a moment's warning".[71]

It is uncertain if any of the guard units moved to Dublin to defend the bridge, but the expected attack didn't materialize.

During the first of September the people of Southwest Virginia witnessed the largest single mass movement of troops that had ever occurred in this section. Gen. Lee had detached Gen. James Longstreet (Lee's "War Horse") and sent him to join Gen. Braxton Bragg near Chattanooga. Longstreet moved his 11,000[72] man corps, including cannon and horses for the cavalry, by rail. In Bristol the general held a troop review for the citizens.

The people of Southwest Virginia had to sacrifice. The government was "Impressing" all grains "...except 5 bushels of grain and 50 pounds of beef or bacon to each adult of the family, and one half of the quantity for those under 14 years of age, for use by Gen. Longstreet's force..."[73] Most people gave willingly.

On September 9, Rebecca Lynch and Elizabeth Murray were with two Confederate soldiers when the thunder storm struck. The four took shelter under a tree. Lightning struck and all four families grieved.

James Longstreet "Old Pete".

The South began strengthening defenses at the saltworks. Eighty slaves were assigned to the task. In addition, on September 16, two Confederate home guard companies were organized at Abingdon.

Toward the last of October, about 200 mounted Yanks and at least one battery of artillery moved from Rogerville, Tennessee through Hunter's Gap to Jonesville, the seat of Lee County. On the way to town they burned Sim's Mill.

Apparently the South was unaware of this movement and sent no troops to oppose the column. They occupied the town on the 27th.

Henry Morgan was the Clerk of the Court. When he heard the Federals were near, he removed most of the papers from the court house.

James Orr recalls that he was at Ben Hur in Poor Valley when he received news that the Yanks were at Jonesville. Orr was wounded at Sharpsburg (Antetium) and was now a recruiter for the army.

He joined a group of about 40 men and moved toward Jonesville on the morning of the 28th.

On that morning the Yanks were busy burning. The Franklin Academy went up in smoke. Apparently the South had used it as a hospital, now there was one less in the department. The courthouse was torched, but thanks to Morgan's actions few records were destroyed.

The group of 40 men moved down the town branch, and they apparently captured a few Yanks without firing a shot. As they moved closer to town a Union picket was spotted. Apparently someone in the group fired a single shot at the Yanks.

The nervous Union commander didn't wait to see the size of the group or form a line. The 200 with their artillery ran toward Cumberland Gap.

Orr and some of the group of 40 chased the Yanks. In the afternoon they sighted the rear guard. It is not clear if any shots were exchanged. Here the South stopped and built a breastworks of "logs and rails"[74] in case the North returned. They didn't.

By the end of the year, Longstreet's corps headed east via the rails in Southwest Virginia. This time it was not a joyous ride. They rode in defeat. The inept Bragg and Gen. Thomas (a Virginian that stayed with the Union) combined to turn a sure Southern victory to a loss.

There was some good news for Southwest Virginia. The Union Gen. Stephen Gano Burbridge from the Military District of Kentucky, was helping Gen. William's recruitment drive immensely. "...Burbridge was actively loathed by a majority of the population over whom he had extensive civil and military powers".[75] His despotic actions when he suppressed civil rights, closed pro-Southern newspapers, burned homes, and persecuted suspected Southern sympathizers, earned him the people's disrespect. One author said it was as if Kentucky seceded after the war was half over.

More and more Kentucky boys joined Williams and John Morgan hoping to take their state out of the Union. Because of Lee's defeat at Gettysburg more troops were moved from Southwest Virginia, and increasingly Kentucky men guarded this section of the State.

As winter approached a certain routine seemed to have repeated itself but with different players. The local children had jobs caring for the cavalry horses. There were no major battles foreseen so the large armies were disbursed. In Tazewell County "Camp Georgia" was occupied by men of the 45th Virginia Battalion (Beckley's Battalion). Food and fodder were more plentiful in the country. McCausland sent part of his horses to North Carolina for the winter.

The blockade had squeezed tighter. There were acute shortages of manufactured goods, but people were making do. The item the citizens seemed to miss most was coffee. The only coffee coming into the Confederacy was small amounts that had been swapped for tobacco between the warring soldiers. People tried to find substitutes for coffee. They used chestnuts, rio, dried apples, toasted wheat, sweet potatoes, rye, seed of the sorghum, and sugar cane.

Yank scouting parties were seen more often in Southwest Virginia. There weren't enough troops to keep them out. Mostly they treated the citizens with respect, but often they stole and burned.

The lack of food was hurting the war effort. Poor rations led to disease and desertion. Letters from home may not have been full of hope and excitement for the war as they were in 1861. Often women wrote begging their husbands and sons to desert and come home to protect and feed them. It was a call many answered. The deserting rate increased dramatically from late 1863 to the end of the war.

"If the diet of the Union soldiers was bad, that of the Confederate was wretched".[76] The Southern soldiers main course was cornbread, fried in a pan, and salt beef ("salt horse" as the soldiers called it). The meat was of poor quality and had to be soaked or boiled to remove the salt before it could be eaten.

Salt was a large bottle neck in the supply line. Without salt and with slow transportation (the railroads were deteriorating because of the lack of labor and manufactured parts) thousands of pounds of meat were rotting before it could get to the soldiers.

The Union recognized the shortage of salt in the South and had tried to increase their enemy's problem. They were doing a good job. Salt was so scarce that the cargo holds of blockade runners may be filled with the precious substance.

George Trenholm was a blockade runner from Charleston in 1863, later he was Secretary of the Treasury. He told of one of his incoming shipments in late 1863 "...the Confederacy got arms, munitions, *salt*, and other necessities of life and war".[77]

The morale of the Southern people was sinking. It had been a bad year and 1864 held no great promises that the people could see. The president, Jefferson Davis, left Richmond on December 10, and traveled to Knoxville and then South. Although no record was found, it is almost certain the president stopped at all major towns in Southwest Virginia as he passed through. He would give a patriotic speech at Dublin, Wytheville, Abingdon, and Bristol. His unshakeable belief in the "cause" and in ultimate victory must have encouraged the people.

President Davis had only left Southwest Virginia when the 16th Illinois Cavalry came in. They pushed from Kentucky to Jonesville in far Southwest Virginia. The 64th Regiment under Col. Slemp was forced to evacuate the area. There was little

Artist's Concept of Bridge over Reed Creek, west of Wytheville.

fighting. It was more numbers and marching. The Federals had the biggest number so Slemp withdrew.

So it was a miserable Christmas in the Department of Southwest Virginia. There were Yanks occupying the Department's territory, food and everything else, it seemed, was in short supply.

Where were those gay boys who marched off to the short, glorious war in 1861? Who are those badly clothed men with sunken eyes and cheeks, who gather silently around the cider bowl? Where are the husbands, friends, and neighbors? Are they shivering in the cold night air at the front? Are they prisoner in some Yankee dungeon? Are they a corpse under foreign soil, or disabled or dying? Or are they missing and God only knows their state?

Christmas 1863 wasn't merry but the men still fought and God would see that their righteous Southern Cause would not fail!

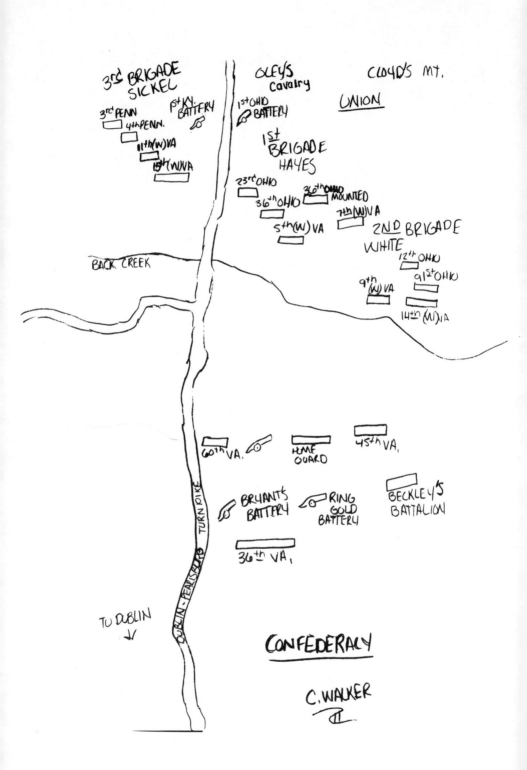

3rd BRIGADE SICKEL

3rd PENN
4th PENN.
1st KY. BATTERY
11th (W)VA
15th WVA

OLEY'S Cavalry

1st OHIO BATTERY

CLOYD'S MT.

UNION

1st BRIGADE HAYES

23rd OHIO
36th OHIO
36th OHIO MOUNTED
5th (W) VA
7th (W)VA

2ND BRIGADE WHITE

12th OHIO
9th (W)VA
91st OHIO
14th (W)VA

BACK CREEK

60th VA.
HOME GUARD
45th VA.

BRYANT'S BATTERY
RING GOLD BATTERY
BECKLEY'S BATTALION

36th VA.

TURN PIKE

DUBLIN · PEARISBURG

TO DUBLIN

CONFEDERACY

C. WALKER

Chapter VI

1864

While some of the soldiers in the Department of Southwest Virginia enjoyed Christmas, others were on the move. Gen. Jones was determined to remove the 16th Illinois from his command.

The soldiers may have received the good news as they traveled toward the Kentucky - Tennessee line, that their pay had been raised by the Confederate government. The privates would no longer receive $11 a month, now their pay was increased to $18. There were similar raises in all grades. This was a help but with an inflation rate of 300% in the South during the war, the soldiers were still far behind.

On the 3rd of January, it was bitter cold as Jones attacked Jonesville with the 8th Virginia and some cavalry. He combined forces with the 64th which was forced out on the 31st.

Because the 64th knew the area, they were Jones' eyes. A group of the 64th under Col. A.L. Pridemore moved along the town branch. When they spotted a Union cannon they withdrew up to the top of the hill, and sent word to Jones.

There were also citizens, women and children, that had fled the town to the hill. James Orr, operating with the 64th, claimed that the Union fired their cannon at the civilians and they "...Scattered like...a gang of geese".[1]

Orr and Bob Woodward suggested to Col. Pridemore that they be allowed to move to another ridge to get a better view of the enemy. Pridemore gave his consent, and the two rode to the ridge. When the Yanks spotted them, the cannon was fired at them. They observed the Union position quickly and moved off the ridge.

Jones felt he knew enough and attacked the town from the east on the Harlan Road.

The action was over quickly. The North didn't offer much resistance. Apparently most of them ran. Maj. Beers couldn't. He was surrounded so he raised a white flag. The South also captured 3 cannons and a number of wagons. Southern loses were put at 4 killed, and 7 wounded,[2] while the Yanks lost about 40 killed and wounded plus those captured.[3] It is likely that the Union dead were stripped of clothing. Everything was in short supply in the Southern army. A good pair of shoes was of great value.

After the battle, Pridemore stood on a stump and gave a speech. He told the men how proud he was of them and their "gallantry".[4]

Besides those lost in action, one or two of Jones' men were "...frozen to death.."[5] The South gave blankets to the captured Yanks as they were being transported to prison at Richmond.

The command was free of the enemy.

Maybe 1864 would be a year of Southern victory; maybe 1863 was the South's "Valley Forge". Maybe the foreign powers would officially recognize the Confederacy, and the war cease, and Johnny could return home in peace. These were the thoughts of many Southerners. All eyes were fixed on Richmond. As long as Richmond held there was hope. The hope of the nation was with Gen. Lee and his Army of Northern Virginia as he defended the capitol. Without Southwest Virginia Lee could not fight. Lee's lead came from Southwest Virginia. Lee's food was preserved with Southwest Virginia salt, so that Southwest Virginia was as important to the cause as was Richmond.

On January 28, the Yanks destroyed another important saltworks at St. Andrews Bay, Florida.

On the financial front the South was not doing well. Gold was the world's standard of wealth. The South started the war with little of the precious metal. A great deal of that amount had been sent overseas to pay for arms.

To try to finance the war effort the government had been forced to borrow more and more from its own people. Taxes were not enough to finance the army. Southerners by the thousands invested all they could afford in government bonds. The price of the bonds fluctuated wildly as battle reports were issued. A major Southern victory increased people's confidence and the price of the bonds would increase. Unfortunately Southern victories were infrequent so the value of the bonds continued decreasing.

Because the central government had little gold reserves it could not issue enough paper money for the economy. Banking laws were established so that local banks could issue paper bills backed by gold, silver, land, or a promise.

Very soon almost every bank was issuing paper money. The denomination of the bills ranged from $1.00 to $1,000.

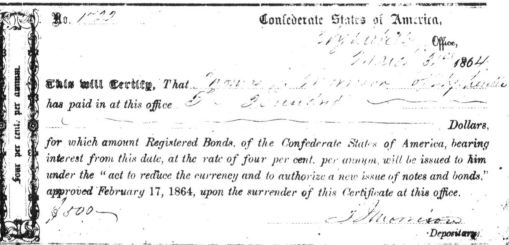

Because of the fluctuation in the bond markets and the tremendous variety of currency in circulation, it was difficult to know what the actual value (buying power) of the money was. The people of the South began to peg the value of their money to the value of Northern currency. (For example: it might take $3 worth of currency from the South-Western Bank of Virginia at Wytheville to equal $1 Yankee money). There was a great deal of Union currency in circulation in the Southern economy.

Because the South had no mints to make coinage there was a shortage of change. The people turned to the post office as a solution. Uncanceled postage stamps were used as nickels, dimes, and quarters to make change. Unfortunately Southern stamp printing facilities could not keep up with demand. So stamps were scarce.

By the end of the war the Post Master at each post office would write the amount he received and his signature on the envelope because he had no stamps.

Times were hard in Southwest Virginia because the men were off fighting. Many of those who were left behind couldn't feed themselves. Over 1,200 in Smyth County alone needed public assistance.

Desertion was an increasing problem. To deal with it, executions were increasing. On February 5, Jacob Mullen of Wise County, met his maker. "He was sitting upon his coffin with his fingers in his ears when the order to fire was given".6

Despite his victory at Jonesville in January, Gen. Jones' critics were too numerous and too loud.

Brig. Gen. John Williams took his dispute all the way to the president. Apparently McCausland felt Williams had not acted with much vigor in opposing Toland in 1863. Jones endorsed McCausland's report and sent it to Richmond. Williams states "...McCausland does me great injustice, but you did me a greater injustice..." The generals in Southwest Virginia were at war with one another.

In October of 1863, Williams sent a telegraph to Jones informing him of 5,000 enemy at his front at Cumberland Gap. To which Jones replied, "If the enemy had 5,000...., they would have driven you away long before this". Williams told the president that Jones thought "...that I (Williams) had not intelligence enough to estimate the strength of an enemy...., or that I had not spirit enough to fight...I was intensely enraged..." Williams said he was "determined to fight...., if it cost my country and the last man..."

Williams went on to accuse Jones of deliberately withholding information about policies and troop deployment in the Department. He said Jones simply didn't forward his reports to the war office "...my report...should have been lost among waste paper..."7

Williams enclosed letters from Col. Bowen, Lt. Peyton, Cap. Everett, and Ruffner supporting his position.

It was abundantly clear to the president from the lengthy report, that Jones wasn't doing a good job. On March 5th, Jones was removed from command. He was replaced by a man who wore many hats during his life, John Cabel Breckinridge.

Breckinridge was a lawyer from Kentucky. At age 35 he was the Vice President of the United States, under Buchanan. He served in the Kentucky state legislature and the U.S. House of Representatives. He was a candidate for president in the 1860 election.

His heart was broken when Kentucky didn't secede. In November 1861 he joined the army as a Brigadier General. Until recently he had been with Bragg and Longstreet at Chattanooga.

John Cabel Breckinridge.

When Gen. Bragg tried to rationalize his poor generalship and defeat, he blamed everyone except himself for the defeat. He accused Breckinridge "of being drunk and unfit for duty..."[8] Breckinridge was sent from Tennessee to take command of Southwest Virginia. His choice was a logical one. Most of the regular army soldiers defending the area were Kentucky's sons. It was logical that a Kentuckian should command. State pride and state's rights were not just empty words during the war.

On April 1, President Davis proclaimed another day of fasting, prayer, and humiliation. The Cause needed God's help.

The Federals were again successful when they destroyed the big saltworks at Wilmington, North Carolina on April 21st. Saltville became more important to the cause. By the end of April, salt from Washington County was being exchanged for food from Tennessee. The South was starving.

Breckinridge hadn't got his seat warm as commander of the Department when he received orders to move as much of his command as possible to the Valley of Virginia to support Gen. Jubal Early.

Gen. Franz Sigel (Union) was moving down the valley and threatening this important bread basket and the railroad that connected it with Richmond and Southwest Virginia. If the North could capture and hold this valley and railroads they would cut off Lee's food, salt, and lead; Richmond would fall!

Lee at Richmond couldn't spare one soldier as he faced the "Great Hammer", Grant. Southern defenses were stretched thin. Southwest Virginia would not be well defended. The Federals were well aware of this fact. They would attack Southwest Virginia and try to destroy the saltworks, lead mines, and railroad. The manpower, the fire power, and odds were in their favor in the spring of 1864.

The command of Southwest Virginia was well aware of Northern desires to invade. Before Breckinridge left for the valley he sent Gen. Lee a telegram on May 1st. In it he stated that he knew Union Cavalry under Gen. Averell was on the Kanawha and believed he would attempt to strike somewhere on the Tennessee Virginia Railroad. He even suggested Averell might follow Col. Toland's path into Southwest Virginia.

The very mention of Morgan's name sent cold chills down the back of any Union soldier that might have to fight his command. No other Southern cavalry general was so hated and feared as was Morgan.

Although Morgan was born in Huntsville, Alabama, he was raised and educated in Lexington, Kentucky. His heart was in the bluegrass country and he was a Kentuckian.

He was daring to the point of being reckless at times. His men were known for their courage and savagery.

Morgan's second in command was his brother-in-law, Basil Duke. Many considered him the brains behind Morgan's success. Together they terrorized the Yanks in Tennessee, Kentucky, Indiana, and Ohio.

On Morgan's most famous raid into Ohio, he seized the union telegraph and sent messages using a fictitious Union officer's name. The Union commanders were confused and disputed instead of consolidating against Morgan. This allowed him to attack smaller Federal units as he laid a path of destruction across Ohio. The people of that state were learning what the war was about.

A small town gave Morgan's brother-in-law, Duke, a very stiff fight before it was conquered. Because the few defenders had fought well and inflicted so many casualties on his men, Duke lay waste to the town and left it in ashes.

As Morgan moved deeper into Ohio he found his escape paths south constantly blocked. As he raced for his life across Ohio more and more of his command was cut off. Many of these cut off units were captured, others made their way south to safety anyway they could.

Morgan didn't make it back to safety. He was captured near New Lisbon, Ohio and sent to the Ohio State Penitentiary. At the Ohio Penitentiary he didn't receive the kind of treatment an officer of his rank would traditionally expect. Officers were treated better than common soldiers as a rule. Morgan was confined in the inner recesses of the prison where the sun didn't shine. His food was horrible and his clothes were soon covered with green mold. His hatred of the Yankees grew.

Morgan and his men didn't like being the guests of the state of Ohio and decided to have a coming out party. They dug 23 feet (six of it through granite walls of the prison) and escaped in a rain storm on November 26, 1863. Morgan's brother-in-law, Duke, didn't escape with him because he was at another prison camp. Duke was later exchanged.

With the help of some Ohio ladies whose sympathies were with the South, Morgan was back in the Confederacy by December 1863.

Morgan and his men had been helping Bragg near Knoxville until the telegraph arrived. So Morgan moved his command by train toward Southwest Virginia at the first of May. The Yanks knew Breckinridge was leaving, but they didn't know Morgan was coming.

John Hunt Morgan.

By May 2nd, Breckinridge established an advanced headquarters at the college of V.M.I. in Lexington, and was assessing the situation that confronted him.

Even though Breckinridge was at Lexington, he was still the commander of the Department of Southwest Virginia, so W.E. "Grumble" Jones informed him of a cavalry build-up that was reported in Logan County.

On the third, Gen. John Echols informed Breckinridge that his "two best scouts"[9] had just returned. They reported that Averell was on the Kanawha and believed the Union was going to strike both at Saltville and the New River bridge at Radford.

On the 3rd, Grumble Jones informed Breckinridge that he was moving to Jeffersonville (Tazewell) that Morgan could defend the saltworks when he arrived.

Also on the 3rd, Jefferson Davis notified Gen. Lee of his official concern over the events taking place in Southwest Virginia. Gen. Lee had been fighting an army many times his size to a stand still in a series of battles known as the Wilderness Campaign. Lee couldn't spare time or men for Southwest Virginia.

By the 4th, Breckinridge had completed his assessment of the situation in the valley. It was desperate. He told Bragg that he was moving "My whole force"[10] to the valley to repel Gen. Sigel. McCausland's command was the largest part of his force he was moving east. McCausland was ordered to withdraw to Dublin and entrain. When he did this, the area from Summers County through Princeton to Dublin was open to invasion. Only Gen. Albert C. Jenkin's small cavalry stood in opposition.

Franz Sigel.

On the 5th, Breckinridge, in effect, placed Gen. W.E. Jones in command of Southwest Virginia when he notified him that he was heading east and told Jones to mind the store. No formal order was issued to the effect that Jones was in command but he did tell Jenkins to inform Jones of any moves in your area. Breckinridge apparently didn't know Morgan was moving toward Southwest Virginia.

On the 5th things were starting to heat up in Southwest Virginia. Cap. James S.A. Crawford, Company F, 17th Virginia Cavalry, reported from Rocky Gap to Gen. Jenkins. He said the North had driven him back from Princeton because McCausland had withdrawn. The Yanks had driven his sharpshooters off the mountain tops. He was sending a detachment of men to Narrows, the rest would fall back on Wytheville. Jenkins must have been upset because he believed the Yanks were heading toward Saltville and Dublin to New River. No attack was anticipated on Wytheville. Now part of the too few troops that could defend Southwest Virginia were uselessly on their way to Wytheville.

Southern intelligence reports were correct. The Yanks were coming and they were going to attack Saltville and the long bridge over New River.

Gen. George Crook was in overall command. He would remain with the main force composed mostly of infantry, and send the head of the cavalry for the Department of West Virginia, Gen. William Woods Averell, to attack Saltville.

George Crook.

Crook had three assembled brigades. The first brigade was commanded by a future president, Col. Rutherford B. Hayes, and was composed of the 23rd, and 36th Ohio Volunteer Infantry; part of 34th Ohio Volunteer Mountain Infantry; and the 5th and 7th Virginia Cavalry (West Virginia) mounted. Another future president served as a lieutenant with the 23rd Ohio, William McKinley.

The 2nd brigade was under Col. C.B. White. It was composed of the 12th and 91st Ohio Volunteer Infantry, the 9th Virginia (West Virginia) Infantry, and the 14th Volunteer Indiana.

The third brigade was under Col. H.G. Sickel. His brigade was made of the 3rd and 4th Pennsylvania Reserve Volunteer Corps, and the 11th and 15th Virginia (West) Virginia Infantry.

There were two artillery units attached to Crook's command. The First Ohio Battery under Cap. J.R. McMullin and the First Kentucky Battery under Cap. D.W. Glassie. They had a total of 12 guns.

Crook's army of 6,155[11] didn't attack the South immediately. He sent several units to the east as if he were going to form a juncture with Sigel in the valley. Southern scouts immediately sent word of these movements to their commanders. Breckinridge must have felt that Crook was going to the Valley of Virginia so he didn't hesitate in ordering McCausland to leave Southwest Virginia and join him.

Because McCausland withdrew to Dublin to entrain east, Crook had an easy time moving from Fayetteville to Princeton. At Princeton he reported running a small band of Virginia cavalry toward Rock Gap. This was Cap. Crawford's command.

Crook didn't have to fight for Princeton like Cox had in 1862, nor did he stop as Scammon did in 1863. He pressed on toward his objective on the New River. Crook knew how few men the South had. He not only wanted to engage and destroy that force; he wanted to lay waste to Southwest Virginia, "So as to render that country untenable to the enemy."[12]

To help him in the destruction of Southwest Virginia, he ordered Averell, a West Pointer, to make a lightning strike against Saltville and, "Destroy that place."[13]

Averell had his 2,479 "pick men" as he left Camp Piatt near Charleston on the Kanawha on May 1st. In Logan County Averell sent the supply wagons toward Charleston. His men carried 6 days rations and 4 days rations for the horses as they continued south. At Logan, Averell's strength was increased as he was joined by part of the 3rd (West) Virginia under Major Conger.

Averell had his first contact with the South in Wyoming County when they chased a Reb scouting party. Averell knew he had been spotted, but would the South guess he was heading to Saltville?

William Woods. Averell (seated) and staff.

Perhaps to decoy the Southern scouts he sent J.H. Oley and 400 men toward Princeton and Crook. Maybe the South would think that the cavalry was consolidating with Crook for an attack on New River. Maybe Saltville would be unguarded.

Averell was following the same route as Col. Toland had taken a year before. Averell came dashing down Abb's Valley with nearly the same results as Toland. Like Toland, Averell was able to surprise and capture the Southern soldiers that were supposed to be watching for the approach of Northern forces. Two companies of the 8th Virginia Cavalry were engaged on the evening of the 7th. When the smoke cleared 20 Reb soldiers were Yankee prisoners.

Averell made camp in Abb's Valley that evening. Col. Abe Cook, the commander of what was left of the 8th Virginia, watched Averell that night and sent information back to Gen. Williams near Saltville.

On the morning of the 8th, Averell continued to move toward Tazewell Courthouse, at a place called Five Oaks. About 15 miles from Tazewell his march was interrupted. Apparently a small band of Southern troops, some of them probably from Kentucky, lay in ambush. Before they knew what had happened 4 Yanks lay dead and 5 wounded. The Southerners apparently high-tailed it before the Yanks could catch them.

(Reportedly one of these Yanks was buried in the garden of C.H. Greever. A neighbor later asked if it bothered him to have a Yank buried in his garden? Greever's reply was "No, ding it, I wish they were all in there".)[14]

Averell met no further resistance as he rode to and through Tazewell Courthouse at Jeffersonville. Averell was at the home of Confederate Cap. W.E. Peery about one and one half miles outside of town by 12:00.

At Cap. Peery's home he captured several Southern soldiers including Thomas Hankins, Alvert Peery, James Freeman, and John Waldren. All except Hankins were released very soon.[15]

It cannot be stated for certain that Hankins or any of the other soldiers talked but someone did talk to the enemy general. The person who gave the information had to be someone who was in a position to know, maybe a well informed Northern sympathizer, or maybe a soldier? Whoever it was that talked, Averell listened.

What Averell heard scared his "pants off". Not only did the Southern commanders know that he was on his way there, and know his strength, but they had invited some unexpected people to greet Averell's force when it arrived. Gen. John Morgan and his "terrible men"[16] were at Saltville. There was now a total of 4,500 men in fortifications and backed by artillery.

He arrived at the Peery home around 12:00 A.M. and didn't leave until 12:00 P.M. That was twelve precious hours that he lost. As a West Pointer he knew that time was a commodity of war and should not be wasted.

It was obvious that an attack on Saltville would be a disaster. Averell was consoled by the fact that Morgan, Jones, and Williams were holding their forces at Saltville to oppose him; they weren't consolidating against Crook who was now approaching Dublin.

The most logical target to attack was Wytheville, for the same reasons Toland had attacked the year before, plus it would separate Morgan from Crook. If Wytheville weren't to be attacked, then Averell should consolidate with Crook. Too much time went crawling by before a decision was made.

Because Breckinridge was in the valley, there was no one man in charge of the Department. The commanders tried to organize as much as possible to meet the superior forces that were marching against both sides of the Department.

Morgan was at Saltville, nothing more could be done there. The home guard units were being called out and assembled near the saltworks.

Meanwhile Jenkins was falling back toward Dublin. This small force of Virginia cavalry, perhaps 200, were no match for Crook's three brigades and 12 guns. Jenkins, on the 7th, notified C.S. Stringfellow, the Adjutant General at Dublin, that military stores there were "in danger".[17]

Stringfellow in turn notified Breckinridge that the enemy was at Rocky Gap and that he had "notified the various post-offices west of this place".[18] That is to say that the home guard had been called out.

Also on the 7th Stringfellow received a telegram from Jones at Saltville. He informed Stringfellow that Saltville was safe from Averell's expected cavalry attack. He told Stringfellow that "Sufficient force should be at lead mines to keep off cavalry. Instruct it to hold houses and *fight to the last...*"[19]

These were the orders sent to the home guard at Wytheville, "Fight to the last". The unit under Kent moved to the mines. No attack was anticipated on Wytheville, but Northern forces were approaching Dublin. New orders were sent to the home guard at the lead mines in Austinville. Proceed toward Dublin. They started toward Dublin and battle.

The hours of May 8 were almost gone. Near Tazewell Courthouse Averell had finally made his decision, he would move toward Wytheville. Maybe he believed that by moving out around midnight, he would give the Reb scouts that were watching his troops the slip. If this was his intent, it failed. As Averell's 2,500 started moving toward Burkes Garden in the last few minutes of May 8, Reb scouts raced to Saltville with the news.

It was the early morning of the 9th when the news arrived at Saltville. The generals knew that Wytheville and the lead mines were Averell's next logical target. If Wytheville were to be saved, every second must count. The generals also knew that a battle was shaping up at Dublin.

Morgan moved his command with great speed and efficiency. At Abingdon he entrained 500 of his men under Col. D. Howard Smith and sent them toward Dublin. That was all the men he could get aboard the train. With any luck the train would be there in time for the battle.

At the same time Morgan was entraining 500 men, he was sending the rest of his command east via the Rock Road at a gallop. The 500 horses that the 500 men on the train couldn't take were probably used as relief mounts for his men galloping toward Wytheville.

Sometime before dawn the train derailed. This was probably due to bad maintenance resulting from the war or to overcrowding on the train. This delay would be critical to the battle shaping up at Dublin.

For some unknown reason Averell didn't follow the course Toland had taken the year before through Burkes Garden to Wytheville. He continued down Clear Fork toward Bland courthouse. This delay would be critical to the battle shaping up at Wytheville.

As Averell was moving toward the courthouse at Bland, Crook was moving in toward Dublin.

On the 6th, Crook received hard intelligence that McCausland had left Southwest Virginia and started toward Lewisburg. This confirmed that the South had gone for the fake troop movement he had arranged at Fayetteville. The path was wide open. His army, mostly infantry, marched 45 miles in the next two days.

The Northern column stretched 3 miles along the valley floor. It's movement only slowed by the 10th of May cold spell (cold rain and wet snow).

Crook rolled along toward Dublin. He pushed Jenkins's small cavalry along in front of him. Jenkins watched Crook but made no attempt to stop him.

The home guard was called out of church in Christiansburg, and told to form. At the Dublin Presbyterian Church the Reverend William P. Hickman "urged his congregation to rally to the Confederate cause".[20] Even though he was over age he left the pulpit to join the volunteers.

By the evening of the 8th, Crook was at Shannon's bridge, 7 miles from Dublin, on the west slope of Cloyd's Mountain. That evening he was joined by Col. J.H. Oley and the 400 men of the 7th (West) Virginia, Virginia cavalry that Averell had detached in Wyoming County.

Oley's command added to Crooks ability to reconnoiter the enemy and out flank him.

While at Shannon's Bridge, Crook received intelligence that the South was massing troops at the top of the mountain. This was not unexpected, the South wouldn't give up its military headquarters and the all important New River Bridge without a fight.

The South was indeed starting to mass its troops. McCausland had made a decision to delay in executing the orders he had received from Breckinridge. McCausland was at the railroad depot with the 36th Virginia Infantry and Col. Benhring Jones of the 60th Virginia while Bryant's artillery was being entrained. McCausland halted the artillery on loading with the command "...to prepare at once to march and to be ready for action".[21]

Adj. Gen. Stringfellow at Dublin attempted to keep Breckinridge at Lexington informed of events occurring in the Department. On the 8th he telegraphed "...we will give them a warm reception here...unless enemy display greater activity and skill, we will not be driven off..."

To set Breckinridge's mind more at ease a telegram was sent saying, "Mrs. Breckinridge left in ambulance".[22] She would be safe.

That evening McCausland moved to the gap on top of Cloyd's Mountain, here he formed a battle line. That evening he was also joined by Ringgold's Battery (4 guns) and Beckley's Infantry Battalion. Some say the Rebs could see the campfires of the Yanks down the mountain.

The men of both sides knew what was going to happen tomorrow.

In the morning Stringfellow sent another telegraph message to Breckinridge "...Pickets been firing two hours,...North fire 6 or 8 cannon shot...it will be two hours before fight open fairly. Our men in splendid spirits, anxious for the fight, and perfectly confident".[23]

What Stringfellow didn't say was that Jenkins moving up the mountain had met McCausland and inspected his line of battle. Jenkins took command and ordered that a new line be formed further from Dublin. A "sharp dispute"[24] took place between the two generals. McCausland was overruled. McCausland may not have agreed with Jenkins, but he followed orders.

It was after 10:00 on Monday, May 9th, a sunny day, when the decision was made to form another battle line. The second line chosen was also on the farm of James Cloyd on Cloyd's Mountain. James helped the South as a scout watching Crook's movements. Now that the battle was here, James moved his family from the farm and joined the Southern line. He would fight for his land and country.

By now a telegram had arrived stating that Morgan was sending additional soldiers. It was hoped that they would arrive before the enemy did.

Jenkins started deploying the troops. The 36th was the reserve force. It was placed to the right of the road (Dublin-Pearisburg Pike) and behind a knoll.

One, three inch rifled gun from the Ringgold Battery under Cap. Crispin Dickenson and the 6 guns of Bryant's Battery under Cap. Thomas Bryant were placed in front of the 36th.

Two, twelve pound Napoleon guns from the Ringgold Artillery were placed on higher ground to the right. They could cover 1,500 feet toward the bottom of the mountain. (See map page 70.)

The 60th Virginia was placed on the right side of the road on a small wooded hill. On this hill Jenkins placed the last 12 pounder under Lt. W.A. Hoge. Lt. William H. Lipscomb and 29 of his men were assigned to defend the gun.

Corp. White G. Ryan commanded the home guard and volunteers along the ridge to the right of the gun.

The 45th Virginia was placed next to the home guard. Beckley's Battalion of 183 men took position on a hill to the rear of the 45th. The line was ready. It stretched about one half-mile.

The North had broken camp at 5:00. With the band playing they marched towards battle. As the army moved up the mountain, Southern skirmishers fell back.

When Crook got to the top of the mountain he said, "The enemy is in force and in a strong position. He may whip us, but I guess not".[25]

Crook used an escaped slave to guide White's 2nd Brigade. The slave's knowledge of the area allowed the brigade to move unseen to the right side of the Southern line.

First Brigade deployed next to 2nd; and 3rd formed on the right of the First Brigade. Oley's 400 cavalry men that came from Averell were kept in reserve.

The 36th Ohio was supposed to assemble behind the 23rd Ohio but got lost in the woods. The 36th found themselves on the line when the battle opened, not supporting the 23rd.

The stage was set. 2,400 regulars, home guard, and volunteers were on the line for the South. They were supported by 10 guns. The North had 6,555 battle seasoned veterans and 12 guns against them. The generals and men knew it was make or break time for both sides. What took place on these few acres of land in the next few minutes would determine whether the Yankee army would flee North for its life, or if its military headquarters for the South and the long bridge would be destroyed. The men on both sides were ready to do their duty. The ultimate struggle, life against life, was about to begin.

Re-creation of Union infantry forming battle line.

Around 11:00 a brief artillery duel began. Then a deathly quiet set in as the North started their advance. The battle was on.

The North's 2nd Brigade attacked with the 14th West Virginia and 12th Ohio. The thick underbrush disrupted the effectiveness of the charge, but the numbers were enough. The Southern defenders were forced back 175 yards to the main breastwork (trench line).

The North laid a heavy volume of fire on the South as they advanced. The 14th West Virginia got to within 20 yards of the breastwork before they were halted. One attacker wrote he "...could distinctly see a sheet of flames issuing from the Rebel works, but could not see a single Rebel, so completely were they protected by their defenses."[26]

Col. Johnson repeatedly ordered the 14th to attack but the troops didn't because the noise was so great they couldn't hear the order. They held their position for one-half hour even though they were taking heavy casualties.

To the left of the 14th the 12th Ohio attacked. The 12th met heavy resistance from the Rebels. The leaves and undergrowth caught fire as the North advanced. As the wounded soldiers fell they cried and begged their comrades in arms to stop and drag them away so they wouldn't be burned alive. These were seasoned soldiers and knew the only way any of them would be safe was to break the Southern line. They didn't stop, but continued to advance on the breastworks.

Re-creation: Union infantry marching to battle.

Approximately 75 yards from the breastworks there was a slight depression in the terrain. The 14th moved instinctively toward it. Although it was only a shallow depression, it did offer some protection. The Union line was taking casualties as it moved into the dip. For some reason Col. Hines halted the attack here. There was not enough depression in the landscape to offer real protection, and the South laid volley after volley of deadly fire into the halted line.

Because the South believed the Yanks would attack straight down the road, their force was out of position when the attack started on the right flank. The 45th Virginia requested aid and McCausland sent orders to move a 6 pounder cannon from Bryant's Battery and a 12 pounder from Ringgold's to increase fire power to support the 45th.

Jenkins, who was in overall command, ordered the 36th (his reserve force) and Bryant's howitzer to the right flank. The 60th Virginia rushed two companies to cover a gap in the line.

It was approximately 11:30 A.M. when the South was redeploying forces to the right, that the 3rd Brigade emerged from the woods and started a direct frontal assault. The South let fly with "...a galling fire of grape and canister."[27] All the Southern guns in that sector were brought to bear on the Union attack. Despite the artillery barrage, 3rd Brigade advanced to within 100 yards of the Reb line. Here Col. R.H. Woolworth, Commander of the 4th Pennsylvania Reserve was struck in the upper leg by shrapnel. It apparently severed an artery. He bled to death very quickly.

Re-creation of Union brigades moving to battle positions.

Regiment flags were the units' symbols. It was a great deed to capture your enemy's flag. It was an honor for the soldier who carried it into battle. It was his responsibility to see that the symbol didn't fall into enemy hands.

The fighting was so intense that flag bearer after flag bearer was needed. The flag traded hands five times as the bearers were shot down. The flag of the 14th Pennsylvania showed 17 holes to attest to furiousness of the fight.

Within minutes the North sustained over 100 casualties. The cannon and muskets from the Rebs position was too much. The attack fizzled, stalled, and died. Panic swept the Union ranks. The men ran for their lives.

The Southern defenders cheered and continued to fire on the fleeing enemy. Two regimental flags could be seen on the battlefield and a third one was with the Yanks as they ran back toward the woods.

At this time the First Brigade started their attack. They came over a rail fence and ran across the field to Back Creek. Crook was with them. He dismounted and waded the creek with his men. His high riding boots filled with water.

The First used a hill to conceal their movements. They advanced to within 20 yards of the 60th Virginia and home guard units before they were discovered.

The home guards panicked and "scattered".[28] The 60th Virginia poured one volley on the attackers before they were engaged in hand to hand combat. Many Southerners were shot through the head behind their breastworks. One Yankee said "... there was no discounting the valor of the Rebs, they fought like tigers".[29]

By now the guns of Bryant's and Ringgold's Batteries were in position. Anti-personal grape shot was the order of the day. The artillery was too much for the penned down 23rd Ohio and 14th W. Virginia troops. They broke and ran. "...Officers lost control so completely that neither regiment participated further in the conflict".[30]

Re-creation of Rebel bayonet charge

Jenkins saw the 23rd and 14th falling back in disarray. He apparently thought the whole Northern line was collapsing. An attack now by Southern forces would prevent the North from regrouping and may provide for a complete victory.

He moved to the front of Beckley's Battalion and ordered, "Charge!" All the men attacked even though only about one-half had bayonets. Over the breastworks they leaped. They captured a few Northern soldiers and continued to advance.

Col. Isaac H. Duval, commander of the 9th W. Virginia, and Col. Turley, commander of the 91st Ohio, saw Beckley's Battalion attacking. They rushed their troops along the ridge line and formed a defense for the fleeing 23rd Ohio and 14th West Virginia. They allowed their panicked comrades to pass through. When Beckley's men came running up the hill, the commands rose and fired "...their deadly volley struck Beckley's men with great effect..."[31] The Southern attack broke and they started retreating.

The 91st Ohio fixed bayonets and retook the ground the 12th Ohio lost. They then breeched the breastworks of the 45th Virginia.

The 9th West Virginia also attacked. The Rebs bayoneted many soldiers as they came over the breastworks. The 9th West Virginia and 45th Virginia were now engaged in savage hand-to-hand fighting. Men used their bayonets to lay their enemy's entrails on the ground. They used their muskets as clubs. They tore each other with knives and fists. This was eye ball to eye ball confrontation. It was kill or be killed. Duval was with 10 of his men as they went over the breastworks. Only Duval was not killed or wounded.

The men of the 45th Virginia rushed trying to capture the flag of the 9th West Virginia. Twelve Southern men died trying to capture it; 25 Northern men died trying to prevent the capture.

The 9th West Virginia attacked with 473 men. In 20 minutes 141 of them lay dead or wounded.

The attack of the 91st Ohio was slowed by Reb artillery, but because the 91st line was so close to the 45th Virginia, the cannonade was stopped. Reb gunners feared they would shoot their own men.

Without cannon bombardment, the 91st renewed its attack with vigor. Southern resistance crumbled.

Jenkins drew his saber and rode forward trying to rally his men. A minie-ball shattered his left arm near the shoulder. He dismounted with the help of his men and sent a message to McCausland, that he was now in command. Enemy General Crook praised Jenkins, calling him "A very intelligent captain of theirs".[32]

McCausland, who was with the 36th, ordered it to form two lines and attack. He knew that the 91st Ohio was weakened. The 36th should be able to annihilate them.

The 36th moved forward, but before they began the attack McCausland received word that the North was pressing hard on his exposed artillery.

McCausland halted the attack just as the lines met. Confusion swept the ranks of the 36th. Why was the attack halted?

The 91st poured fire into the standing ranks. The confused men of the 36th started a disorganized retreat.

When the 36th fell back, it allowed the 9th West Virginia and 91st Ohio to bring their full weight to bear on the 45th Virginia.

The 45th was in a dangerously exposed position. With sword in one hand and revolver in the other, Col. Edwin Harman tried to rally the 45th. His attempt didn't last long. A Yankee bullet ripped into his chest and lung. He fell dead almost instantly. "Heaps of their (Confederate) dead were lying behind their works mostly shot in the head".[33]

Re-creation of Confederate massed infantry firing on Union, note Union casualties in foreground.

The Southern right flank was turned. The line was collapsing. The army was falling back toward Dublin.

Hoge's Napoleon was cut off and the North was closing in fast. He gave the order "...Boys, take care of yourselves as best you can!"[34] A moment later he lay, mortally wounded.

As the Rebs found themselves cut off and surrounded they began to surrender. Many of the surrendering men and officers were bayoneted by the enemy.

The right of the Confedrate line was collapsing, but the left still held. When the attack by 1st brigade had been beaten back by the Confederate left, the 15th West Virginia which had been in reserve, moved forward. They pressed the Reb artillery. McCausland sent orders to Thomas Smith with the 36th to send men to cover the artillery. Before he could execute the order, he was shot dead. Maj. File succeeded Smith in command, but knew nothing of McCausland's order. So no troops were sent.

Without protection Bryant's Battery had to retreat. The Yanks were within 75 yards when the last cannon was moved. Without artillery the left side of the line could no longer hold. The entire Confederate army started to retreat.

To prevent a rout, McCausland deployed the 36th Virginia. He made a skirmish line and allowed the artillery and wounded to pass through. One gun from the Ringgold Battery under A.B. White, helped shore up the line. Parts of what was left of the 45th and 60th Virginia fell in along the line.

With the Rebs retreating, Crook knew it was time to use his cavalry. The 400 men under Oley which Averell had sent, charged the fleeing Confederates. The charge was a brief one. The stubborn Rebs controlled a small hill and they weren't about to give it up.

Cap. Glassie, with the Northern artillery, quickly brought his battery forward and formed a ring around the base of the hill. His guns let lose on the Rebs with a deadly hail of canister fire.

Union artillery pound Confederate position.

The partly surrounded Rebs saw an opportunity. The artillery was only protected by disorganized cavalry. Apparently acting without orders from above, the Rebs raced down the hill through minie-ball and grape shot, toward the lightly protected guns.

Future president Col. Hayes, saw the danger. His 23rd Ohio had been mauled severely in the fighting earlier. He moved his troops toward the guns.

When the South saw Hayes men moving toward them the charge stopped. While falling back, the Rebs, mostly members of the 36th and 60th took heavy casualties.

McCausland knew it was over. Most of the artillery and wounded were safely falling back on Dublin. To try and hold the line longer would only increase casualties, the battle was lost. Retreat!

Rutherford B. Hayes

The common soldier knew that death or capture awaited him if he fought on. They obeyed their general's order quickly. One observer stated, "One 18 year old boy won the blue ribbon as the fastest runner that ever struck Southwest Virginia."[35]

When Crook realized he had won, he was overcome with "excitement and exhaustion."[36] He had been moving about the field with his boots full of water. The strain was too much and he fainted. His staff worked to revive him. Even in his dazed condition, he ordered the army forward.

Crook was pressing his army forward trying to destroy McCausland. McCausland was moving toward Dublin trying to preserve his command. McCausland, going east, was met by Col. D. Howard Smith (22nd Kentucky) and some of Morgan's "terrible men." They had just arrived from Saltville.

They formed a skirmish line. "A slender line of heroes retard(ed) the Federals."[37] Cap. Christopher S. Cleburne had a premonition that this would be his last fight. "Bury me where I fall," he told his comrades. They did, and now that little piece of ground near the airport off Route 100 will forever be Kentucky...consecrated with his spirit and bones.

Speaking about the furiousness of the battle, Crook later said, "...the enemy kept up a grave yard whistle with their artillery everywhere we made our appearance."[38]

Military headquarters and the supply depot at Dublin were wide open. The Confederates fled through the town and toward New River; Crook's army took possession of the town including a considerable "accumulation of military stores."[39] The Reb army carried very little with them as they fled; they were almost out of gunpowder.

Private homes, including the Guthrie's house, were converted into temporary hospitals, and the doctors started their bloody work. Many an arm and leg were piled up outside the door as the surgeons amputated limbs to try and save lives. Not only was amputation the quickest way to treat minie-ball wounds of the extremities, it was the only way. Because of the large size of the bullet (usually 52 or 58 caliber) and the slow speed which it traveled, bones would be shattered and no medical treatment was available to treat such an injury.

What follows is the official Union casualty count.

	KILLED		WOUNDED		MISSING		TOTAL
	OFFICERS	MEN	OFFICERS	MEN	OFFICERS	MEN	
1st Brigade							
23 Ohio	2	19	2	76	0	24	123
34 Ohio	0	4	1	22	0	1	28
36 Ohio	0	4	0	17	0	0	21
5 W. Va. Cav.	0	0	0	0	0	0	0
7 W. Va. Cav.	0	0	0	0	0	0	0
2nd Brigade							
12 Ohio	0	9	5	63	0	10	87
91 Ohio	1	1	0	25	0	3	30
9 W. Va.	1	42	3	125	0	15	186
14 W. Va.	0	13	6	56	0	13	88
3rd Brigade							
3 Pa. Reserve	0	3	6	29	0	1	39
4 Pa. Reserve	1	5	5	28	0	2	41
11 W. Va.	0	1	3	11	0	1	16
12 W. Va.	0	1	3	5	0	2	21
Artillery							
Ky. Light							
1 Battery	0	0	0	5	0	0	5
Ohio Light							
Battery	0	0	0	0	0	0	0
Cavalry							
7 W. Va.	0	1	0	2	0	0	3
Totals	5	103	34	474	0	72	688[40]

Because military headquarters of Southwest Virginia was captured and destroyed, Confederate figures are less accurate. Crook stated, "We buried over 200 of the enemy dead..."[41]

	KILLED		WOUNDED		MISSING		TOTAL
	OFFICERS	MEN	OFFICERS	MEN	OFFICERS	MEN	
36 Va.	0	18	3	55	0	35	111
60 Va.	4	16	9	59	1	64	153
45 Battalion	0	4	2	9	0	15	30
45 Va.	5	21	7	89	0	52	174
Bryant's Batt.	0	3	1	3	0	0	7
Ringgold's Batt.	0	0	0	4	1	2	7
22 Ky.	1	4	0	18	0	30	53
Totals	10	66	22	237	2	198	535[42]

The South suffered a casualty rate of 23.3%, including Gen. Jenkins.

The North suffered a casualty rate of 10.5%.

Crook was so "excited"[43] when he won the battle that it contributed to his loss of consciousness, but by night fall his elation had turned to depression. It was a great victory that afternoon, but now all he could think about was rapid retreat. The whole picture changed after he received two pieces of information. He now believed the high commands grand strategy was falling apart. The only safe thing to do was retreat.

The high commands strategy called for Gen. Grant to apply so much pressure on Richmond that Lee would be forced to move troops from the Valley of Virginia. With the food producing valley undermanned, Gen. Sigel with 15,000 would march South and threaten the railroad. This would force the South to move troops from Southwest Virginia to the valley. (If the plan had worked, Breckinridge would be in Lexington and McCausland would have been there also but he decided to delay in following orders so he could meet Crook on Cloyd's Mountain).

Crooks part in the grand strategy was to take Dublin and the long bridge over New River. By this time Averell would have destroyed the saltworks, lead mines and joined with him. Together they would move east toward Salem and on to Lynchburg, destroying the railroad. Then moving up the Valley of Virginia, they would form a pincer movement with Sigel moving south. They would occupy the valley and cut the rail line. Lee would be cut off from his salt, lead and food. The Army of Northern Virginia could not continue to fight. The fate of the Rebel capital would be sealed.

Crook wrote that he had engaged 14 different units. One of those units was from the command of Gen. John Hunt Morgan. Morgan was supposed to be in Tennessee. Crook had to be concerned because Averell was riding straight toward Morgan at Saltville and didn't expect to meet major resistance. Morgan had the advantage because he knew Averell was coming and was no doubt ready to meet him. Why, Morgan would chew him up and spit him out!

There was little doubt that after Morgan finished with Averell, he would turn his attention toward Crook's army. Morgan's cavalry would stand no chance against Crook's fine infantry in the open battlefield, but Morgan may do considerable damage to the spread out column as it snaked through the mountain valleys.

The other piece of intelligence Crook received at Dublin was a Reb telegraph message. It was found when the North captured military headquarters.

The telegram stated that Lee had handed Grant a severe defeat and that Grant was in full retreat.

On the 7th Grant lost over 17,600 men in the Battle of the Wilderness. Lee lost 7,500 that couldn't be replaced. Grant was only faking retreat. His real plan was to flank Lee and get between him and the city of Richmond. Some of the Reb high command believed Grant was retreating when they sent the telegram. Lee was not fooled. Lee and Grant would meet again shortly at Cold Harbor and the bloodiest 15 minutes ever experienced in the Western Hemisphere.

Crook believed Grant was retreating. With the pressure off Lee, troops would be sent to the valley and to Southwest Virginia. The only prudent course was to retreat.

That night Rebel forces moved to the other side of New River. Most of the infantry crossed on the railroad trestle but the artillery could not. They followed McAdam Road to the Ingles Ferry bridge and crossed there. The South destroyed the bridge after crossing to prevent the Union from following.

Remains of Ingles Ferry Bridge near Central Depot (Radford).

Sometime during the night or early morning hours of May 10, orders reached the old men and boys that were the home guard unit from Wytheville. First they were ordered to Austinville to guard the lead mines. Then they were ordered to march toward Dublin and the forthcoming battle at Cloyd's Mountain. Before they arrived the battle was decided. Now they were told to move back to Wytheville and join Morgan. Their knowledge of the area might be needed. So the tired guard moved as fast as possible so they could defend their town.

As the morning sun rose, Crook advanced toward the New River Bridge at Radford (Central Depot) about 7 miles from Dublin.

The South positioned their artillery and the 45th Virginia Regiment at the bridge. The Union brought up their troops which out numbered the South's. The Union couldn't cross the bridge because of the Reb artillery. Soon the Yanks brought their guns on the line. An artillery duel ensued with the infantry of both sides mostly as spectators. The guns boomed and the shells fell but the Union couldn't advance over the bridge.

The Rebs had used most of their gunpowder the day before on Cloyd's Mountain and not having time to replenish their stock as they fled through Dublin toward New River; the Yanks were now firing Reb gunpowder and shot at the South. As the gunpowder ran low it was apparent that Southern guns couldn't stay on line.

Without counter artillery fire the Yanks would try to cross. With their superior numbers the South would lose. The order was given and the unhappy task fell upon the 45th. The South burned their own bridge, severing rail service, to keep the Yanks from taking it.

By 12:00 it was all over. It cost the North one dead and ten wounded.[44] The wooden bridge of over 400 feet, "Collapsed with a great hiss of steam from the river...A fine scene it was..."[45] recorded Col. Hayes in his diary. Though later president, he was most proud that he "...was one of the good colonels."[46]

Similar to "Long Bridge" over New River at Central Depot (Radford).

Sometime on the 10th Crook received a message from Averell. He said he wasn't going to attack Saltville because it was defended too strongly. He was going to march on Wytheville.

Crook no doubt returned a courier informing Averell of his change of plans. He was not going toward Salem, but was retreating north. Crook wasted no time waiting on Averell, but started retreating.

It was raining on the 11th as Crook retreated. He had a skirmish with "Mudwall" Jackon near Narrows. "Mudwall" was driven back. Crook claimed there were 1,500 Rebs with him.

Also on the 11th, Gen. Lee telegraphed Breckinridge "Just heard that Averell has cut Virginia - Tennessee Railroad at Dublin. It may be necessary for you to return to protect Lynchburg..." If Lee had one weakness it was not issuing direct orders. He told Breckinridge "You must judge."[47]

Not only was "Mudwall" pressuring Crook's army, but the road under their feet was turning to quagmire. The wagon train was strung out. Some wagons were buried up to their beds in mud. Near Salt Pond, on the 13th, some wagons were abandoned and supplies were removed. Others were destroyed to prevent them from falling into the enemy's hands.

Crook was moving North, as Averell moved out of Tazewell around midnight of the 8th and early hours of the 9th. He pushed the 8th and 16th Virginia Cavalry, who were stationed in Tazewell, ahead of him. The Rebs were too few to offer a serious fight, but they did slow the column. Undoubtedly, a Reb or two would wait until the head of the Union column approached and fire a shot. Because of the harassment and threat of a Reb ambush, Averell couldn't push his troops at top speed.

The retreating Rebs performed another service for the civilians. With the main body of troops near the head of the Union column, slowing it, outriders were sent ahead. They spread the word that the "Yanks are coming." This advance news allowed civilians some time to prepare and protect property. Cabin floor boards were pulled up. Sheets were laid on the ground. Wheat, hams, and other foods were placed on the sheets. The boards were replaced. Usually a ham or two was left in the smokehouse so the Yanks would think they were stealing the last bit of the Reb's food and would search no further.

Livestock was driven to the mountain.

As the Yanks moved, they stole every horse they could lay hands on. They apparently moved through Bland Courthouse before dark on the 9th. It appears that the 2,500 Yanks didn't camp in one central location, but strung out along the road. The Yanks occupied houses and barns. They stole food and took water as they wished.

When the Yanks entered the Davis house, they were told that the fat lady in bed had smallpox. They decided not to stay.

They apparently didn't enter Nancy Compton's house but spent the night on her place, sleeping in the barn. Marion Compton, a small, curious boy, watched and talked to the Blue Bellies. The Reb boy offered no threat and reminded them of happier times of their childhood, or maybe of their children back North. They didn't mind his company and didn't watch him too closely. When the Yanks left in the morning one didn't have his gun and the boy had a souvenir of their visit.

When the Yanks mounted they spotted the Compton's flock of geese. They made sport of decapitating the Reb geese and shouting, "On to Wytheville."[48]

Still pushing the 8th and 16th ahead of them, they reached the intersection with the Raleigh-Grayson Pike at Rocky Gap. Before leaving Rocky Gap they discovered a church with Reb supplies inside. It was burned to the ground.

The North pushed south toward Mechanicsburg. One story states that Dr. Nye was on his porch when the Yanks approached. Dr. Nye flashed the Mason's distress signal to the Yanks. Apparently the Yank commander was a Mason. Mechanicsburg was spared any real damage.

The Reb outriders spread the word that the Yanks were coming. In the Cove area of Wythe County, the families prepared for the unwelcome visitors. Some families sent their livestock to a cave near the intersection of Rt. 603, Cove Road and Rt. 600, now located on Cave Spring Farm. The cave is less than 100 feet from the Raleigh-Grayson Pike, but it's entrance couldn't be seen from the road. The cave's opening is just large enough to allow the cattle to pass inside. The floor is remarkably level, with a fine spring wrapping around one side. The cattle were herded inside and cared for by a boy named Elisha Adams, about age 9. The noise of the cattle was muted by the ground. Both boy and beast, within feet of clashing armies, remained safe.[49]

Morgan had been moving his cavalry over the Rock Road toward Wytheville since the 9th. It was probably after 1:00 on the 10th that the head of the column was entering Wytheville from the west. At about the same time the outriders from the 8th and 16th were entering Wytheville from the Raleigh-Grayson Pike. They were spreading the news.

Morgan reversed the outriders and sent them back to their units with orders to inform their units that he was coming, and to form a battle line. The dust must have flown from the streets of Wytheville as Morgan pushed his command and the three pieces of field artillery, which he had brought from Saltville, through. He later wrote, "...If I had been one hour later this place (Wytheville) and the lead mines would have been lost."[50]

It was around 4:00 in the afternoon of Tuesday May 10, that Averell received his first shock. The 8th and 16th Virginia Cavalry he had been pushing ahead of him had stopped running and had formed a battle line.

The Reb line was established across the tops of a series of hills that looked down on the Raleigh-Grayson Pike (now on Cove Road Rt. #603 and Rt. #600).

When Averell saw the line he knew he couldn't circumvent it. Even if the enemy held the higher ground, their numbers were far too few to stop him. The column halted as Averell began to organize his troops to attack. What Averell didn't know and couldn't see because of the rough terrain, was that Morgan was moving his men along the line.

Some of Averell's men had visited Wytheville with Toland the year before. They were ready to avenge those bad memories. The 34th Ohio Volunteer Infantry was back as was the 2nd West Virginia Cavalry. Col. Powell was commanding the 2nd West Virginia just as he had done the year before when he was "mortally wounded", and imprisoned. He rejoined the 2nd on March 11, after being exchanged.

Averell hadn't come this far to run. He started the plan of attack. The 3rd West Virginia Cavalry (probably dismounted) was on the far left. Then came the 34th Ohio (dismounted). On the right was the 2nd West Virginia mounted.

Re-creation of Union cavalry forming a skirmish line.

The attack was commanded by Col. Schoonmaker, 1st Brigade, leading the 14th Pennsylvania and the 1st West Virginia Cavalry. The 14th and 1st were placed in three rows and made a general advance along the entire Reb line. As they pressed the Reb positions their lines began to break up due to fences they encountered. Because the formations collapsed and because of the fire from the Rebs on higher ground, the "vigor of the attack gradually decreased."[51] The Yanks charge was halted when the South "poured a withering fire into the charging Yanks."[52]

The sounds of the battle could be heard by the fearful citizens in town.

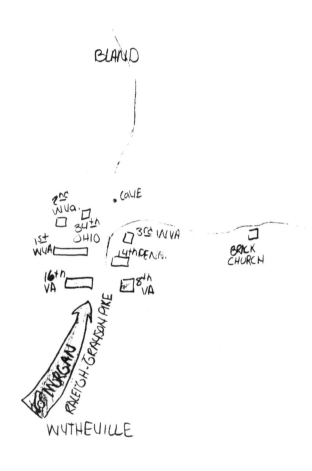

C. WALKER
'74

As the 14th Pennsylvania and 1st West Virginia fell back, the South attacked. It is unclear if Morgan, himself, ordered the attack or if Col. Grimes of the 16th, who spear headed the attack, did so on his own. The 14th and 1st "Received the shock of the battle, while the 2nd and 3rd West Virginia Cavalry and 34th Ohio Mounted Infantry established a line which the enemy had reason to respect and remember."[53] The 8th Virginia moved to cover the gap in the line when the 16th attacked.

Morgan was "hungry for revenge for the indignities he had suffered in the Ohio Penitentiary."[54] He wrote later about his 750 men, "My men fought magnificently, driving them from hill to hill. It was certainly the greatest sight I ever witnessed to see a handful of men driving such masses before them. Averell fought his men gallantly, tried time and time again to get them to charge, but our boys gave them no time to form."[55]

Morgan attacked and kept on charging...this rattled"[56] the Union.

Re-created battle scenes.

Re-created battle scenes

Because the South kept attacking, Averell was too busy trying to form a line, so he couldn't assess the situation properly. Averell probably felt that his troops were outnumbered, when the reverse was true. If he had known how weak the Reb attackers were, the battle may have ended much differently. Because of the hilly terrain it was difficult to ascertain the enemy's troop strength, when only a small part of the battlefield could be seen at a time.

The center charge of the 16th Virginia forced the attacking Union (14 Pennsylvania and 1st West Virginia) to fall back toward their line. Morgan poured more men and artillery into the battle. He began pressing the right of the Union line (the 2nd West Virginia). The 16th Virginia moved eastward (left of the Union line) to a ridge line to regroup after their attack.

With Morgan pushing on the right of his line, Averell saw an opportunity to out flank Morgan and move men around the left of the line. Averell sent a part of the 3rd West Virginia to flank the Rebs and attack from the rear.

The 16th had no idea the hill they chose to regroup on afforded a good view of the Yanks trying to sneak around their lines. From their vantage point on high ground, they cut the sneaking Yanks to pieces. The dismounted cavalry turned tail toward their line.

About the same time Morgan almost broke the Union line. Gen. A.N. Duffié, 2nd Brigade commander, wrote "My thanks to the 2nd Virginia Cavalry, who, under the leadership of their gallant Col. (Powell), while retreating under a galling fire from the enemy, preserved their rank unbroken...saved the left..."

But "...when the 2nd Brigade gave way in some confusion...the 34th Ohio...held the enemy...gave time for the broken column to be reformed...thus saving the division from a shameful rout."[57]

It is not known when Averell received his head wound stopping Morgan's onslaught. The wound, though painful, didn't cause a change in command.

Averell now knew his dreams of an easy ride into an undefended Wytheville, were only dreams. The men in front of him weren't just a couple of cavalry units and a worn out homeguard unit. He had the infamous Morgan staring him in the eye.

Col. Alfred N. Duffie.

Averell felt he was outnumbered, the enemy "Devil" Morgan had artillery support. The best course was to retreat. The sun was low, the cover of darkness might afford him the opportunity to escape from Morgan.

Averell formed an "echelon"[58] as he began to withdraw. That is, the units were staggered in a stairstep like formation. This allowed each unit to provide covering fire for itself and the unit directly in front. The unit in front would withdraw to the rear of the entire formation. The process repeated so that the army withdrew orderly, not allowing the South an opportunity to charge isolated units. Averell withdrew from Morgan.

Morgan later wrote his wife, "If we had two more hours fighting, would have captured the entire force."[59]

Darkness came and Averell started his escape. He paused at the "Brick Church"[60] in the Cove. Here the wounded that couldn't stay in the saddle on their own were placed in the church. Their blood stained the floor of the house of worship. Those wounded would slow the column. Averell never wanted to meet Morgan again.

Part Two

As Averell started toward Dublin and a link-up with Crook, he left 114 officers and men killed or wounded. This is not the "Heavy loss"[61] that some reported. He retreated down Walker Creek by Shannon to Peppers Ferry.

After viewing Averell's report he could be described as a man who held the truth so precious that he seldom used it. He quoted an alleged Southern newspaper as stating that Morgan and W.E. Jones had "5,000"[62] men against him. He went on to state that most of the troops were infantry. He must have known he was fighting almost exclusively cavalry units. Reading his report gave little indication that he had lost the battle, in fact, the reverse may have been assumed.

To get some of the facts of what really happened through to the Union high command, Averell's subordinates had to resort to subterfuge. While not denying Averell's account of the battle, they added comments, such as "Powell...saved the left...this saving a shameful rout."[63]

Because military headquarters at Dublin was burned, no official Confederate reports of the battle were filed. No Southern casualty figures are available, but losses are believed to have been light.

Morgan apparently had a better assessment of the Union's strength than they did of his. He decided not to pursue the Federals, less they turn on his much smaller force.

The weary home guard joined the Southern forces on the battlefield that night. They serve who only march and march.

Morgan secured the area just in case Averell's retreat was a fake and that he would attack again at dawn. Only later the next day were the Federal wounded and dead found in the brick church.

Averell raced toward Dublin, perhaps not knowing Crook was in full retreat North.

There was confusion in the Southern ranks as well. Apparently the South believed that Crook was pursuing them east from Dublin along the railroad. On the 11th, Stringfellow wired Breckinridge that they were in Salem and still retreating. He also informed Breckinridge that he heard "in vague reports of a battle and our success."[64] (Wytheville).

Modern view of "Brick Church" where Union wounded were abandoned by Averell.

When Averell arrived in Dublin on the 12th, he found that Crook and the infantry were gone. Averell moved on to Christiansburg. Reb defenders fled the town leaving two three-inch guns. While there, Averell burned the depot, shop, and damaged about four miles of track. Also while there he learned that some Southern forces were not retreating. He decided it was time to follow Crook north.

Averell moved but he moved too slow. The Rebs, defeated at Cloyd's Mountain, were not dead. Part of the cavalry of the martyred Jenkins, commanded by Col. William H. French, combined with troops under Col. William J. Jackson. They chased Averell through Blacksburg to Newport in Giles County on the 13th. There, in a gap in the mountain, they caught him.

The south said they beat and scattered Averell's forces before dark set it, but McCausland lamented "...but the small cavalry force I had sent out has not been heard from since."[65] This indicates that there were casualties taken on both sides but no figures were given.

French apparently fell back on Narrows and Jackson continued to pressure Averell. At Greenbrier River another skirmish occurred. Jackson stated he had driven some of Averell's men and horses into the water, "drowning and killing some of his (Averell's) men." Apparently men of both sides fought hand to hand, shooting and cutting in the river. Because Jackson said, "...we have to mourn the loss of many brave officers and men."[66] Averell confessed he lost a few men (between 15 and 20) and horses by drowning. Once again, no official body counts were given.

It was a beat up, exhausted column of Yankee Blue's that joined Crook at Union (West) Virginia in Monroe County on the 15th. Their ammo was almost gone. Apparently they had been beaten in each encounter with the enemy.

As information came into Stringfellow, the Adjutant Gen. now at Salem, he kept Breckinridge, near New Market, informed. On the 14th, he wired Breckinridge that the "lead mines and salt works were safe"...that "Morgan certainly whipped Averell badly on Tuesday near Wytheville...French and Jackson repulsed him severely near Newport yesterday."[67] This was some comfort to Breckinridge who was preparing to meet Sigel at New Market.

The Yanks had visited Southwest Virginia in strength. They had accomplished one of their three major goals in Southwest Virginia, cutting the Virginia - Tennessee Railroad. They had handed the South a sizeable defeat, occupied, and destroyed military headquarters.

The destruction of the long bridge over New River caused delays in the movement of salt, lead, and soldiers, and other materials of war and commerce. Trains were off loaded, supplies ferried to trains on the other side and reloaded as soldiers, and civilians labored frantically to rebuild the bridge. This was another strain on the already failing economy of the South.

McCausland tried to put the best face possible on the events in Southwest Virginia. He admitted "...they have destroyed New River Bridge and some smaller ones and stolen some Negroes and other property...(But, Their)...movement (of the enemy) was a great failure..."[68]

At least 52 of the stolen Negroes escaped and returned.[69]

McCausland was acting temporary commander of the Department of Southwest Virginia.

Although Breckinridge was the commander of the Department, he was at New Market. He had Wharton's and Echol's brigades which he had brought with him. He had a hastily assembled hodge - podge of regular and irregular units, including the Corps of Cadets from V.M.I. Some boys were less than 15 years old. Breckinridge was inferior in every respect to Sigel's finely clad, well equipped, well trained, 15,000. Logic called for defense or retreat. Breckinridge attacked.

This mob masquerading as an army broke Sigel on May 15.

It was an unbelievable David and Goliath event. The Valley was safe. Richmond was safe. Grant was livid. He demanded, and got, Sigel's removal.

Aerial view of "Twin Forts" overlooking Saltville area. Shown are two forts approximately 80 yards apart connected by trench with rifle pits at the tree line. (Photo courtesy of Tom Totten: all reproduction rights reserved to the Totten Collection.)

Part Three

As the smoke cleared in mid-May, many more Yanks than Rebs lay dead on the battlefield. Lee was as invincible as ever and Richmond remained unconquered.

The temporary troop movements that avoided disaster for the South, became permanent. There was some reshuffling of troops but Breckinridge, McCausland, and the 36th remained in the valley.

McCausland finally got his promotion to Brigadier General. He had blamed the president for his lack of grade. He believed Davis, a Mississippian, blamed him because he escaped from Fort Donelson at the first of the war. He escaped and didn't bring the Mississippi troops out with him.

The defense of Southwest Virginia fell more on Kentucky's son's shoulders and their leaders, Morgan was now the commander. The name was changed from the Department of Southwest Virginia to the Department of Southwest Virginia and East Tennessee.

Morgan's feet may have been planted in Southwest Virginia, but his eyes and heart were fixed on his bluegrass state.

Because the headquarters at Dublin was destroyed, and it was now the Department of East Tennessee also, and because it was closer to Kentucky and the provisional government of Kentucky in exile was there, Morgan moved his headquarters to Abingdon. No sooner had he moved to Abingdon, than he was busy plotting another raid into Kentucky. Although he was a brilliant general, and a savage fighter, many in the Confederate high command structure feared Morgan because he was too independent.

To try and prevent the Yanks from burning the long bridge at Radford again, the South built permanent artillery fortifications that commanded each end of the bridge.

Morgan's command, like all armies in the Confederacy, was in a state of decline. New recruits were few, and disease, death, desertion, and disability were taking their toll. There were shortages of everything, food, shelter, clothing, guns, etc. One European observer (today they are called military attache) reported that the Confederate armies looked nothing like an army. There were few uniformed men. They appeared to be a mob, not an army, to the observer.

Desertion was a growing problem. Each night the enemy won a victory. More men left the rigors of army life, some because of the miserable conditions, some to return home to help the destitute family. Husbands and sons were needed; families were starving. Not since colonial days had so many men worn lace. Outfitted in a long dress and sunbonnet, the deserters worked the fields.

It is not known when Lt. Thomas Walker, with the 36th, got his working furlow. He could go home for a visit to family (his house literally was divided by the Tazewell - Bland County line), but he had to return a deserter. The deserter was a man Walker knew, perhaps from his own outfit, perhaps a neighbor and friend. He had to bring the deserter back. When he did, the deserter would be imprisoned, perhaps shot.

No doubt Walker's mind was burdened as he rode home. He must do his duty, but he didn't want the deserter punished. Walker devised a plan. He went to a store nearest the deserter's house. He remained there most of the day, telling everyone why he had come. Only after he was sure the neighbors and relatives of the deserter had borne the news of his presence, did Walker go to the deserter's house. Now he could report back that he had searched diligently but couldn't locate the deserter.

Jack Musser, who had helped to recruit at Musser's Mill in Wythe County, was home too. He, like so many others, was on crutches.

There was no date given for the following story that occurred in Wytheville, but it was probably in 1864. "One day a blue streak appeared in the road and it moved toward town. Bedlam broke loose, women screamed, children cried, the dogs barked. It was confusion worse confounded. The Yankees were on us again. I think now that it was a sober second thought that quieted things down...that it did not move with the impetuosity of an avalanche which would have been the case had this been a company of Yankees assaulting the town...It transpired that a company or regiment of Rebel cavalry had raided a Yank wagon train loaded with overcoats or had made a raid on some commissary stores...needed the coats and proceeded to wear them."[70]

Seeing Union clothing on Reb soldiers was nothing uncommon. There were thousands of Union blue overcoats on Rebel backs.

Because the South was desperate for troops a new conscription (draft) law was passed. Men up to age 50 were called up. Many men didn't go willingly. They deserted before they entered the army. Some took their case to court. In Wythe County, Anderson Ledgerwood said he couldn't go because he was a Negro overseer. The court agreed. William Cassell "of the poor house..." didn't have to go.[71]

William Stave was arrested by the enrollment officer but he explained that he had been captured and paroled at Knoxville. He didn't go.

J.P. Vermillion's father got him out of service. The father claimed the boy was under age when he signed up and that the army said he would stay at Dublin. When the troops moved to the valley, the army broke its contract. The judge agreed and the army lost a son.

The enrollment officer caught a healthy male but he appealed to the judge. He told the judge he was the Post Master at Knoxville which the Yanks now controlled, but he was still Post Master. The Confederacy had not conceded Knoxville as a permanent loss, nor had the Post Master's job been declared "vacant". Even though no Confederate mail was being delivered in Knoxville, the South needed a Post Master even if he was in Southwest Virginia. C.W. Charlton was exempt.[72]

The court examined Mr. Crockett's case. He was found to be in good health. Just because he didn't want to be a soldier was not good enough. He was ordered to Richmond.

A storm was brewing and heading for Southwest Virginia. Gen. Stephen Gano Burbridge, Military Governor of Kentucky, was assembling an army, estimated to be 6,000 to 8,000 in number. They were going to pay a visit to Morgan and Southwest Virginia.

Morgan believed his forces in Southwest Virginia and East Tennessee were too small to stop Burbridge. He decided to strike first before the Union consolidated and started to move.

Morgan moved with approximately 2,100 men, half of them dismounted. Col. Giltner commanded the mounted men; Col. D. Howard Smith commanded the dismounted troops. Morgan hoped to secure mounts for all his men when he left.

As Morgan left his Department of Southwest Virginia and East Tennessee at Lebanon, he informed high command in Richmond that he was gone.

At Pound Gap on the Virginia - Kentucky border, he struck his first serious opposition. Two regiments of well entrenched Yanks, approximately 700 men.[73]

Morgan overran the enemy and captured the stores and horses. Fewer men were walking as he entered Kentucky.

He moved toward Lexington. Thirty miles away at Mount Sterling he encountered stiff resistance from the town defenders. Morgan took Mount Sterling too. He captured 400 men "and immense quantities of military stores,"[74] which were destroyed because they couldn't be transported.

No casualty figures were given only "he lost some valuable officers and a good many men."[75]

Morgan cut the railroad at several points.

On June 9, Morgan was back in his beloved Lexington. He captured the city and took enough horses to mount all his men. He destroyed the depot, Union supplies, and stables.

At Cynthiana about 30 miles north of Lexington, Morgan suffered his first defeat when the defenders entered the houses and fired on Morgan's men from their protected positions. Morgan lost many men and burned part of the town before he took control. At Cynthiana he learned that Gen. Hobson was coming to attack him.

Col. Giltner, with about 1,000 men, met Hobson. Hobson had 2,000 men and fought for about 3 hours. Hobson may have had twice as many men but they were no match for Morgan's terrible men. Hobson surrendered his command. Hobson was paroled on the condition he would try to get as many of Morgan's men who were in prison exchanged South as he could.

By the 12th of June, Burbridge decided to call off his attack on Southwest Virginia and concentrate on pushing Morgan out of the state. Morgan's plan had worked and the pressure on Southwest Virginia was relieved.

Burbridge pursued Morgan with 6,000 men, but Morgan returned safely to Virginia with "Two thousand seven hundred prisoners and a large number of wagons (loaded)."[76]

There were scouting and raiding parties throughout Southwest Virginia and East Tennessee that summer but no major Union force wanted to take on Morgan.

Morgan wasn't content to sit and defend Southwest Virginia. He longed for Kentucky and to raid the Union which earned him "...the undying animosity of a large segment of the frightened North."[77]

Apparently Morgan didn't have the permission of the high command when he left his Department early in September. He sent word to Richmond only after he started.

He was heading to Knoxville to visit the Union troops garrisoned there.

Morgan bivouacked in Greenville, Tennessee on the night of September 3. The Greenville area of East Tennessee had divided sympathies from the first of the war. Most of the people there would have preferred to remain in the Union. Their state may have left the Union but their hearts were still there.

After placing his troops around the town, Morgan took lodging for the night in Mrs. C.D. William's house.

Morgan didn't know that Mrs. Williams was a Northern sympathizer. She left the house that night and rode to the Union lines. She informed them that Morgan was her house guest and gave the strength of his forces.

At dawn approximately 2,000 Yankee cavalry came to call on the sleeping Morgan. The Yank surprise was complete. Before the Confederates knew it the Yanks were upon them. The house where Morgan was staying was surrounded. Only a few troops of the Morgan command realized they were under attack. Some shooting took place as Morgan and his staff ran from the house into the garden.

Mrs. Fry whose husband was Col. David Fry (Union) saw Morgan and the Rebs run into the garden. She informed the Yanks of Morgan's location. Over 100 shots were fired until "...at last the fatal ball pierced the bravest of the brave."[78] All the staff members with Morgan were captured except Maj. Gassett who hid in Fry's basement and escaped later.

Morgan vowed he wouldn't be taken prisoner again. He wasn't, Campbell (perhaps a private) shot him dead.

The Yanks also killed six to eight Rebs, took one cannon, and about 50 prisoners.

D. Howard Smith was bivouacked south of town and came toward Morgan's position, but found there were too many Yanks to attack. He withdrew, not knowing Morgan was dead.

Morgan's body was paraded through the streets. Then to show their hatred they dumped the body in a mud hole.

Cap. J.J. McAfee of Morgan's command came under a flag of truce and retrieved the body. The Union withdrew toward Bulls Gap to spread the word, the "Devil", the man "whom the Yankees dreaded," the "terrible Morgan" was dead.

The body was returned to his wife, Mattie, at Abingdon. There on the 6th of September at 4:00, Rev. Cameron, Brigade Chaplin, preached Morgan's funeral. It was the largest funeral held in the county up to this time. Mattie "...young and devoted wife is crushed with anguish, a nation condoles with her."[79]

Morgan's body was entered at Sinking Spring Cemetery.

Gen. Morgan's body remained in the ground less than one week. He was too important to the "cause" to just let him die. The nation was fighting with little more than raw courage. Morgan was a hero, he died a hero's death, he would be given a hero's funeral. His example would encourage others and help the morale of the nation and its soldiers.

His body was taken from the train station around 10:00 "...to the capital of the country, where, ten months before a joyous assemblage of citizens had met to signalize his triumphant presentation to the Congress of the Confederate States and the legislature..."(After his escape from the Ohio Peniteniary). The body lay in state under a Confederate flag until around noon. Hundreds of ordinary citizens passed the flag draped "Plain pine box...(covered) with wreaths and flowers."[80]

At 1:00 the funeral procession began. "The publick (sic) guard under Cap. Gay" in front, then the fire brigade under Cap. Charters followed by "Several hundred soldiers from the fortifications of Richmond" under Col. Atkinson. Then came the hearse "Drawn by four gray horses; a carriage containing Cap. Calvin Morgan and other relatives of Gen. Morgan (wife not mentioned); the Kentucky delegations in Congress; the Secretary of War, Governor of Virginia, Generals Ewell, Kemper, and the Mayor and City Council of Richmond; the members of the Husting Court of Richmond..."[81]

Gen. Ewell couldn't stay for the entire funeral. Lee recalled him abruptly because of an attack by Grant near Petersburg.

Other notables present were Brigadier Generals Preston, Gardner, Smith, and Lawson; Colonels Cox, Augest, and Smith and Major Gassett (who alone escaped) were also there.

Morgan, an Episcopalian, was interred a second time in Hollywood Cemetery in Richmond, the honored "National" cemetery for the Confederacy.

While the nation wept at Richmond, the Department of Southwest Virginia and East Tennessee was reorganized. Basil Duke, Morgan's brother-in-law, took command of Morgan's brigade.

Duke was woeful about Morgan's death when he said "the glory and chivalry seem gone from the struggle, and it became a tedious routine, enjoined by duty, and sustained only by sentiments of pride and hatred."[82]

Gen. Echols assumed temporary command of the Department.

1. Lt. Henry H. Brogden, 2. Lt. Col. Joseph T. Tucker, 3. Lt. H.H. Smith, 4. Cap. Hart Gibson, 5. Lt. J.J. Andrews, 6. Brig. Gen. R.B. Vance, 7. Lt. Col. Cicero Coleman, 8. Rev. I.W.K. Handy, 9. Pvt. B.P. Key.

10. Brig. Gen. M. Jeff Thompson, 11. Col. R.C. Morgan (Gen. Morgan's brother), 12. Col. W.W. Ward, 13. Cap. C. H. Morgan (Gen. Morgan's brother), 14. Gen. Basil W. Duke, 15. J.A. Tomlinson.

Part Four

As the South wept, the North rejoiced. No one was happier to see the terrible Morgan dead than Burbridge who was at Pikeville, Kentucky still licking the wounds Morgan had inflicted on him in June. Now that the famous or infamous Morgan was dead, Burbridge felt he could strike hard at Southwest Virginia and revenge his humiliating defeat. He sat about his plan at once.

Secretary of War, James A. Seddon, was worried about a possible attack on Southwest Virginia. He wrote Lee of his concern stating the area was "almost denuded of troops."[83]

Gen. Lee knew the important area was not properly defended, but he had no one to spare. The whole South was not properly defended at this point in time.

The South was worried about an attack that Burbridge was preparing, but not all of the Union high command and field generals believed a push on Southwest Virginia was the best course at this time.

Gen. William T. Sherman wrote Maj. Gen. John M. Schofield "...I doubt the necessity of your sending far into Virginia to destroy the saltwork, or any material interest, we must destroy their armies."[84]

Sherman was in Atlanta. He had been pushing eastward since his and Grant's big victory at Vicksburg in July, 1863.

Gen. Joseph E. Johnston, whom Lee succeeded in command of the Army of Northern Virginia, had opposed Sherman every step of the way. Sherman had over 100,000 troops to Johnston's approximately 50,000. Johnston knew he couldn't defeat Sherman head on, on the field of battle. Instead he destroyed bridges, felled trees, and attacked with hit-and-run raids on Sherman's flanks to slow him. He inflicted a high casualty rate on Sherman by fighting his men only when he had the advantage. The men respected him because they felt he was concerned that they not become cannon fodder. He was nicknamed "Uncle Joe."

Despite the fact that his men respected him and that Sherman respected him, the people of the deep South could see Sherman coming and Johnston constantly retreating. Johnston had planned to make his stand on Peach Tree Creek outside of Atlanta. But because of the poor relations with the president, Johnston didn't communicate his plans.

On July 17, President Davis relieved Johnston from command and appointed John B. Hood of Texas, commander of the Army of Tennessee. Hood was a brilliant, gallant and courageous corps commander under the masterful hand of Lee. Most historians agree the qualities that made him an outstanding corps commander, made him inept as an army general.

The Southern people cheered because at last they had someone who would fight. Sherman cheered because at last he had someone who would fight.

Outside of Atlanta, at Ezra Church on July 28th, the Army of Tennessee bled profusely under Sherman's guns. Atlanta was beseiged. On September 1, Atlanta was evacuated.

As Atlanta burned, Sherman occupied the city and ordered the entire civilian population (that had remained) out of the city at gun point. He sent the elderly, the sick, the young, the blind, and crippled out into the countryside with no food, or shelter. It was part of his punishment policy. He and Grant knew and used a total war concept.

Many historians believe that Sherman's major victory, the taking of Atlanta, took the punch out of the peace movement. The peace movement, or Copperheads, believed that total victory was too costly and far off. Sherman's victory may have re-elected Lincoln.

Sherman, in Atlanta, was collecting men and supplies before breaking out to the interior of the deep South. Sherman opposed Burbridge's invasion of Southwest Virginia because he wanted Gen. Alan Cullem Gillem and his crack command shipped to him. He wanted none of Burbridge's colored soldiers. There was no room in Sherman's army for Negro troops. Sherman was overruled and the operation was approved by high command.

In late September, Burbridge's plans were completed and his men started to march. It was designed as a pincer movement on the Preston saltworks at Saltville. Gen. Jacob Ammen was to attack from East Tennessee with 1,500 men, while Gen. Burbridge marched south. Gillem would apply pressure from Bulls Gap. Based on numbers, supplies, and fire power, the South had to lose.

On September 23, Jonathan Echols reported back to his commander at Dublin, John Echols (probably a relative). (Military headquarters was moved from Abingdon after Morgan's death). Jonathan reported that 8,000 Union men had been spotted at Pound Gap, it was his guess that they were going toward Saltville.

The following day he reported that the Union had cut the railroad in two places and that there were "Bushwhackers" operating between Bristol and Abingdon.

On the 25th further details came in from a scout. There were 8,000 to 10,000 men, 3,200 pack mules, and 40 flat boats of provisions at Pound Gap and the mouth of Beaver Creek. The North looked so good because the South had so little. Echols added almost wistfully, "I hope that the arms that I have telegraphed to Richmond for, will be sent at once."[85]

On September 27, Special Order #229 was sent "Maj. Gen. J.C. Breckinridge, Provisional Army, C.S., will assume command of the Department of Southwest Virginia and East Tennessee."[86] Gen. Echols was out; Breckinridge was in again. One of the first orders was to inspect fortifications at Saltville. Gen. William E. Jones and "Mudwall" Jackson stated "Saltville well protected..."[87] Gen. Breckinridge didn't have time to warm his desk chair; he had a battle to fight.

When Burbridge started out of Kentucky, he was "easily the most roundly despised man in the state (Kentucky)."[88] The people hated him because of the heavy handed tactics he used as military governor. Harsh reprisals were inflicted on the civilians because of Confederate guerrilla activity, and he forced the people to sell their produce below a fair market value to the government. He even "ordered the arrest of anyone suspected of opposing the re-election of Abraham Lincoln."[89]

Stephen Gano Burbridge.

Burbridge had the following units under his command, the 13th Kentucky Cavalry, 35th Kentucky Mounted Infantry, 36th Kentucky Mounted Infantry, 45th Kentucky Mounted Infantry, 40th Kentucky Mounted Infantry, 26th Kentucky Mounted Infantry, 30th Kentucky Cavalry, 37th Kentucky Regiment Mounted Infantry, 39th Regiment Mounted Infantry, 12th Regiment Ohio Volunteer Cavalry, 11th Regiment Michigan Cavalry, 5th U.S. Colored Cavalry, and 3 sections of Mountain Howitzers. A total of 5,200 men.

There was racial dissension in the ranks as the army moved south. Col. James Brisbin, commander of the 5th U.S. Colored Cavalry, complained "On the march, the colored soldiers, as well as their white officers, were made subject of much ridicule and many insulting remarks by the white troops, and in some instances petty outrages, such as the pulling off of the caps of colored soldiers, stealing their horses...insults, as well as the jeers and taunts that they would not fight..."[90]

Echols suspected the troops under Gillem at Pound Gap were heading toward Saltville, but the Rebs definitely knew that Burbridge from Kentucky was heading there. A "housewife"[91] rode from Salyerville, Kentucky, to Abingdon to warn the South.

Breckinridge had Echols oppose Gillem at Pound Gap. He sent Gen. John Crawford Vaughn's command of 600 to fight Ammen's 1,650 in Tennessee. The only troops to defend Saltville were under the past-temporary commander, John Echols. He was a big man, 6'4" and weighed 260 pounds. There were 400 men under Col. Henry Giltner and less than that number in the 13th Battalion Virginia Reserves, less than 800 to oppose Burbridge's 5,200.

Jacob Ammen.

While Breckinridge was rushing every man he could find, some unarmed, to Saltville, Echols and Vaughn were doing outstanding jobs. Echols watched Gillem at Pound Gap. While Vaughn fought delaying skirmishes at Rheatown, Tennessee on September 28, at Jonesborough and Watlauga River on the 29th, at Carter Station on September 30 and October 1st. General Gillem and Ammen never made their rendezvous at Saltville.

Burbridge moved from Pikeville up the Big Sandy River, then to Grundy, crossed the mountains into Tazewell County along the Kentucky - Tazewell Courthouse Pike, and moved through Richlands by the end of September.

John Crawford Vaughn.

Gen. Echols ordered Giltner's 400 to move out of Saltville toward Burbridge. Giltner must slow Burbridge if Saltville was to be saved.

The South had to leave some men at Abingdon because there were not enough rifles.

The first troops to reinforce Saltville were the home guard units. From Tazewell County came Col. Robert Smith, from Montgomery County came Col. Robert Preston, from Washington County came Col. James Preston, from Wythe County came Maj. Joseph Kent. There were approximately 700 men in all. They were placed under Col. Robert Trigg.

There was some difficulty moving troops to Saltville because of the civilians fleeing. "The roads were crammed and blocked with cattle, sheep, Negroes (There were over 2,000 slaves working at the saltworks), wagons, buggies, and great numbers of citizens with their families."[92]

Small Southern units operating as guerrilla units harassed Burbridge's rear and interrupted communications back to Pikeville.

When Southern forces learned that colored troops were coming with Burbridge, the talk seemed to focus on them. The Southerners knew that the colored troops, today, were Southern slaves yesterday. There was much resentment that their slaves would turn and fight against them. Although they knew many slaves were forced north. Many left willingly, but to return and fight against them was unpardonable.

Because the home guard units were mostly composed of boys under 17 and men over 45 who had little military training, and because of their very poor showing at Cloyd's Mountain, the generals were concerned that the men might not fight well and might run at the first sound of battle. Gen. Alfred Jackson asked Co. Trigg "...Do you think your reserves will fight Niggers?" To which Trigg replied, "Fight 'em...by damn, sir, they'll eat 'em up!...By damn, sir, we'll cut 'em up!"[93]

It is not known why Union High Command decided to call off the attack, but orders to retreat were sent by Gen. Schofield to the three invading units, Ammen, Gillem, and Burbridge.

By the night of September 29th, Burbridge was starting up Laurel Mountain. One Yank wrote, "The horrors of that night march eclipsed all previous experiences...."[94] At least 8 men were killed when their horses stepped off the mountain road and they were thrown. It is not known how many were injured.

On the morning of September 30, the first contact was made. About 150 Rebs of Giltner's command under Col. Edwin Trimble, skirmished on Reese T. Bowen's farm near Cedar Bluff. The South fought and fell back. Giltner was not trying to stop Burbridge, just slow him. Burbridge occupied the Bowen home and remained there throughout the day as his men pushed the Confederates up the mountain. "Due to the bravery and the ingenuity of one of Bowen's daughters, several of the officers lost their rifles."[95]

In was morning of the first, when Burbridge started up Clinch Mountain. At about 2 miles from the Bowen farm, approximately 300 Rebs ambushed the forward units. These were Kentucky troops fighting Kentucky troops. The South held the road and fought about one-half hour before retreating toward the top of the mountain. They felled trees across the road as they went, to slow the Yanks.

Around 12:00 the North moved on the summit of the mountain. Part of the command dismounted and left the road in an attempt to out flank Giltner and cut off his escape route. Giltner discoverd the Union movement and rapidly withdrew from the summit of Clinch Mountain to Laurel Gap.

Laurel Gap was a good defensive location with a narrow road and high cliffs. It took the entire brigade to scale the cliffs and attack Giltner. It is not known how long the battle lasted or what casualties were taken. Giltner knew his 400 couldn't hold Burbridge's 5,200 men very long. There was a real danger that Burbridge would overrun his rear guard when he retreated if the entire command retreated toward Saltville over the narrow road. Giltner divided his command and retreated. Approximately one-half under Dr. E.G. Guerrant went toward Poor Valley; Giltner and the other half under Col. Pryor moved toward Saltville.

Burbridge didn't know it, but Saltville was wide open. There were only 700 home guard, less than 400 in the 13th Battalion Virginia Reserve and the approximately 200 retreating men of Giltner's command to defend against Burbridge's 5,200.

Maybe Burbridge remembered the horrors of the night march of the 29th, and decided to wait until morning to attack the saltworks. He camped at Laurel Gap.

Gen. Jackson, who was now in command at Saltville, recognized the desperation of the situation. He sent a telegram stating, "If reinforcements are not sent tonight, it will probably be too late."[96]

That night 300 "raw recruits" arrived from Abingdon. Some of the raw recruits may have "volunteered"[97] against their will.

That night Jackson, with Trigg's help, organized the defenses as best he could, but believed the battle was a foregone conclusion. He positioned his 8 cannon and erected stone and log

William Lowther
"Mudwall" Jackson.

walls. His belief that the Negroes wouldn't fight was a little comfort.

By Sunday October 2nd, Schofield's orders to retreat were received by Ammen and Gillem, but Burbridge received no orders because of the guerrilla activity at his rear.

On that morning, fighting started about 3 miles outside of town as the forward units, the 12th Ohio, 11th Michigan, and 5th U.S. Colored tangled with Giltner's men again. The North had "...three small Mountain Howitzers but excellent cannon (that) opened fire on our troops."[98] They pushed the South back until about 9:00 where Giltner halted Burbridge's advance north of the river at Saunders Hill, near the residence of "Governor" Saunders. Giltner was just outside the breast works that Jackson had erected.

At approximately 9:30 John Williams arrived. He had been temporarily detached from the department. He and his troops were sent against the Yanks at Knoxville. They had little success against the defenders there, so they returned earlier than expected to Southwest Virginia. They rushed into Saltville with two brigades and some artillery, approximately 1,700 men in all. One brigade was under a 25 year old, Gen. Felix H. Robertson, the other under Gen. George G. Dibrell. Also with Williams was some cavalry under Cap. Champ Ferguson whom the North considered a "notorious guerrilla, bushwhacker, and brutal murderer."[99]

Re-creation: Rebs show off captured Mountain Howitzer.

At 9:30, the third command change occurred when Williams assumed responsibility.

Southern forces were deployed from left to right as follows: North of the road on the left was the 1st Kentucky under Col. Griffith, then came the 9th Kentucky Cavalry under Col. C.P. Breckinridge (maybe a relative of Gen. Breckinridge).

The Giltner brigade deployed as follows: 4th Kentucky under Col. Pryor, Johnson's Battalion under Col. Thomas Johnson, Jenkins Battery under Cap. Jenkins, Clay's Battery under Cap. Clay. Then the 64th Virginia Regiment under Col. A.L. Pridemore, 10th Kentucky under Col. Edwin Trimble who was near the ford at Governor Saunders. (The family didn't leave their home but "barricaded themselves in the spacious fireplace."[100] Bullets penetrated the house during the battle but no family members were wounded. James "Governor Saunders" was taken prisoner after the battle).

Then came the home guard units under Trigg and Preston, apparently Kent's men from Wythe County were toward the front, followed by Robertson's Brigade under Gen. Robertson, and Dibrell's Brigade under Gen. Dibrell.

Six pound artillery under Cap. John Barr were placed on Church Hill above the road behind the 10th Kentucky.

Cap. Hugh McClung's Tennessee Battery of four six-pound guns was placed behind Robertson on Chestnut Ridge. (It may have played no part in the battle.) (See map page 124.)

Because the terrain was so hilly and the fords over the Holston River so few, Burbridge couldn't fight his army as a single unit. Col. Hanson was placed near a ford on the Confederate left, Hobson in the center, and Ratliff on the Confederate right.

At 11:00 the battle opened on the Confederate left when Col. Charles Hanson moved on the ford, but Giltner and the 9th Kentucky kept the Yanks pinned on the north side of the river.

Shortly after Hanson opened the battle on the left, Col. Ratliff attacked on the South's right.

Ratliff formed three lines in each of his attacking units. The colored troops were on the South's far right, 12th Ohio in the center, and 11th Michigan on the left.

The North pressed Robertson and Dibrell who moved to the west side of the small stream, Cedar Creek. Here Southern resistance stiffened and the Union attack halted. The North regrouped and swept the field with "murderous"[101] fire (Spencer Rifles?). They continued their advance which was slowed because of a dense "jungle of briars, bushes, and wildcorn."[102] The growth was too low for cover, but high enough to slow the advance to a crawl. The Northern troops reached the creek and jumped over. The troops fought hand to hand for about two minutes.

Robertson and Dibrell retreated to the stone and log breastwork half way up Chestnut Ridge. When the South retreated this "encouraged"[103] the colored troops to attack with more vigor. Both sides fought hard as they went.

When Robertson retreated to the breastworks it left Kent's home guard unit exposed. Kent believed Robertson's retreat was cowardly. Robertson felt Kent was inexperienced and didn't know enough about battle to retreat when his position couldn't be held. Kent "...for sometime and without assistance,

Felix Huston Robertson.

maintained the contest against overwhelming numbers, suffering the loss of a number of excellent men, Maj. Hounshell himself exhibiting a bravery never excelled..."[104] Cap. Gallager had a bullet pass through his canteen. The home guard would fight. Kent and the reserves also fell back.

As the Union attacked up Chestnut Ridge a Confederate went after the regimental coloreds of the 12th Ohio held by Sgt. Jeremiah Davis. Both men had lost their guns. In the contest over the flag, Davis used the flag pole as a spear. "It passed clear through the unfortunate Confederate and came out between his ribs on the other side."[105]

Near the Confederate breastworks Ratliff reorganized his men for a final attack. He put the colored cavalry in front "and drove (them) through the briars."[106]

"The Yankees put the Negroes in front and forced them to attack...enraged Southerners on one side and the sharp point of Yankee sabers on the other."[107]

Cap. Charles Baumgardner wrote later, "This raised the anger of the Dixie boys and they covered the ground with niggers."[108]

Dibrell's Brigade "...being especially effective in mowing down the advancing enemy;"[109] Preston's reserves never got their chance to shoot the "Nigger soldiers."[110]

Gen. McLean who was in overall command of the 5th Colored Cavalry stated that the South opened with a "terrific fire...(but)...Negroes rushed upon the works with a yell..." They killed and wounded some defenders. The Negroes would fight. McLean wrote, "I saw one man riding with his arm off, another shot through the lungs, and another shot through both hips."[111]

George Gibbs Dibrell.

The Union advanced to within 50 yards of Dibrell's 8th Tennessee Regiment. The Tennesseans jumped from behind their breastworks and attacked the Negro troops "...so great was their contempt and anger."[112] The colored troops fired back as the Confederates left their protection.

The Yanks brought their three cannons forward. Cap. James W. Barr ordered his battery to fire "...from one eighth of a mile or more...with one shell bursting among them, put them out of commission."[113] Three hours of "Heavy combat" took place with the colored troops receiving much concentrated fire.

Dibrell's men left their breastworks and moved up the hill without orders or without informing Robertson on his left, that he was moving. Robertson's flank was exposed and the 12th Ohio poured into the gap.

Ammunition was low on both sides. The Tennessee troops were using pistols because their powder was gone. The North began to push them back toward the artillery. The artillery was moved to town. By 4:30 Ratliff's Union forces owned the hill. The town was in clear view. Robertson and Dibrell had formed a new line on the edge of town, but with almost no ammunition, and with the enemy on high ground, there was little hope of holding the position.

Ratliff looked down on Saltville from the hill which had cost him 38 killed and 213 missing or wounded. Saltville was his for the taking, but he was so low on ammunition he couldn't attack.

Even though Hanson had opened the attack on the Confederate left at 11:00, he had made litte progress all day. He made serious blunders as he tried to attack with his men through water sometimes 10 foot deep, and charged bluffs 10 feet high. "Above them, the Confederates with their long range Enfields, inflicted terrible damage on the struggling Federals with little loss to themselves."[114] One of the casualties was Hanson who was wounded about 4:30.

Southern forces taunted the enemy by hollering "Come right up and draw your salt."[115] The North took about 100 casualties.

Hanson attacked the Confederate left at 11:00. Ratliff attacked the Confederate right shortly thereafter, but Hobson didn't receive orders to attack until 1:00.

He attacked the Confederate center but the artillery fire from Barr's Battery of Church Hill was so intense, that he had to divide his forces and attack in three directions. By dividing his forces he lost much of his power.

He crossed at the ford held by the 10th Kentucky under Col. Edwin Trimble, and attacked up the cliff. "Every field officer of the 10th Kentucky"[116] was either killed or wounded. The 64th Virginia and 10th Kentucky Rifles came to the aid of the 10th Kentucky.

Giltner saw the situation and told Col. Trigg commanding the home guard units to send aid. Two companies, one from Wythe, one from Carrol County, were placed under Kent and moved forward. By the time Kent arrived the North had started to retreat. The home guard joined the fight for about 15 minutes, "not much of a fight for us",[117] Col. Preston recalled.

It is uncertain if Col. Trimble was leaping for joy or chasing the enemy, but he leaped "five feet"[118] in the air. When he hit the ground, he was dead from a bullet in the head.

By 5:00 the battle was over. Gen. Basil Duke and Col. Cosby came on the scene as the battle noise was fading. Also approaching Saltville was Gen. Vaughn. When the North broke off his contact at Carter's Station, Vaughn immediately pushed his command to aid Saltville.

As darkness covered the battlefield, the sound of musketry and cannon ceased. In the dark, the only sound coming from the field was the groans and moans of the wounded, mostly Northerners, including Corps Commander Hanson. The South rested and reinforced their lines as they kept a weary eye on the Union campfires across the river. In the morning the Union would probably attack again, they thought.

Burbridge knew the battle was over. He was too low on supplies, especially ammo, to attempt another attack. Also by now the orders from Schofield had gotten through. Campfires were kept burning for men who weren't there. Burbridge was retreating north under the cover of darkness.

In the darkness the South began counting their wins and loses. They didn't take the flag of the 12th Ohio, but they did capture two other regimental colors.

Also in the darkness Sam McClure had a vision. He saw his brother dead on the battlefield. He went to his captain and asked permission to go to his brother. The captain denied permission, telling McClure that he was just dreaming. McClure said he hadn't slept.

In a bit of grave-side humor a Confederate came upon a Union corpse with no head. He pulled some salt from his haversack and poured it into the head cavity saying, "there, you came for salt, now take some."[119]

When a burial detail was formed the next day, McClure went to the place he had seen in his vision and recovered his brother's body.[120]

At dawn on the 3rd, George Musgrove with the 4th Kentucky, heard shooting on his right. Thinking the attack had been resumed, he went to the line. With light he could see no enemy anywhere, but the firing continued all along the line to his right. He went to assess the situation. He reported, "...the Tennesseans were killing Negroes."[121]

Private Henry Schocker of the 12th Ohio was wounded on the field. He said he saw Cap. Champ Ferguson shoot a Negro and heard his screams. He also said he heard Ferguson ask another wounded Yank, "...why he came up there to fight with the damned Niggers?"[122]

There is no evidence to indicate that Robertson or Dibrell ordered the Negroes shot, but there is also no evidence to indicate they ordered the killing stopped.

"After the battle, there were several Negroes left wounded on the field and some so scared they stood on their knees and begged for mercy as several Southern ruffians waded into them with their swords—whacking them down..."[123]

Gen. Breckinridge had by now arrived on the scene and the command changed for the fourth time in two days. He ordered the killing stopped and rode off to find Robertson and Dibrell so they could restore order to their commands. Some additional killing may have taken place after Breckinridge left.

"The dead Negroes were gathered and dumped into a sink hole...and scantily covered with earth."[124]

While the dead and wounded of both sides were being taken care of, Echols reported to headquarters that "...we are in hot pursuit"[125] (of Burbridge's army). Gen. Burbridge reported the "...enemy being too badly crippled to follow..."[126] Neither side reported any major engagement as Burbridge moved north.

When Burbridge retreated, he not only left his dead and wounded on the field, but also the staff and wounded in the field hospital. The Union medical staff and wounded became Confederate prisoners. Medical personnel were not usually treated as prisoners of war. In a few days they were released and allowed to rejoin their units.

When William H. Gardner, a surgeon with the 13th Kentucky Infantry, (Union) was released, he filed a report with headquarters which read in part, "...on Monday morning, October 3, there came to our field hospital several armed men, as I believe soldiers in the Confederate service, and took five men, privates, wounded (Negroes), and shot them."

On Friday evening, October 7, at Emory and Henry College Hospital,"...to which place our wounded had been removed, several armed men entered the said hospital about 10:00 P.M. and...shot two of them (Negroes) dead in their beds."

"...on Saturday, October 8, at Emory and Henry College Hospital, several armed men wearing the Confederate uniforms,...about 4 P.M., overpowered the guard (Confederate) that had been placed there by the surgeon in charge,...and shot Lt. E.C. Smith, 13th Regiment Kentucky Cavalry, dead in his bed..."[127]

Northern newspapers angrily reported the massacre at Saltville. They called for revenge. 155 Negroes were massacred, they reported. The papers also decried the fact the dead and wounded were stripped of arms, valuables, and clothing. Because of the South's inability to supply its army, the army was supplying itself from any Union source it could.

Brig. Gen. N.C. McLean, commander of the 5th, suggested to Burbridge that he ask the South to turn over to the North those people responsible for the slaughter. If the South didn't, then order "Immediate retaliation be enforced upon said Confederate prisoners as we have...".[128]

The Union high command was not about to order retaliatory executions. It had a deliberate policy of punishment and starvation for Southern prisoners, but executions were too extreme. Besides, there were more Yanks in Southern prisons than Southern prisoners in Yankee prisons. It was more of a strain on the South to maintain and feed their prisoners than on the North.

It is unclear why, but Cap. Champ Ferguson became the focal point of the massacre. A Northern reporter named him as the killer. Northern newspapers charged that he "alone"[129] killed 14 Negroes. Ferguson was accused by the North of the murders in the hospital, and also said he wanted to kill the wounded Col. Hanson.

In response the South said Burbridge was "determined to sacrifice the Negroes in order to protect his white soldiers."[130]

Southern official reports are silent on the issue. Although Ferguson was apparently never charged or tried for any Negro killings, he was jailed at Wytheville. Although others were involved, only he was imprisoned.

Burbridge knew losing generals didn't stay in command long. Morgan had soundly defeated him in June. What appeared to be a Reb victory to all present on October 2, turned into a Reb defeat by October 10. Once safely back in Kentucky, Burbridge wrote a fairytale to Union high command. Instead of starting with "Once upon a time", in his official report, he opened with "We whipped the Rebels..." The South had more men and more artillery. He fought "...Echols, Williams, Vaughn, and it is said, Breckinridge." While he had only 2,500 men, the South had between 6,000 and 10,000 plus 4,000 more from Lynchburg. He lost "about 350, the enemy more." Also "some of the outer salt works were destroyed." He used the truth when he said that he had pushed the Rebels back from the main fortifications, but his ammo "gave out." His night retreat became a "Withdraw(al)."[131]

A Union surgeon's report listed Northern casualties as follows:

UNITS	KILLED	WOUNDED	MISSING
13 Kentucky Cav.	4	13	1
35th Ky. Mont. Inf.	3	11	21
45th Ky. Mont. Inf.	0	2	0
40th Ky. Mont. Inf.	0	1	0
26th Ky. Mont. Inf.	1	3	0
30th Ky. Mont. Inf.	5	2	0
30th Ky. Cav.	0	10	0
37 Ky. Reg. Mont. Inf.	2	9	0
39 Ky. Reg. Mont. Inf.	1	10	0
12 Reg. Ohio Vol. Cav.	5	31	12
11th Mich. Cav.	11	61	16
5th U.S. Colored Cav.	22	190	53[132]

(statistics show a higher casualty rate for Negro soldiers. The number of killed and wounded reflect conditions at time of retreat. The number of killed increased after the massacre).

Rebel sources state that there were 104 white soldiers dead on the field. The number of colored ranged from 156[133] to 165.[134]

Gillem only reported 4 casualties, three were wounded when a shell burst accidentally. William H. Norton was "severely wounded in the head by the accidental discharge of his own gun...."[135]

The number of prisoners said to be taken varies from 300 to 1,200.[136]

Although no official report on Southern casualties was found, all other sources agree that Southern figures were miraculously low. It appears that only 8 Rebs died and only 51 were wounded. Two of the 8 dead were Col. Trimble and Lt. Crutchfield of the 10th Kentucky Regiment.[137] Of the 51 casualties, it appears that the home guard units under Kent suffered the most. They took 24 casualties including Cap. L.G. Shockley, 1st Lt. W.C.H. Bolt killed, and Private William McGee missing.[138]

The Department of Southwest Virginia and East Tennessee could report with pride to Lee at Richmond, "We whipped the enemy badly...the reservest and detailed men acted splendidly..."[139] Not a word was said about the Negroes killed after the battle.

After the battle on the 8th, a Confederate telegram stated that 61 prisoners were being sent to Lynchburg, including the surgeons and attendants from Emory and Henry Hospital. No mention was made of other prisoners. Also the telegram stated that 5 coloreds were being sent to the hospital. Two other coloreds were being sent to Abingdon "...to be tried for desertion...abandoning the Confederacy and joining the Federal service. One is a clear case of desertion from his own admission."[140] He must have told his captors that he was once a slave. The life expectancy for the two was not good.

The South had won a major and miraculous victory over an enemy that was much larger and better equipped. The saltworks, lead mines, and railroad were still intact; Lee could breath easier.

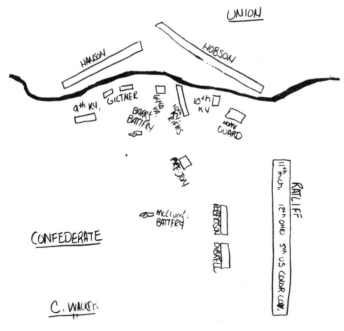

Part Five

As the winter of 1864-65 set in the common soldier believed that only devine aid could save the "cause." There was never any doubt in the soldiers mind that the Confederacy was a just and righteous nation, but as the cold wind blew through their ragged uniforms they knew the enemy was much stronger. They were sure God would intervene and save them and the "cause". This bleak night would give way to a glorious, victorious dawn.

As one Southern lady put it, "...that...soldiers pray; that prayer was the weapon of the South, as well as the bayonet."[141]

Revivals sprang up in every army of the South. Tent meetings were occurring somewhere almost every hour of the day, every day of the week. Many prayers included, "Bless and help Gen. Lee."

Gen. Lee, who's stature and legend had grown since the first of the war, was now almost deified. The soldiers knew that as long as Richmond stood there was hope. Lee had fought Grant's hordes to a standstill. A David against Goliath. Lee must be God's appointed one. That winter Lee moved a step above being a superior general and Southern gentleman, to the position of a super-human being. A position his memory still occupies.

Of course, not every man's mind was looking above. There is a story of an officer returning to camp from Richmond. He passed a tent revival. The officer didn't know what was occurring in the tent. A soldier called to him as he rode by, "Come in, Sir, we have just what you need inside." To which the officer was alledged to have replied, "No, thank you. I just came from town, where I already got a little."

As the winter set in, it became more apparent that the economy was collapsing. The blockade was strangling the South. Less cotton was going out and less war material was coming in. The ships and boats were generally smaller in size because the Yanks occupied most major Southern seaports. The Reb blockade runners were using rivers to hide. Rivers are more shallow, therefore the vessels were smaller.

Some estimates state that 50% or more blockade runners never returned. The South couldn't get raw materials or manufactured goods. The South didn't have the industrial base to manufacture, so the people did without.

The South seemed to be short of everything except hunger and biting cold.

Gen. Vaughn complained to Breckinridge that he needed arms, saddles, and other equipment, especially pistols. "My command is absolutely destitute of clothing and blankets,...and barefooted...Many of my men have not been paid their salary for 15 months..."

Gen. Williams also told Breckinridge, "My horses are entirely broken down. I have quite a number of men almost naked and barefoot. Couldn't some clothes be found in the Department for immediate use?"[142]

There wasn't much Breckinridge could do. Many horses were sent to North Carolina to the Mt. Airy region for the winter. Food was more abundant for them there. There wasn't much that could be done for the men.

"Salt had been scarce in the Old Dominion for 2 years. Now it would be practically non-existent." There was no salt for "what little meat they could lay hands on..."[143]

"Scanty rations were reduced or not issued at all. Troops went for days without food;..."[144] Without pay, food, clothing, and ammo, no wonder the disease and desertion rates were high.

The lead from Austinville could meet only half of the South's needs. People donated "pipes, window weights, rooks, cistern lining, common utensils... Battlefields were gleaned for the indispensable material..."[145]

Although the map of the Department of Southwest Virginia and East Tennessee covered alot of area, Breckinridge only controlled a narrow corridor along the railroad. There wasn't enough manpower to maintain effective military control in the Department.

Re-creation: Union scouting party.

By late 1864, Union scouting parties were almost as frequent in the area as Southern troops. A group of Federals occupied the barn on the Huddle farm at Black Lick in Wythe County. The boy took the livestock and hid. The mother and daughter were not molested in their home. The Union seemed to be waiting, to pass the time they took target practice on a large tree in the yard. They finally left. When the boy returned he dug the lead out of the tree and turned it over to the Confederate Quarter Master.

In November a Mr. G. Moore, probably with the home guard, sent a telegram to Breckinridge. He said Johnson County Tennessee was "Infested with several bands of bushwhackers, murderers, and deserters...(some equipped)...with guns of the best quality." They were terrorizing citizens in Virginia, Tennessee, and North Carolina. Many of the iron workers who were under contract to the Confederacy couldn't leave home without an armed escort, while "...the Union (Northern sympathizers) men seem to be in no danger..." Moore said that there were only 20 men from age 14 to 60 to defend the area.

He told Breckinridge "...you will not suffer any portion of your military Department to fall into the hands of the enemy if it can be avoided..." He asked Breckinridge for help. He then added, "We will try to hold this county (around Mountain City, Tennessee)..."

About the same time Samuel S. Glenn of Washington County wrote Breckinridge about the bushwhackers saying, "(They were) in danger from a party of robbers...who make their rendezvous in the mountains bordering on Johnson County, Tennessee."[146] He also asked for help.

The battle at Saltville, and the loss of control, made many civilians in the area nervous. One was George Robertson's father. Robertson wrote in his book *A Small Boy's Recollection of the Civil War*, that the father decided to move the family further south to Ashville, North Carolina, where they would be safer. The father was apparently well off because he bought a whole wagon load of salt to send with the family. It was hoped that the bushwhackers that might be encountered on the way, could be bought off with salt. Robertson recalled that he didn't see a single Confederate soldier after they left Wytheville until they arrived in Ashville. There was little protection for the populous. Fortunately they never encountered bushwhackers.

Breckinridge sent one company of men under Cap. Cantrill to help in the rural area, but they were to report back in 7 to 10 days.[147]

Breckinridge didn't have enough soldiers and some of them would be leaving, but not everyone was sad to see them leave. Gen. Vaughn was upset because Gen. Robertson had not helped him as he felt he should have in the recent battle at Saltville. Vaughn told Breckinridge that Robertson and the Tennesseans (who were involved in the massacre) had been ordered to join Hood "...and the sooner they are ordered from the Department, the better..."[148]

Hood and the Army of Tennessee had taken great casualties and lost Atlanta, but Hood still had the ear, and confidence of President Davis. Hood got Davis's O.K. for an operation north.

It was Hood's belief that Sherman would leave Atlanta if Union troops in Tennessee were pushed back. So it followed that if the Union was pushed out of

Tennessee and the Ohio River area threatened, Sherman would abandon Atlanta to stop the Southern invaders on Union soil. Lee had used this technique many times to reduce the pressure on Richmond, by attacking near Washington. The North was not unaware that troops were being sent from Southwest Virginia to Hood.

Gen. George Stoneman, operating around Knoxville, sent a letter containing a proposed attack on Southwest Virginia to Maj. Gen. Schofield, and asking for permission to strike Southwest Virginia. "I owe the Southern Confederacy a debt I am anxious to liquidate, and this appears a propitious occasion."[149] He may have been referring to the time he had spent in a Southern prison camp after his capture earlier in the war. He was exchanged north and now commanded an army of 9,000 to 10,000 "effective men." The South only had 3,000 to 6,000 between New Market and Bulls Gap, Tennessee. He wanted to "force him (the South) across mountains to North Carolina and maybe destroy the saltworks."[150]

Stoneman's plan called for Burbridge to move south out of Kentucky and join him in Tennessee.

Schofield gave Stoneman the nod to start planning, equipping, and organizing, but no attack could be launched until they knew what Hood was up to.

The eyes of both nations watched as Hood moved north into Western Tennessee. This was supposed to keep Sherman penned in Atlanta, but Sherman didn't read the script. With virtually no troops in front of him, Georgia was wide open to invasion. Sherman decided to abandon his supply line and take what he needed as he went.

Major-General George Stoneman.

The rape of Georgia remains a black spot on history. When a reporter questioned Sherman about the wanton destruction of Southern properties, (military, commercial, and private), the stealing, raping, and murdering, Sherman made his remark that is so widely misquoted, "War is hell." His soldiers were on a picnic and they were eating Georgia. The war was hell to the innocent civilians.

While both sides watched Hood, Stoneman was collecting his forces around Bean Station not far east of Knoxville. Stoneman believed he could surprise the Confederates in Southwest Virginia. Historically speaking, major offenses are conducted in the spring and summer, winter weather usually fights on the side of the defender. Cold, bad roads, poor communications and transportation, are considered a handicap for the attacker. Because of the lack of strength of Southern forces and their shortage of weapons, ammo, food, shelter and clothing, the winter weather would fight with the attacker.

Stoneman took many steps to try and conceal his intentions from the South. He collected supplies and cattle. His troop movements were designed to fool the South into believing that the army was consolidating to move north as the cold December weather set in.

Stoneman organized his army as follows: Under Gen. Burbridge was the 11th, 12th, and 13th Kentucky, the 10th and 11th Michigan, the 12th Ohio, and the 5th and 6th Colored Cavalry.

Under Gen. Gillem was the 8th, 9th, and 13th Tennessee and Battery E Kentucky Light Artillery, about 1,500 men.

Gen. Ammen controlled the rest of the artillery, the 2nd Ohio Heavy Artillery and the 1st U.S. Colored Artillery approximately 1,000 men.

About one half of Burbridge's men were equipped with "carbines".[151] The carbines were probably Spencer Repeating Rifles. They held 7 shots. Whereas the standard musket could be fired 3 times a minute, the Spencer rate of fire was 15 times a minute. It could put a slug 13 inches deep in pine boards at 50 yards.[152]

Although the South captured thousands of these weapons they couldn't be used against the North because the South didn't have the expertise or manufacturing facilities to make the cartridges for the weapon.

Stoneman felt he was deceiving the South as he collected troops and equipment. Although some tools were carried with the army, Stoneman packed a large number of sledge hammers with him.

Stoneman thought he was deceiving the South, but on December 2, Duke sent a telegram to headquarters from Morristown stating that there were 1,500 to 2,000 Yanks at Bean Station. He questioned, "Perhaps a movement on Bristol?"[153]

On the 3rd Vaughn started a stream of telegrams to Breckinridge. He said that "information received from Union resources..."[154] said part of the men were there to guard a wagon train. He suggested that the area around Saltville be strengthened.

On the 4th, Vaughn said there was no doubt the Union was going for Saltville.

On the 5th, Vaughn reported Burbridge had 7 regiments.

On the 6th, Breckinridge sent Duke toward Rogersville.

On the 7th, Vaughn reported from Greenville, "This country is full of parties from the Federal army - bushwhacking."[155] He said Duke was attacked today while foraging about 5 miles from Greenville and lost two men.

Vaughn suggested that Breckinridge order an attack on Stoneman's supply line, and thus stop the expected attack. Breckinridge issued no such orders.

Maj. George W. Day was fooled by Stoneman's movement. He reported that Stoneman retreated to Bean Station with 3,500 men. "He takes all horses, cattle, hogs,...."[156] Stoneman was not retreating.

On the 9th, Vaughn sent Breckinridge some hard intelligence in the form of a letter from Cap. Messick. Messick had been captured by Burbridge a week before and escaped. By talking to the guards and fellow prisoners, Messick learned much about the Union forces. He stated that Burbridge had 3 brigades; First under Col. Brown, 2nd under Col. Buch Buckley, and 3rd under Col. Wade of the 6th U.S. Colored. There were 9 regiments that he knew of; the 11th, 12th, 13th, 54th, (39 or 50), Kentucky, the 12th Ohio under Col. Bently, the 11th Michigan, 2 Negro (5th and 6th U.S. Colored Cavalry). He saw 5 guns and thought there were 3 more. One gun was a 12 pounder, the others were 6 pounders. He estimated there were between 5,000 and 6,000 cavalry and mounted infantry.

There was no doubt in Vaughn's mind that the Yanks were coming. Vaughn added that Stoneman was just waiting to see what Hood was doing.

Despite the telegrams from Vaughn, Breckinridge did not react. He wrote later "...Although it was known that Gen. Burbridge had not returned to Kentucky, the intelligence from the front looked to a retrograde movement, and I had no uneasiness until I received the news; ...a possible combined movement by Burbridge and Gillem..."[157]

Hood's Army of Tennessee, struck the Yanks at Franklin Tennessee on November 15. Charge after charge on the Union lines left thousands of brave Southern men killed and mangled. Twelve Southern generals and 53 regimental commanders were killed, wounded or captured. The Army of Tennessee was reduced to impotency. There was a futile attempt on Nashville, but everyone knew it was over. Unlike Joseph Johnston's (Uncle Joe) very favorable casualty rate, Hood had bled the army dry. The Army of Tennessee was broken as it retreated south. The survivors rephrased the "Yellow Rose of Texas" and sang it openly to their Texas general to voice their resentment of his mishandling of the army.

It went in part:

> "and now I'm going southward,
> for my heart is full of woe,
> I'm going back to Georgia
> to find my 'Uncle Joe.'
> You may talk about your Beauregard
> and sing of Gen. Lee,
> but that gallant Hood of Texas,
> played Hell in Tennessee."

As Hood moved out, Schofield gave the orders and the attack on the Department of Southwest Virginia and East Tennessee began.

It was cold on the 12th when Gillem came from Knoxville and joined Stoneman and Burbridge at Bean Station. The combined army marched all night and was at the edge of Kingsport by daylight of the 13th.

Duke's Brigade of 250 men were there, but Duke was in the hospital at Bristol. There were 14 wagons and 4 ambulances with the brigade.[158]

John McAllister Schofield.

The foraging efforts of the men had paid off. They had made a big catch of whiskey. A large part of the command was drunk.

Stoneman sent the 13th Kentucky Mounted Infantry and 13th Tennessee two miles above Kingsport, and crossed the river at Possum Ford. Gen. Gillem sent the 8th Tennessee directly toward Kingsport.

The drunken command was surprised "...sustained a severe defeat."[159] There were 18 killed and 84 captured, including Col. Morgan.[160] The rest fled for their lives. One man "...was so drunk that he danced a jig when captured."[161]

By nightfall the Union held Kingsport. The prisoners were sent back toward Knoxville on the captured Reb wagons.

Duke heard about the attack and left his sick bed at Bristol to join his command.

At Dublin, Gen. John Echols was assembling the reserves, but said it would take 3 or 4 days to complete.

While the action was occurring at Kingsport, Stoneman sent Burbridge ahead toward Bristol. This move cut Vaughn off from a direct road link with Bristol. Vaughn was at Greenville with 1,200 men. His horses were in poor condition.

Stoneman used one of Morgan's tricks. He sent a telegram to Bristol stating that the Union had been defeated, signing a Confederate officers name. This caused confusion in Bristol so that proper defensive measures were not taken.

Breckinridge sent orders to Vaughn and Duke to delay the enemy.

Burbridge built large campfires so that Vaughn could see them. He wanted Vaughn to think that he was camping. At 3 A.M. he launched his attack on Bristol. The 11th Kentucky Cavalry "Charged into the place with drawn sabres."[162]

Vaughn was caught off guard. He attacked toward Bristol and was repulsed. Once again the North held the main road (Rock Road, Rt. 11), and kept him detached from the rest of the department.

Burbridge set about the task of destroying the town. He destroyed the railroad, round-house, Masonic Lodge and burned churches. Much of Bristol went up in flames. His men looted at will. About 60 towns-people were made prisoners, including J. Austin Sperry, the editor of the "Bristol New's on Register." Sperry was a firey Southern editor that Burbridge wanted to "Hang"[163] personally. Sperry was captured but Burbridge didn't know it, and continued to search for him.

Stoneman recalled there was a "Dense fog"[164] when he and Gillem joined Burbridge at Bristol on the 14th. In Bristol, Stoneman found a telegraph message from Breckinridge to Vaughn asking if the railroad was still open. Stoneman sent a reply that the railroad was safe.

Breckinridge sent two train loads of reinforcements forward. There were about 500 men in all. The track in Bristol was destroyed. As the trains passed toward Bristol, the tracks behind them were also destroyed.

When the trains stopped because of the track, the 500 found themselves surrounded. There was some shooting but the South quickly realized their situation was hopeless. The 500 and the two trains were captured. One train was a mail train from Richmond. There was a dispatch containing valuable information on bridge repair in the Richmond area. It and the prisoners were sent toward Knoxville. There were about 1,000 guns and much precious ammunition aboard the trains.[165]

After Vaughn was unable to enter Bristol he moved toward Bluff City and started toward Abingdon on a parallel road. He hoped to rejoin the command there.

Breckinridge didn't have many forces to oppose Stoneman. The 34th Virginia Battalion under Lt. Col. Vincent A. Witcher had been operating against Union Head Quarters on the Kanawha. It had been ordered to Saltville after the raid began, and was only now approaching Centerville in Monroe County. The unit marched 90 miles in 25 hours to Tazewell County by the fifteenth. Brig. Gen. George B. Cosby was in Marion with a small brigade from the Valley of Virginia. At 3:30 P.M. on Wednesday the 14th, he was at Seven Mile Ford. He moved toward Saltville that night. Lt. Col. Robert Smith was at Wytheville with one company of reserves. Col. Henry J. Giltner moved from Russell County toward Saltville (maybe with the 4th or 2nd Kentucky). Brig. Gen. John Echols was in Dublin assembling the reserves. The home guard was activated. The unit at Wytheville under Col. Kent (promoted from Major after his gallant stand at Saltville in October) apparently headed toward the lead mines at Austinville. The 3rd Tennessee, 2nd Kentucky Cavalry, and 58 North Carolina Infantry were also operating in the area.

Breckinridge decided to consolidate at the major target of the raid, Saltville.

Stoneman waited at Bristol for Burbridge to complete his destruction of that place. Burbridge was then ordered forward to Abingdon to cut the railroad and prevent Southern reinforcements from moving on Stoneman.

Duke had "a strong picket"[166] posted at Abingdon and felt he could stop Burbridge.

Burbridge's men met little resistance. Duke's strong picket fell back and "...the home guard threw down their arms and fled into the houses."[167] Burbridge continued the destruction of the railroad. He captured one 16 pound Napoleon, one locomotive, 12 cars, and lots of stores. Duke moved toward Saltville.

Burbridge was in Abingdon two hours before Vaughn arrived. Vaughn realized he was cut off again and started toward Marion.

On the morning of Thursday the 15th, a cold drizzle fell. Stoneman was unsure where the Southern forces were and what their intentions were. He would seal off Saltville and then test its defenses. He knew that Vaughn was separated from the command and would try to prevent Vaughn from making a junction.

Stoneman conferred with Generals Gillem and Burbridge. Gillem was to cut the railroad at Glade Spring, while Burbridge was given the task of fending off Vaughn. Stoneman took two regiments (the 11th Kentucky under Col. Boyle, and the 11th Michigan under Col. Brown) to strengthen Gillem. Stoneman took part of Burbridge's command and advanced on the saltworks.

Gillem ordered Maj. Harrison and the 12th Kentucky Cavalry to cut the railroad at Glade Spring.

In the early morning of the 15th, Breckinridge was coming down the railroad headed to Saltville. He was with a company of reserves under Col. Preston, and a battery of artillery from Wytheville. Breckinridge passed Glade Spring only 20 minutes before Harrison cut the line. (Harrison missed Breckinridge, but he caught two supply trains that followed later. Many valuable supplies were burned).

Vaughn made another attempt to join Breckinridge at Seven Mile Ford. Again Vaughn was too late. The place was occupied. After a brief exchange, Vaughn headed toward Marion, hoping to cross the Rock Road before the Yanks sealed it off also.

Stoneman moved toward Saltville. Duke confirmed the Yanks were coming by the Glade Spring Road, the Abingdon Road, and Lebanon Road. "The enemy made decided demonstrations against the saltworks, but did not attack them."[168]

Breckinridge realized the Union had cut the railroad at Glade Spring when his supply trains didn't arrive. To avoid further loss he sent a message to Maj. J. Stoddard Johnson (Quarter Master) at Wytheville, informing him that the North was at Glade Spring.

He told Johnson to send troops and horses to Seven Mile Ford and then over to Saltville. Johnson was to see that the men coming had arms and ammunition. Breckinridge didn't know where Vaughn was nor that Gillem was pursuing him toward Seven Mile Ford and Marion.

As the Union moved toward Saltville and Marion, they left some buildings smoking in Abingdon. Hurt's store, Sinon's Wagon Shop, Musser's Wagon Shop, and the Confederate barracks across from the jail went up in smoke.[169] No private residences were burned.

One Union soldier, Cap. James Wyatt, Co. M. 13th Tennessee, didn't advance with his unit. This was his town and now was his time for sweet revenge because "Noble I. McGinnes, a prominent citizen of the town and member of the court, had sometime previous to war, punished him for an offense of which he was not guilty."[170]

He forced a Negro slave to hold his horse while he went inside and set the courthouse on fire. Then he mounted the horse and rode into all the buildings on the south side of Main Street, setting them on fire, and rode out.

He stopped at the intersection of Main and Court Street, swung one leg over the saddle and unholstering his rifle, dared anyone to try and stop the fires; he sat and watched the fires of his revenge.

Little did he know that he was being watched by another man in a Yankee uniform. He was a Reb from Mississippi. Many Confederate men were using parts of Union uniforms and equipment because the South had none to supply them. Apparently the Mississippi soldier was with a small unit of cavalry wintering in the area, and not attached to the department.

He rode back to his unit outside of town and informed them of Wyatt's actions and of a few Union men at the blacksmith's shop having their horses reshod before they rejoined their units.

The two Findlay boys (John and Samuel) of Holly Spring, Mississippi, must have been at the front of the small group. They asked a young boy, who burned the town? The boy pointed toward Wyatt.

John Findlay and the others went toward the blacksmith's shop; Sam went toward Wyatt. When Wyatt saw the man in the Yank uniform fire his pistol at him from some distance, he thought it was a mistake. Wyatt called for the soldier to quit firing at his own, but Findlay kept on shooting.

Wyatt raced toward Findlay going west out of town. Findlay kept firing. As Wyatt's horse turned left, Wyatt fell to the ground, mortally wounded.

Sam Findlay captured Wyatt's horse, while John and the rest overran the few Yanks at the blacksmith's.

Wyatt's desire for revenge cost him his life.[171]

Rumors began to circulate among the Union troops about Wyatt's death. They believed a local citizen had shot him because he had left the area to join the Union. Union soldiers from the South became nervous at the thought of being captured and executed.[172]

By dark Breckinridge was joined in Saltville by Duke from Abingdon, and Cosby from Marion. Cols. Giltner and Witcher were on their way.

Gillem had chased Vaughn until the afternoon, when he stopped to rest about 14 miles east of Abingdon. Around dark he started after Vaughn again.

Around 11 P.M. the head of Gillem's army - the 13th Tennessee, struck the rear of Vaughn's column under Col. Gillespie at Marion. The North pushed Vaughn out of town. Because so many Confederates were wearing Union uniforms, there was confusion in the ranks of the North as they dashed into town in the dark. Apparently Cap. William Gourley mistook Col. Gideon for a Reb and attacked him. Gideon lived to explain the confusion.[173]

Gillem knew Vaughn was just outside of town at the heights, but explained that he couldn't attack because he could find no guide (a traitor, Northern sympathizer).

The night of the 15th, several houses were burned in Marion, as the Union patrolled the streets.

Vaughn knew he couldn't move his men to join Breckinridge at Saltville. He divided his command. He ordered Gillespie to harass Gillem, while he and the wagon train moved through Rye Valley toward safety.

The early morning light of the 16th, revealed the body of Col. Bean of Gillespie's command, dead on Main Street in front of the courthouse. There was a Northern and Southern officer dead between the courthouse and the bank.

As dawn broke, Gillem attacked Gillespie. A sharp skirmish ensued. Gillespie gave Gillem all he could handle. Both sides charged and counter-attacked. When Gillespie saw troops from Burbridge arriving on the field, he knew he could hold the line no longer.

He began his retreat east over the Rock Road. He left 15 men killed and wounded, and 75 prisoners as he pulled back.

He sent a message to Breckinridge informing him "...my force is falling back in some confusion..."[174] but the artillery was safe. Gillespie had 7 or 8 pieces of artillery, 4 of which had been captured from the Union at Bull's Gap and Morristown, Tennessee. His horses were worn out.

Re-creation: on the firing line. Note Confederate in mostly Union uniform.

As Gillespie fell back, he began to reorganize his forces as best he could. Because his jaded stock was given out, he believed the Union would overtake the small wagon train and artillery. He decided to make a stand at Mt. Airy on the Rock Road, just north of Rural Retreat.

The South hastily formed a line, they didn't have to wait long for the Union to arrive.

It is uncertain how long the battle at Mt. Airy lasted. Gillespie made effective use of his artillery on Gillem's left. No Union casualty figures are available.

After Gillem established his line, he ordered the 13th Tennessee to attack directly upon Gillespie's artillery. The 13th broke through and took possession of the artillery; Gillespie knew it was all over.

He sent a message to Maj. J. Stoddard Johnson in Wytheville. Johnson was about the only military man left in town. He was the quartermaster for Southern supplies. Apparently Johnson sent a message to Kent informing him that the town was in danger. It is not clear if Kent and the home guard had reached the mines yet.

Gillespie informed Johnson that he was falling back from Mt. Airy. The enemy was pressing him hard and that he would avoid a fight if he could.

Gillespie left 198 men captured, and 7 or 8 guns in Gillem's hands as he fled. Gillem overtook the few wagons and ambulances Gillespie had with him. Gillem was unaware that most of Vaughn's wagon train left through Rye Valley and was now near Cripple Creek getting ready to cross over New River. Gillem thought he had captured it all.

Gillem continued to pursue what little was left of Gillespie's command toward Wytheville.

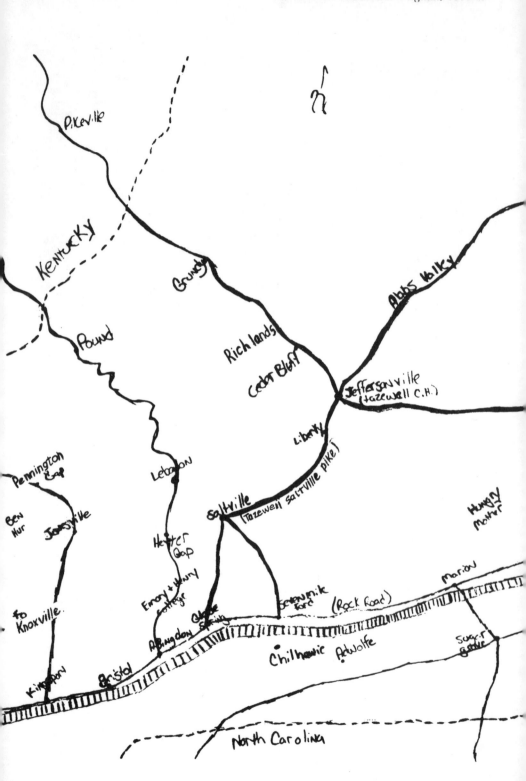

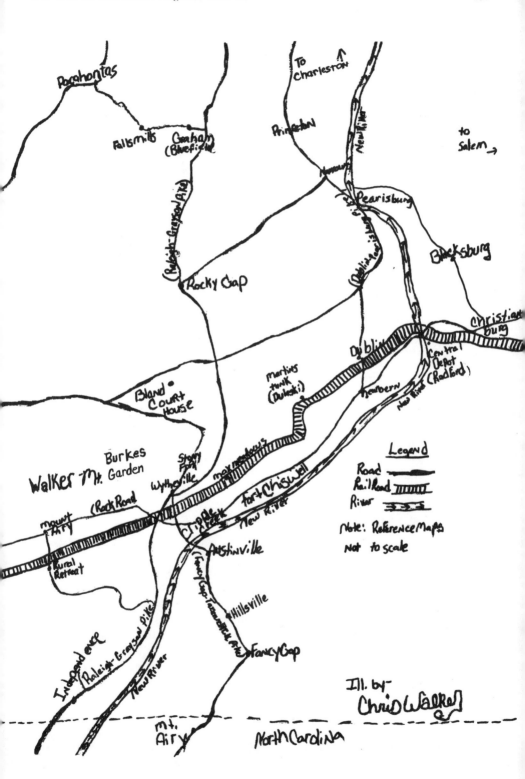

At Wytheville Johnson was hastily loading what supplies he could on the 14 railroad cars he had, so they could be moved toward Dublin and avoid capture. He complained that if the railroad had given him more cars he could have loaded more supplies. He also set about the task of defending the town with only a few men. One source said there was Johnson, his clerk, 3 other officers, and "one drunk private."[175] Johnson indicated he had 8 men to stop Gillem's army.

Upon receiving the news that the Yanks were coming, Kent started toward Wytheville, leaving the mines unprotected.

At Wytheville Johnson prepared rifle pits for men that weren't there. He knew that Gillespie's men would help defend the town when they arrived.

While Johnson was preparing at Wytheville, there was confusion in Marion. William Sexton, who was Clerk of the County, was at his farm in the Rye Valley area when told about the Yanks. He rode to town and secured a wagon and Negro driver. At the courthouse he quickly loaded as many files as possible, covered them with dry goods, including several bales of calico material from Thursman's Store. He just started out of town when Maj. Harrison and the 12th Kentucky Cavalry rode in.

Stoneman had ordered Harrison to Rye Valley. Had Harrison known Vaughn's wagon train was spread out through the valley, he would have had a field day. Harrison was not after Vaughn; he had come to destroy.

Sexton was sure the Yanks were going to Wytheville. When the Union followed him, he knew he couldn't outrun them. He warned the people in the nearest house about the approach of the North. He told them what was in the wagon. He unhitched the wagon, and fled on horseback into the mountains. "Several shots were fired at him,..." but he escaped.

The Yanks set the wagon on fire and approached the nearest house, the Killinger's. The youngest daughter, Elizabeth, met the two Yanks at the door. They asked politely for water which Elizabeth gave them. They also asked if any Rebs were in the area. She replied no. When the Yanks asked if there were any guns in the house, Elizabeth's oldest sister replied and brought in "dad's old gun." She was afraid that Elizabeth would tell about the two new guns that had been captured from the Union.

The Yanks laughed at the dilapidated old gun, and said "I hear that calico is scarce in the South now. There are several bales of it burning in the wagon at the foot of the hill. Go down and help yourselves." Then they left.

Elizabeth's mother and sister didn't want her to go, but she knew what was in the wagon and how important it was. Alone she went down and removed the court books one at a time. They were charred at the edges but apparently few records were lost.[176]

Harrison's command destroyed his major objective, the "great iron works,"[177] Thomas' Furnace near Sugar Grove. They also discovered 75 salted beefs in a barn. What they couldn't carry, they burned. People for miles around could smell the burning meat. Harrison continued "...burning right and left as he went..."[178]

Stoneman was headquartered in Seven Mile Ford at the Preston house. He allowed his men to use the Preston's mahogany table as a slaughter board for Rebel beef.

Stoneman had a telegraph operator with him. The operator was listening to Reb messages. He rushed to Stoneman with the news that the South was sending reinforcements from Lynchburg. Gillem, who was pursuing Gillespie, was riding into an ambush with "700 to 800"[179] Southern infantry. Stoneman left Seven Mile Ford and rushed to Marion to confer with Burbridge.

The troops referred to were probably about 400 convalescent and "...detail men, and would not be able to make a march."[180]

There was no help coming to Breckinridge. "...He will either defeat them or will be defeated himself before we could render him any aid..." Even the bridge at New River was "uncovered."[181]

At Wytheville, Johnson was still working on his rifle pits when Gillespie's men entered the town. He thought Gillespie's men would help defend the town; he was wrong. "All my efforts to rally Gillespie failed; they kept on to New River without halting at Wytheville."[182] Johnson wasn't giving up his town yet.

Gillem had been chasing Gillespie since Mt. Airy. He captured about 50 more men as their horses "gave out." Some of Gillespie's men left the main road and fled into the mountains to avoid capture.

Gillem also learned the South had 700 to 800 men at Wytheville. Gillem was apparently some distance back from the head of the column. At 4 P.M., Col. Brown and the 11th Michigan halted the column about one mile west of town to regroup and reconnoiter the Reb position. Brown sent Col. Boyle north of town; his group's assignment was to ride north around town to the Pepper's Ferry Road, then go east to the railroad at Max Meadows. By destroying the railroad they would prevent additional reinforcements from reaching Wytheville.

As Brown watched, he saw Johnson "...showing myself with 6 or 8 others at different picket posts (rifle pits)."[183] He also saw several cannons Johnson had placed along a line. These were cannons unfit for service that had been brought to Wytheville to be repaired or smelted down. Brown didn't know that, of course. All he could see were the cannons. Brown watched. He saw the 6 or 8 men, but couldn't see the 700 or 800 others.

During the delay Gillespie's men made good their escape as did more Rebel supplies. All but 4 of Johnson's men joined them.

Brown watched and reorganized his command for two hours. He then sent a "flag of truce" to Johnson and "...an unconditional surrender was demanded. I (Johnson) agreed to give up the town, but required half an hour to withdraw my troops."[184] Johnson had "brass."

Brown talked to the flag bearer who had seen no troops and sent word that he would not accept Johnson's terms, but would attack immediately. Johnson knew that the show was over; he and his four men ran for their lives toward Dublin where he had sent the supplies.

When Brown attacked he was still not 100% sure of the enemies' strength. He was surprised when he took the town "...without seeing our enemy firing a shot."[185]

The Yanks burned Barrett's Foundry which was one of the few places in the Confederacy that made percussion caps. Charles McWane's Foundry went up in flames. It made wagons, gun stocks, and reconditioned railroad cars.

The depot burned, several cars and two locomotives were destroyed. A large number of saddles were burned.

The Mt. Tabor Presbyterian Church and several other buildings that stored Reb ordnances were destoyed, "...consider that it's sacred character did not protect its war-like contents..."[186]

The 13th Tennessee was still west of Wytheville when they heard the ordnance exploding. They assumed the Rebs had attacked Brown. Not knowing the situation, and it being dark, they decided not to join Brown. They moved further west from Wytheville and established a defense line and camped for the night.

The Yanks destroyed 8 guns, but the South said the guns were "condemned"[87] anyway. Johnson used them as decoys. Strangely headquarters of the quartermaster was not burned.

Having "...completed the destruction of Wytheville..."[188] by 12:00 midnight, the Yanks moved east along the railroad tracks toward Max Meadows. They were looking for Boyle, who had reached Max Meadows, burned the depot, and a medical supply building; apparently doing little damage to the tracks and had headed west toward Wytheville. They met Brown about 3 miles east of Wytheville and camped there for the night.

The South didn't know how far east the Yanks intended to come. The populous was panicked as far as Salem.

By nightfall Stoneman and Burbridge had moved their forces from Marion to Mt. Airy, to reinforce Gillem who they believed had by now struck the 700 to 800 infantry coming from Lynchburg.

The day of the 16th, Breckinridge had spent consolidating and organizing. Colonels Giltner and Witcher had arrived. Breckinridge deployed his artillery and strengthened his defenses, which the Yanks described as "very strong fortifications."[189] The largest earth fort was named in honor of the commander, Fort Breckinridge. Also on the 16th, Breckinridge realized that Saltville was not the only objective of Stoneman's raid: the enemy had threatened the works, but had made no serious effort to attack them. He had only limited information about what was occurring in the rest of his department, but knew the Yanks were causing havoc. It became evident that he couldn't remain stationary and preserve his department. He must come out and attack. "...it would not be creditable to remain there (Saltville) and surrender the whole department to the enemy... I supposed the lead mines to be quite as important as the salt works."[190] He would move at dawn, hoping to form a coordinated attack with the forces of Vaughn. He didn't know Vaughn had split his command. The wagon train was well on its way to the lead mines at Austinville, via Rye Valley to Cripple Creek. Part of Vaughn's men were beaten, scattered, and running east from Wytheville. He would leave the reserves, "Some dismounted men, Barr Artillery company, a few men of Kain's Artillery, and some pieces in position, all under the command of Col. Robert Preston."[191] These 400 men were left to guard Saltville.

Re-creation: briefing the company before the battle.

Breckinridge was hoping to repeat his spectacular victory of New Market. There his forces were inferior also, instead of retreating or defending, he attacked.

By dawn of Saturday the 17th, Stoneman and Burbridge had guessed that the lead mines should be lightly defended. Burbridge said, "Here I detached Col. Buckley with his brigade, (10th Michigan - 600 men) with instructions to move as rapidly as his horses would carry him, to the lead mines,..."[192] He was to return by Seven Mile Ford. Burbridge was anticipating attacking Breckinridge at Saltville, via Abingdon, Glade Spring, Seven Mile Ford, or maybe by all three. He wanted Buckley to return as quickly and directly to the main body as possible.

Buckley left Mt. Airy and apparently stopped in Rural Retreat. Most of the population hid as the cavalry approached. A Northern major asked one citizen who did not run, if there were any Rebs near. Yes, was the reply, about 15,000 behind the Lutheran church. The Yanks knew better and questioned the lying Reb no further.

They moved toward the depot. "When they arrived they found Tom Buck near the depot. They gave him a match and told him to set the baled hay on the platform of the depot afire. He obeyed, scared badly. He was quite young. Don't know when he stopping running when he got away. So Tom Buck burned the depot. (sic)"[193]

On the morning of the 17th, Brown moved west through Wytheville toward Stoneman and Burbridge at Mt. Airy. Brown, of Gillem's command, was going to succeed where Toland and Averell had failed, "...having sent a portion of his command to Reedy (sic) Creek,..., destroyed the important railroad bridges over that stream..."[194]

Joe Staley's house was near the crossroads (Staleys) near Rural Retreat. He made whiskey and was worried the Yanks would get it and get drunk. A drunk Yankee with a gun was not a good house guest. The soldiers ransacked his home, but didn't find the liquor closet under the stairway. His slaves ran to the mountains, because they knew the North was forcing slaves into the army.

On the morning of the 17th, Breckinridge moved out of Saltville with Col. Witcher and the 34th Virginia in advance. At Marion Witcher learned the last Yank had headed east toward Wytheville, two hours before. Witcher also learned "...the enemy's horses were very tired and worn out."[195] Witcher chased them toward Mt. Airy.

As Witcher closed in on the Yanks at Mt. Airy, Buckley was closing in on his target, and lead mines. He passed through Cripple Creek community, and took the Blue Springs Road to Thorn's Ferry at Austinville. He didn't realize that Vaughn's wagon train had already passed over. Vaughn, who had been so courageous at the action around Saltville in October, seemed to have lost his nerve. With the river as a natural barrier, he still informed the people that he couldn't stop the Union. He wouldn't even try. He told the populous to run. He took his own advice and continued toward Hillsville. He fired not a single shot in defense of this critical facility.

When Buckley arrived on the north side of the river around 2:00, the ferry boat was tied on the south side. Buckley scanned the shore for Reb soldiers, but only saw civilians, mostly Negro mine laborers.

Re-creation of Confederate brigades moving toward battle.

      As the Yanks eyed the cold December waters of New River, they called across for someone to bring the ferry boat over. Then they tried a bribe. The amount reached "...$500 to anyone who would bring the ferry boat..."[196] There were no takers.

It is to be remembered that these were the days before penicillin. Pneumonia was a dread disease. A December swim was a good way to get the disease. There is no such thing as getting used to the December ice cold river water. It has a numbing, paralyzing effect on the body.

It is not known how Buckley picked those 25 men that would go over. They may have volunteered. They were extremely brave men. It is not clear if Buckley joined them.

The brave 25 and their horses plunged into New River and started swimming over, not knowing if a Reb unit might appear suddenly and cut them down in mid-stream. No doubt the soldiers on the north shore watched for Rebs as the 25 swam.

Vaughn with his 400 could have easily stopped the Yanks and saved the mines, but once the Yanks came over, William Kohler, Superintendent of the mines, hoisted a white flag. He asked the Union not to destroy the town. Apparently they honored his request. One report states that only the furnace was destroyed. Another stated, ..."the ore washer, and partially destroyed the smelting plant. A mule stable and blacksmith shop, a windlass and other hoisting equipment, a crushing machine, bellows, shop utensils, a furnace, and a grist and sawmill were also destroyed by fire."[197]

The raiders spent less than two hours on the south side of the river. The ferry boat was burned as they headed back toward Cripple Creek.

Cap. Henry T. Stanton, Assistant Adjutant General, estimated the mines would be in production in 8 days. Superintendent Kohler said it would be two months. One source states that full production was not started until March 22, 1865. The Yanks claimed they had completely destroyed them.

About the same time as Buckley struck New River, Witcher struck the rear of the enemy at Mt. Airy.

Witcher's 300 surprised the North and gained some initial advantage. Apparently Stoneman temporarily relieved Burbridge of command because Burbridge's forces were so disorganized they couldn't effectively oppose Witcher.

Stoneman reorganized. Burbridge brought the artillery on line, and soon joined the fight.

Witcher's men began retreating toward Marion. Burbridge was doing an effective job on them with the artillery.

The 11th Michigan was sent to chase Witcher whose retreat was rapidly turning into a rout.

About two miles east of Marion, Gillem sent the 8th Tennessee under Patton, along with some artillery from Burbridge, in for the final kill.

Witcher retreated across the Holston on one of the two bridges near the Allen place. They ripped some boards off the floor to slow the Union.

Apparently Breckinridge was preparing a defensive line for Witcher.

When Witcher's men struck the line, there was panic and confusion. Witcher's men spread the highly contagious battlefield disease of fear to Breckinridge's troops. The entire army almost panicked. Breckinridge and his officers were able to prevent the spread of the disease and the line firmed.

Col. Mannagan, probably with the 11th Kentucky Cavalry, along with the 53rd Kentucky Infantry and part of the 8th Michigan, chased Witcher. As they moved on the bridge, they hastily replaced the boards the Rebs had removed and advanced up the road the Rebs had taken. They were surprised when they struck Breckinridge's solid line. The South loosed a "torrent of shot and shell."[198] The North ran back to the covered bridge, but it was in range of Confederate guns. Southern guns knocked large timbers loose onto the Yanks while Reb "...sharpshooters riddled it like a sieve."[199] The bridge was a shambles by the time Col. Mannagan withdrew across the river.

Duke, "the little whale bone," stabilized the right of the Confederate line and the Union advance stalled.

Duke was one Southern general that was not intimidated by the Yank's new Spencer Repeating rifle. In fact he said, "...(we) met the troops carrying Spencer rifles with more confidence than those armed in any other way."[200]

Duke believed that stopping to reload made his men "...comparatively cool and steady..." While those with repeaters would "...fire fast but will fire wildly..."[201]

As darkness approached, both the North and South brought four guns each on line, men began digging trenches, and the fighting died down.

Apparently the 5th and 6th U.S. Colored Cavalry were to the left of the bridge, while the 11th Kentucky, 11th Michigan and 12th Ohio were in front of the bridge. They were backed by the 5th Kentucky Battery under Lt. Judd.

It is believed that this story of a Southern atrocity took place on the 17th. Apparently a sick Union soldier was captured by an unidentified band of Rebels. The Rebs didn't need a Yank prisoner, especially a sick one that would slow them down. If he had been an officer with information, the story may have ended differently. The Southern officer decided to shoot the prisoner. The Billy begged for his life, but saw it was futile. He then asked that he not be shot in the road. His body would be trampled by Reb horses. His final request was not honored either. He was shot in the road. His body was stripped except for trousers and shirt.

Mr. Snavely and Phillip Pickle had been watching from Snavely's store. They went out and asked what should be done with the body. The reply was to leave it lay and let the hogs eat it.

The Rebs rode off.

The two men buried the body in a hole two feet deep along the road. On the body were papers indicating the Union soldier was from Tennessee.[202]

Because Breckinridge was in Saltville and cut off from communications, M.S. Langhorne from Lynchburg took it upon himself to assume command of the department.

That night at Marion the Allen family, near the bridge, was trapped between the lines. Apparently Mrs. Allen, her daughter Susan, and one year old son Ferd, along with a neighbor's daughter Betty Killinger, decided to move to Betty's father's house. Michael Killinger's house was a short way back through enemy lines.

While the band moved to Michael's house, Mrs. Allen kept pinching the baby, Ferd, so he would cry. That way the Yanks didn't fire on them by mistake as they moved.

Once at Michael's they barricaded themselves in with feather ticks.

Apparently Breckinridge spent the night at James Sheffey's house in Marion, as each side waited for light to do battle.

It was gloomy on the 18th, with a cold rain falling at dawn. It was Sunday, but no one was going to church. About dawn the fighting of the day before resumed. It was mostly pickets firing at each other from their trenches. Stoneman began probing Breckinridge's defenses, looking for weak spots. As he looked and estimated the Reb strength, he soon realized he was facing most, if not all, of Breckinridge's army. Breckinridge was estimated to have around 1,000 men.

If Breckinridge's army was in front of him, who was minding the saltworks? He guessed correctly that it was either defended lightly or not at all.

Stoneman's plan was simple. He would keep Breckinridge occupied with over 3,000 troops while Burbridge moved around Breckinridge's left flank. He would either capture the saltworks, or at least cut Breckinridge off and force a very uneven fight on open ground.

Stoneman did a good job of concealing Burbridge's move from Breckinridge. Burbridge took an estimated force of over 1,000 men, and Breckinridge was apparently unaware of the movement. It was early morning when Burbridge started flanking Breckinridge.

By the early morning of the 18th, Col. Buckley's Brigade of 600 was at, or approaching, Seven Mile Ford. He was returning from Austinville where he had destroyed the lead mines. He moved through Adwolfe, then to the Rock Road west of Marion. He apparently didn't know that Breckinridge and his army was at Marion. He was following orders as he moved west toward Seven Mile Ford, where he camped.

It may have been Reb scouts, but most probably it was a citizen that rushed toward Breckinridge at Marion with the news that the enemy had a force of "900 to 1,200 strong"[203] on his right flank, blocking the Rock Road to Saltville.

While the troops were deploying around Marion, H.T. Stanton, Assistant Adjutant General, was relocating military headquarters for the Department to Max Meadows. The telegraph and railroad were open from that point east.

He informed Gen. Lee of the destruction of the lead mines and gave him what little information he had on the movements of Breckinridge and Stoneman. Lee had to be gravely concerned about events in Southwest Virginia. He knew without the salt and lead, the Army of Northern Virginia couldn't hold Richmond. Without the capital, the Confederacy was doomed.

Stanton also attempted to coordinate troop movements toward Breckinridge. Maj. Bozang was coming from Martin's Tank (Pulaski) with a small force. Col. Kent was near Fort Chiswell; he knew the mines had been attacked. Stanton was gathering crews to repair the railroad and telegraph to Wytheville. Stanton said, "Vaughn's brigade...scattered to the four winds."[204] Vaughn and the train were heading to North Carolina. Gillespie and his few men were heading toward Dublin. Many of Vaughn's men simply left the main roads and disappeared into the mountains to avoid capture.

In the morning at Marion there had been much shooting, but few casualties taken on either side. Breckinridge was in a very strong position, but by afternoon Stoneman thought he had found a weakness. Whether by coincidence or by policy, he began to assemble his colored troops for a direct frontal assault. The sector Stoneman chose to attack was commanded by Duke, "...the coolest and always most self possessed officer that we encountered during the war..., the more danger involved, the more quiet and composed and undisturbed was this brilliant cavalryman."[205]

Duke was considered the brains behind Morgan. Here at Marion he would get to try a new defense. It wasn't the inflexible straight line that was standard. Duke's line consisted of two strong wings with a thin line of men in between. The line was concave toward the rear. As the attackers advanced they would naturally avoid the strong wings and move toward the weaker center of the bowl. As they moved past the wings and deeper into the bowl, they were exposed to fire from both the front and sides.

Stoneman found Duke's line devastating. Duke only had 220 men and some reinforcements Breckinridge had sent from Witcher's brigade, but Duke estimated 187,[206] mostly colored troops, lay dead in front of his line before the day was over (the official Union count was 143).[207] There was hand to hand combat as men attempted to kick, stab, and gouge their enemy to death.

This was "one of Duke's proudest moments..." he later recalled "...that troops never fought more resolutely and bravely then did those I commanded on that day."[208]

Before the day was over, Col. Boyle of the 11th Kentucky Cavalry, lay dead at Duke's line. He destroyed the depot and railroad at Max Meadows east of Wytheville.

It may have been Duke's men that charged Stoneman's line, or it may have been others who could charge because of Duke's action. In either case, the South almost captured part of Stoneman's wagon train. The South was desperate for supplies.

Stoneman knew he was lucky to prevent a break in his line. He halted the attack and sent Cap. Roberts toward Burbridge with orders to stop his advance on the saltworks and return as fast as possible to aid him.

Stoneman pulled his men back to the trenches. Rumors were circulating that Stoneman was preparing to surrender. Many of his men who had come from East Tennessee and Southwest Virginia began deserting. They feared that the Southern citizens would kill them as they had killed Cap. Wyatt at Abingdon.

During the day of fighting, the Allen women and baby were at Michael Killinger's house, with him and his daughter. The women took cover, but old Michael "refused to get behind anything but calmly sat before the fire smoking and chewing tobacco and grumbling because he was too old to get in the fight."[209] He wasn't hit but a bullet struck his chair.

By nightfall Breckinridge had learned of Burbridge's move around his left flank, but didn't know that Burbridge had returned to Stoneman by sunset.

Re-creation of battle. Note Reb on right removing the end of paper cartridge with his mouth.

Breckinridge believed that the road to Saltville was blocked by "900 to 1,200" troops and that a strong enemy force had rounded his flank and blocked entrance to Saltville in that direction.

Although they had taken light casualties while inflicting considerable losses, and although they occupied a strong position, they would have to retreat. Breckinridge reported that there was only an average of 15 rounds of ammo left per man. They couldn't stop another assault by Stoneman.

At 11:00 P.M. Breckinridge moved his army south through Rye Valley out of Marion. "It was difficult for horsemen and deemed impracticable for artillery, but by the energy of Maj. Page and Cap. Burroughs, the guns were got to the top of the mountains before daylight."[210]

Shortly after dawn on the 19th, Stoneman discovered that Breckinridge had slipped away during the night. He sent Lt. Col. Bentley and the 12th Ohio Cavalry after Breckinridge. About six miles south of Marion, he "charged with the sabre,..."[211] upon the last of Breckinridge's wagon train. He captured two wagons and one artillery caisson. He could pursue no further because the Rebs had felled trees to block the road.

He returned to Stoneman. Because the road Breckinridge traveled lead south, Stoneman assumed that Breckinridge was running to North Carolina.

Breckinridge spent the day circling through the mountains to reach the Rock Road east of Stoneman near Mt. Airy so he could resupply.

Breckinridge was gone from his front so Stoneman began to move his troops through Marion toward Glade Spring. Here he would regroup and plan his attack on Saltville.

Burbridge was the last to leave toward Glade Spring. He said "...my instructions to the rear guard were to reduce the country to such a condition as to render it difficult for the enemy to follow us in any force."[212]

The first order of business for a small rear guard group was the easy destruction of the bridge near the Allen home. The Yanks set a fire on the bridge and rode off. Mrs. Allen's daughter, Susan, an early teenager, ran with a bucket to the bridge and doused the flames.

The Yanks were not far away and saw what Susan had done. They returned, set the fire again, and told her not to put it out again.

They left, she scooped water from the stream and doused the fire a second time.

The angry Yanks returned and "threatened to do all manner of things to her...and run their bayonets through her."[213] They were sure they had scared her. They set a third fire and rode off.

No sooner had they left than she doused the fire a third time. The Yanks didn't come back, and the battle scarred bridge was saved.

As the Yanks moved west they stopped at the Greever house. Mary Poole was a young slave at the time. She recalled later that she waited on the Yanks. The officers discovered a barrel of apple brandy in the basement. They broke it open on the floor to prevent their men from getting drunk. She recalled the North camped up and down the road as far as she could see. They pulled the rail fences down to make campfires. They "cought...all the chickens, hogs, and what cows was on the place and killed them and was cooking them for their supper."[214] (sic)

Burbridge confirmed they stole plenty of food for men and animals.

The colored soldiers were resented and hated by the Southern population. "The terror aroused by the presence of the Federal troops in Southwest Virginia was increased by the atrocities committed by Cap. Cole's Regiment of Negro soldiers."[215] They shot an unarmed citizen, Lafayette Snavely, in the doorway of his home a few miles from Marion. The colored troops behavior was considered "Barbarous" toward prisoners. Some Negro soldiers thought they were just getting even for what Southern soldiers had done to other coloreds in Union uniform.

While the North was moving toward Glade Spring, a courier from Breckinridge was approaching Wytheville.

By 2 P.M., Stanton was on the telegraph trying to get help. The telegraph was now working to Wytheville. Stanton sent word that Breckinridge would be at Mt. Airy by night fall. He requested that ammo be sent at once. He stated that "Saltville may be besieged at any hour, and troops must go to its relief." Trains could come to three miles west of Max Meadows. "For God's sake...", he pleaded that troops and supplies be sent. He begged and then threatened, "If Langhorne persists in refusing to let the Lynchburg troops come, I would telegraph...General Lee."[216]

Ammo was moved forward.

Breckinridge struck the Rock Road near Mt. Airy by night fall, where he camped.

By morning of the 20th, Breckinridge was resupplied with 6,000 rounds of ammo. He moved his exhausted army west along the Rock Road toward Marion in the cold. He knew that Stoneman could move his whole force at will against the saltworks.

Gen. Lee, himself, ordered Early, in the valley, to send a brigade of infantry as fast as possible to try and save Southwest Virginia.

It is unclear what the defenders at the saltworks knew about the action the day before. It is unlikely they knew Breckinridge's location on the morning of the 20th, because they were expecting reinforcements from him at any time.

At Wytheville, Echols was trying to move reinforcements to bolster Breckinridge. Kent, with a reserve battalion of 270 men, was sent forward. Four hundred men, probably from Lynchburg, were expected that night. They would be sent forward also. Supplies were being sent, "Wagons to be impressed for (that) purpose."[217] Echols also informed Breckinridge that Mrs. Breckinridge was safe at Mrs. Cloyd's.

At Marion in the early morning hours, Stoneman started his troops in motion to capture the saltworks. His major concern was that Southern troops from Lynchburg might suddenly appear.

Stoneman divided his army. Burbridge was apparently to attack via the road from Seven Mile Ford, while he and Gillem moved over the road from Glade Spring toward the target.

As Stoneman and Gillem advanced they were greeted by Southern pickets. They acted as an early warning for the main body at Saltville. The pickets fell back as Stoneman advanced. They delayed the Union movement as much as possible while sending information to the rear on the enemy's strength.

Col. Robert Preston, with his few reserves and artillery, manned the forts (earthworks) with "stationary guns"[218] on high ground, as they waited for the large Northern army to close in on them. By 2 P.M. the wait was over, and the head of the Union column came in sight.

Preston was as ready as he could be. Barr's and Kain's Batteries were positioned to cover the area where the enemy was expected to advance. Men were in the forts, rifle pits, and ridge lines. Preston was still hoping for reinforcements from Breckinridge. The fate of the Confederacy was on the line, held by only 400 reservists.

When Gillem arrived he started positioning his men. The 9th Tennessee was placed on a hill to the right of the road. Next Gillem deployed artillery support on the hill. At this point Southern riflemen cut loose and the battle was on. While peppering the Union position on the hill, Preston sent troops down a ravine. He hoped to surprise the 9th and capture the artillery before more Northern troops arrived.

However, Gillem observed the Southern troops movement. He quickly ordered the 8th Tennessee Battalion to dismount and move through the woods and intercept the Rebs. When the Rebels met the 8th they knew their plan was discovered. They fell back to their line.

The sky looked threatening as Gillem and Stoneman studied the Confederate line. The artillery and big earth forts (which they called Fort Breckinridge) in front of them, presented major obstacles. They deployed troops left and right, and searched for weaknesses. Col. Stacy and two battalions of the 13th Tennessee, swung wide of the line as they looked for a weak spot.

In the late afternoon word arrived from Burbridge that he was going to attack. He did. The attack fizzled.

By dark it was raining and foggy. The 9th Tennessee moved forward, but they too were soon rebuffed by the defenders. The 400 were more than holding their own against the 5,000.

With rain, fog and dark, activity ceased along the line. Apparently Southern defenders moved to a shelter to eat, rest, and prepare for the next day. The sentries would maintain their vigil and alert the command if the Union were to try anything during the night.

About 9:00, Stacy and the 13th Tennessee had found a big hole in the Confederate line. They had swung wide of Saltville and entered from an area where there had been no fighting. When the sentries saw the blue uniformed column at a distance, they weren't alarmed, but happy. There were many blue overcoats in Confederate service. This column was the promised reinforcements sent by Breckinridge.

Apparently Stacy advanced to the base of Fort Breckinridge before they were recognized. There was some shooting as the 13th "dashed" up the hill and swamped the unprepared defenders. Stacy lost no men, and only 2 horses, as they easily overpowered the Rebs. They captured several men, including two officers. They took the fort and two guns, before the South knew what hit them.

At the sound of firing, Stoneman and Gillem put their armies in service. They moved forward to help secure Ft. Breckinridge and advanced on the two smaller forts. "Because their artillery was stationary it was of little use against the Yanks pouring through from Fort Breckinridge." The confused defenders started running for their lives in all directions.

Cap. B. Dyer was sent to attack the town, itself. Some "brave Confederates"[219] attacked Dyer, but he soon dispersed them and began destroying the town. Private J.M. Butt (South) was there and remembered "we retreated south to the railroad east of Glade Spring, before we reached top of the hill the flames leaped in air from furnaces and buildings making light all about us. (sic)."[220]

By 11 P.M., Stoneman was in possession of the last of the three major targets in Southwest Virginia, (the railroad, the lead mines, and saltworks).

It is unclear if Burbridge had to overcome Reb resistance, or if he simply failed to advance. Whatever the reason, he didn't arrive in Saltville until 4 A.M. of the 21st, much to Stoneman's disgust.

By dawn of the 21st, there was no Reb resistance left. The Yanks had captured all the artillery and a large amount of powder.

There was little rest for the Union generals and army. With the morning light, Stoneman examined Ft. Breckinridge and two other earthworks. He observed the rugged terrain and concluded, "Had he (Breckinridge) remained...it would have been very difficult if not impossible for us to have taken the place."[221]

Stoneman was not too concerned about Breckinridge, but he worried about reinforcements from Lynchburg. Union troops now stood where the Southern defenders had stood.

Shortly after dawn the first of Breckinridge's troops under Duke arrived. They skirmished with Union pickets but could find no unguarded entrance to Saltville. They knew too well the strength of their old position, no major assault would be tried. Duke lost one man.

On the 21st of December, Stoneman attempted to destroy what William King had started in 1790. King's small saltworks was now huge. Over 2,000 slaves labored there to produce salt. Shafts had been drilled and water poured in. After the water had dissolved the salt it was pumped up and into evaporating kettles. The fire never went out under the large kettles. The brine was reduced to salt. The salt was shipped out to preserve meat all over the South.

Most Confederate states east of the Mississippi had set up their own evaporating works at Saltville to get some of the precious mineral for their states.

Because South Carolina had seceded first and because they fired first, Stoneman selected their works for first destruction.

Now the Union soldiers realized why they had been dragging those heavy sledge hammers around with them since Knoxville. All that day the sound of hammer against iron kettle was heard. There were 788 kettles destroyed; 128 were too thick to break.

One civilian that fell into Union hands was the chief engineer for the saltworks, "Who undoubtedly had Union sympathies..."[222] He helped destroy the wells, some of which were 160 feet deep. It was found that 12 pound cannon balls filled them well. The Yanks added railroad track and trash. The engineer said it would be easier to drill new wells than to attempt to open the old ones. The engineer knew his life would be forfeit if he remained in Saltville, so he withdrew with the enemy. Many of the slaves also accompanied the Union army.

Southern flour was poured on the ground at Saltville, and the rain turned it to dough.

Stoneman destroyed the town, the wells, pumps, engines, and most of the kettles on the 21st. That night his army rested in strong Southern defenses.

The rain turned to snow, and the 22nd it turned bitter cold.

"Gen. Cold" took command of the Southern army. Because they and their animals had less to eat, and because they had less good clothing and blankets, the weather was harder on the Rebs.

As Stoneman withdrew on the 22nd he was troubled more by "mountains slippery with ice and covered by snow"[223] and high water, than he was by Rebels. Some of the cavalrymen's boots froze to the stirrups in the bitter cold.

Vaughn who had finally quit retreating, wanted to pursue the Union, but because of "the intense cold...it is an impossibility to move the men."[224]

Breckinridge said "I deeply grieve that it was not in our power to punish the enemy more severely..."[225]

Stoneman withdrew without much Rebel pressure.

Back in Knoxville Stoneman listed his accomplishments for the high command. The Union moved 870 miles in 20 days.

He engaged Breckinridge, Vaughn, Giltner, Cosby, Witcher, Duke and the reserves. He destroyed all railroad bridges west of New River, 13 railroad depots, all foundries, mills, factories, storehouses, wagon and ambulance trains, turnpike bridges, towns of Bristol, Abingdon, Wytheville and Saltville, 2,500 rounds of artillery ammo, small arm ammo also, 2,000 new pack saddles, large amounts of artillery, 19 field artillery caissons (11 extra large), 2,000 horses, 100 mules, large numbers of Negroes, salt (between 50 and 100,000 bushels), lead works, saltworks, furnaces, kettles, machinery, wells and shafts filled with shells, railroad iron, buildings burned down,...harness, large amounts of subsistence and medical supplies, several hundred wagons and ambulances (serviceable and unserviceable), 2 locomotives, several cars..."[226] He also was proud that the chief engineer from Saltville was with him.

He destroyed "Four destiferous secession printing presses." He captured two editors, (one was J. Austin Sperry from Bristol) "these last were sent as a Christmas present to the proprietor of the Knoxville (Reb) Ventilator."[227] He captured 34 officers and 84 men. No estimates of Reb casualties were given, nor did he give Union figures. Breckinridge stated that over 200 Union wounded were left in Southern hands. Three hundred Yanks were frostbitten, but there was no complaint in Stoneman's command.

Stoneman concluded "East Tennessee is free from any organized body of the enemy; Eastern Kentucky is free from the fear of any large raiding parties."[228]

Stoneman who came to "liquidate" a debt to the South said, "I regretted the necessity of giving orders that may cause suffering to non-combatants..."[229]

The South went to work trying to restore the telegraph, the railroad, and getting some production for Gen. Lee and the rest of the South out of the lead mines and saltworks. It would take many weeks and much scarce southern material and labor to start partial production and transportation. The wells at Saltville were reopened.

Stoneman had struck a serious blow against Lee and the Army of Northern Virginia.

Burbridge sent his report in on December 28; by January 3, 1865 Breckinridge had a copy of that report. This shows not only that Southern intelligence was excellent, but that the hatred of Burbridge extended to his personal staff.

It was a bad winter, and the worst Christmas that has ever occurred since white man entered Southwest Virginia. At no time in history has there been such universal suffering and grief. The soldiers longed for their homes in Kentucky, Tennessee, and other parts of Virginia. The citizens there longed for their soldiers who were with Lee and Hood. Citizens in the countryside feared for their lives because of bushwhackers and deserters. People along the railroad feared that the Union would invade again.

Many were homeless; burned out by Federals. Many were temporarily unemployed because the railroad, lead mines, and saltworks were under repair. Few had enough Confederate, Union or gold dollars to keep up with inflation.

Many homes mourned that Christmas. A father or brother had been killed. Many anguished over loved ones in a far off Union prison. Many dreaded what they would learn about their loved one, missing in action. Many dreaded that they would never learn what happened to their loved one missing in action.

Most all were hungry and cold. Disease stalked the land. There were massive epidemics of smallpox. Many men cowered inside and never went outside without a dress on, the deserters.

Few could remember the glitter and sparkle of the first war Christmas. Many couldn't remember what it was all about. All longed for the old times before the war.

There was very little to be joyful about in Southwest Virginia that Christmas of 1864.

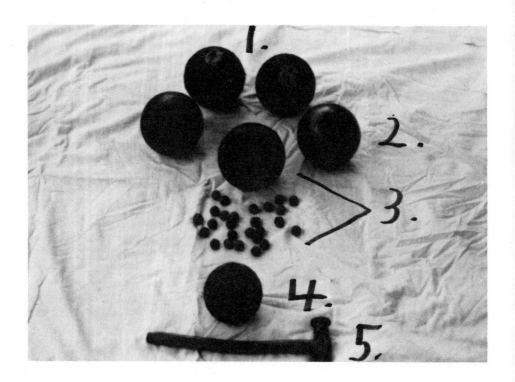

Row 1 — 12 pound shells with Bormann fuses, fired from Union Mountain Howitzer.
Row 2 — 12 pound Confederate shells.
3 — 12 pound case shot with grape shot contents.
4 — 6 pound Confederate solid shot.
5 — Confederate artillery hammer. All were recovered from Saltville battlefields.
(Courtesy of Harry R. and Donald C. Haynes.)

Chapter VII

1865

The bells that rang in the new year were not joy bells, but death bells. More of the Confederacy was in Union hands or in dispute than was controlled by the central government.

No matter how the "cause" was viewed, it was a dying cause. Foreign recognition was it's only hope, and that hope was very faint. The only bright spot was the seemingly invincible Gen. Lee and his army of heroes. Richmond still stood. Grant seemed as far away as ever at Petersburg. Lee knew looks were deceiving. Every day an irreplaceable Reb fell, and Grant's trenches extended further. Everyday Lee's line was stretched thinner.

Not only was the Confederacy being challenged by the Union, but in Southwest Virginia it was challenged by Washington County. When Wyatt burned part of Abingdon in December, one building to go was the courthouse. The court needed a building. At the end of December, a contract to rent Dunn's Store for $1,500 a year was signed. There was only one problem, Cap. J.G. Martin, commander of the military forces in Abingdon, was using the building as a guard house. He refused to vacate.

The court ordered him out in January, but he said he would hold the building by force of arms if necessary.

The county then appealed "Requesting that a sufficient force be ordered out by the governor to enforce the order of the court..."[1]

There was no mention of violence, Reb against Reb, or of how the dispute was settled.

The economy was terrible and breaking down at an increasing rate. It was strangled by the sea blockade. Major rivers and rails were in enemy hands. Coastal cities were occupied. Sherman had cut a path of destruction from Atlanta to the sea. Raids like Stoneman's had destroyed factories, rails, and communications across the South.

There was less land that could be safely cultivated and less labor to work it. The South was starving, and being bled white.

In Russell County, Thomas Davis was the agent in charge of buying food for the families of the soldiers. The court allowed him to pay up to $6.00 for a bushel of wheat or corn, and $2.00 a pound for fat back, but he reported, "that commodities could not be bought at any price."[2] Summers stated in his book about Washington County, that even earlier in the war "The condition of affairs was such that the people of the county were threatened with a famine for bread,..."[3]

Some Southerners could see the handwriting on the wall. They knew what it said. The price of slaves fell. Joe Staley, who lived near the crossroads at Rural Retreat, was accused of only being interested in money when he sold his slave and her baby.

Confederate money was exchanged for gold or U.S. money. It took many Confederate dollars to buy a Union dollar, but it was hard to find anyone who would trade. The money was no good. One hundred Confederate dollars equalled one dollar in gold. It took $150.00 to buy a barrel of flour, $200.00 for a pound of bacon, $15.00 for a pound of beef, $20.00 for a pound of butter, $50.00 for a chicken, $12.00 one yard of calico, and boots cost around $200.00.[4]

The Southern people and army were starving. The thin lines were held by scarecrows.

Because of the lack of supplies and salt, Lee reported that his men went into battle not having meat for three days. He predicted, "...calamity unless the men get more food quickly."[5]

Not only was there not enough food for people but the animals were gaunt. In Southwest Virginia horses were sent to the Mt. Airy, North Carolina area to winter because there was no fodder for them.

Duke reported, "He tried to re-equip the men, but the Confederacy had little to offer. There was no underwear, overcoats or blankets."[6] There was not enough food, medicine, guns, bullets, horses, saddles, railroad cars, locomotives or rails, to keep them moving.

Basic government services were breaking down. Communication, both telegraph and mail, were deteriorating.

The story is told about a Southern girl who came down to breakfast dressed in a ball gown. When the father saw here, he berated her for dressing so elegantly when the soldiers were starving and naked, when the common people had nothing but home spun to wear. "But..." the tearful girl explained, "I have nothing else." Her entire wardrobe was worn out.

The South was existing on little more than raw courage. Heroes and martyrs were used to sustain the peoples morale. On January 17, the Smyth County Court officially recognized Elizabeth Killinger's "heroic efforts" for saving the county's records. She also received a $500.00 reward.[7]

Breckinridge who had been a Kentucky Senator, Vice-President of the United States, a presidential candidate on the Southern ticket, and a general, was ordered to Richmond. He was to wear one more hat for the Confederacy. He became the last Secretary of War on January 27.

It is unclear because of faulty communications but Gen. Echols, the most senior general from Southwest Virginia, probably took over command of the department.

As raids became more frequent in Southwest Virginia, people began to recognize that Yanks weren't all devils. The story is told of a party that visited the Huddle farm on Blacklick in Wythe County. One raider noticed the boy was about his own son's age. He wanted to give the poor Reb boy a gift, but knew the boy would probably refuse Northern charity. The Yank saw a tin star the boy had made. He bought the star for $5.00 Union money, "good money."

In Russell County the court could not meet at times because the enemy was too near.

The courts seemed to be responding to the need for soldiers. No longer did it dismiss very many men from service as it had done in 1863. In the court records for Wythe County only two men were allowed out in 1865. On February 20, Francis Allison, Jr. was let out because of sickness. On March 23, Elijah Dotson was excused because he proved he was too old.

Now that Lee was not only general of the Army of Northern Virginia, but Commander-in-Chief of all Southern forces, he relieved Hood of command of the Army of Tennessee and reinstated "Uncle Joe" Johnston. Johnston moved to oppose Sheman along the Carolina coast.

Sherman (destroying as he went) was moving up the coast to link up with Grant. This was more pressure than Lee could handle and Lee knew it.

Lee was desperate. He suggested drafting the slaves. He needed every man he could get. Skilled labor was drafted. The South would reduce already low production further, in order to put more bodies on the line. Eighty-four men were drafted from the saltpeter caves of Rich Valley and from the iron works near Sugar Grove in Smyth County (the works were partially destroyed by Stoneman).[8]

It was March 21st when Stoneman started another raid from Morristown in East Tennessee. He was to attack western North Carolina. By doing so he would keep Gov. Zebulon Vance from shifting troops to Johnston on the coast. Johnston only had a handful of bedraggled veterans to oppose Sherman's thousands.

Gillem and many of the same troops that invaded Southwest Virginia in December were with Stoneman. Their exact number is not known, but they were more numerous than the defenders. They had four pieces of field artillery with them.

Col. Miller, of Gillem's command, struck Gen. "Mudwall" Jackson at Bulls Gap. Jackson fell back leaving some dead. The Yanks captured some stragglers and deserters. Because Jackson was pushed back, this left the path wide open. (Boone, North Carolina learned of the Federals approach from either outriders or from a citizen). This allowed time to call out the home guard. At 10 A.M. on March 28, Gillem struck the home guard defenders. Maj. Keogh of the 12th Kentucky Volunteer Cavalry, lead the attack. They killed 9 and captured another 68. Before 12:00 the Union possessed the town.

At Boone, Stoneman decided to split his army. He knew the South didn't have enough men to oppose him even if he fragmented his troops. Smaller units could reap more havoc than a single large army. Stoneman stayed with the 2nd Brigade.

The 1st Brigade under Col. William L. Palmer, and 3rd Brigade under Col. John K. Miller, were placed under Gillem. At 1 P.M. Miller's orders were to take 500 "picked men" and go by "Porter's Ford, on New River, to Wytheville and destroy the railroad bridge over Reedy (sic) Creek and at Max Meadows, together with the department of supplies at Wytheville."[9]

They rested until 7:00 that evening before they moved north. They hadn't moved far until they came upon Patterson's Factory "..., at the foot of the Blueridge."[10] Here they found a large supply of corn and bacon. (North Carolina was the only state in the Confederacy with supplies. Vance had been hogging his supplies and troops for North Carolina's use only). The Yanks feasted and looted. What they couldn't carry they burned.

It rained most of the night of the 29th.

Citizen riders spread the word of the Union column moving north. This helped those people and towns immediately ahead of the Yanks, but there was no direct telegraph link to Wytheville. There was no advanced notice that the Federals were on their way.

News that the Northern forces were coming arrived at Mt. Airy on April 2nd. A wagon train loaded with supplies started up the mountain toward Hillsville at 3 P.M. to avoid capture.

At 10:00 that night Gillem reached Mt. Airy. There was no mention of Rebel resistance as they took the town. It was probably from a Northern sympathizer that Gillem "Learned" of the wagon train "...going in the direction of Hillsville, Virginia."[11]

It is unclear if Gillem sent Col. Palmer and the 15th Pennsylvania Cavalry under Lt. Col. Charles H. Bettes after the train that night or waited until morning.

On the 2nd of April what Lee knew was inevitable, happened. The entire South was shocked that it did happen. Lee's line around Petersburg was stretched too thin. At Five Forks the Union began to pour through. Lee sent an entire brigade (though undermanned) with orders to hold at all cost. The brigade gave its all that day, and was completely wiped out, but the Yanks kept coming.

Lee informed the president, and Richmond was evacuated that day.

Because the government was collapsing, and because of bad communications, it is not clear when the soldiers and citizens in Southwest Virginia received the news of Richmonds fall.

Word of the Union raid from North Carolina reached Gen. Duke. He apparently didn't know the enemy's strength or direction of travel. He knew his men needed their horses from North Carolina. There were only about 50 mounted men in his command. He sent part of his brigade to North Carolina on foot after the horses.

Near Hillsville on the 3rd, Palmer caught the wagon train. He captured and burned 27 wagons. No reports of casualties on either side.

It was probably on the 3rd or 4th that Palmer intercepted Duke's band of unmounted cavalry, heading toward Mt. Airy. Duke reported that his men fought as infantry and lost. Gillem reported that some Rebels attacked the main body, but they were quickly dispersed.

While the Federals were moving toward Wytheville, President Davis and his cabinet were moving south. They carried some necessary government documents and the Confederate treasury. It was mostly Confederate notes and bonds, but it also had the last of the gold, about $50,000 worth.

Gen. Lee was moving west, hoping to turn south and make a juncture with Gen. Johnston in North Carolina.

It was probably the 5th or early morning of the 6th when the Union arrived at the lead mines at Austinville. It appears that the home guard from Wytheville under Col. Kent, had chosen to remain at Wytheville. There were no reports of resistance as the Union column rode in. They were in no rush this time. "...Northern raiders hit it again. This time the mines were put out of action...".[12]

From what little information that is available, it appears that the home guard, Gen. Jackson, and some other troops from the department, were stationed at Wytheville.

The Yanks crossed over New River and did some damage in the Porter's Cross Roads area. Perhaps burning a house or two.

They must have arrived at Wytheville in the morning hours of the 6th. There are few details of the battle. The Yanks were not overly proud of it and the Confederates had no capital to report to.

Col. Miller and 3rd Brigade attempted to take the town. There was a "...brisk skirmish." Miller seemed surprised that the Rebs attacked "...with infantry and cavalry."[13]

No Reb casualty figures were given but Miller admitted he lost 35 killed and wounded, and a number made prisoner. From what Miller didn't say it appears the Yanks never entered the town itself. Wytheville escaped being burned a third time.

After being repulsed the Union moved on the railroad depot south of town. Here they burned a "large deposit of commissary, quartermasters, and ordnance supplies, among which were a large amount of ammunition and 10,000 pounds of powder...".[14]

Railroad bridges both east and west of town, were burned again before the Union drew off toward Porter's Crossroads. Here they waited as messengers were sent to Stoneman. He seemed pleased with the results of their raid and confident that the South could pose no serious opposition in his sector. It is not known if the Yanks knew that Richmond had been taken. Stoneman ordered Gillem to advance on Lynchburg, destroying as he went.

From what little information is available it appears that most of the troops from the Department of Southwest Virginia and East Tennessee were moving after Gillem as he destroyed the railroad. At Radford he tried to burn the long bridge again, but the timber was too green. (It was rebuilt after Cloyd's Mountain).

On the 9th of April at a little railroad depot called Appomattox, Lee realized it was over. The Army of Northern Virginia had less than 28,000 men, all hungry, weary, and out of supplies. Grant had 100,000 chasing him. Lee knew he couldn't make a junction with Johnston. Lee surrendered.

It was probably late on the 10th when the news arrived in Southwest Virginia. Duke recalled, "Men looked at each other as if they had just heard a sentence of death and eternal ruin passed upon all."[15]

The entire command was in a state of shock for two days, and remained in the Christiansburg area. There was no capital. There was no Gen. Lee. Was the war over? Were they civilians or soldiers? No one in authority had given orders to surrender. Were they still to fight? Who could give the orders and where was this person?

While the officers and men debated what to do, the 84 laborers that had been recently drafted from the saltpeter caves and ironworks, hadn't reached Richmond before its fall. They knew exactly what they wanted. They disbanded and started toward Smyth County. For them the war was over before they had to fight.

At Wytheville local authorities knew the end was near. On their own authority they released guerrilla Champ Ferguson. He had been imprisoned but not charged after the massacre at Saltville. The South knew his life would be forfeit in Union hands. Ferguson began running in the confusion that engulfed the South.

On the 12th a meeting was called, Echols probably commanded; Vaughn, Witcher, and Duke were present. The entire effective fighting force of the Department of Southwest Virginia and East Tennessee were assembled. They numbered close to 600. Only 600 out of the 10,000 that once ranged by the Kanawha near Charleston through Southwest Virginia.

They were tired, hungry, dirty, unpaid, ill-clad, and ill-equipped. Their officers had decided to put it to a vote. Should they disband and return home? Home, there is no sweeter thought to a soldier. Or should they move south and try and locate President Davis and keep fighting? Each man must vote his conscience.

The war was ending somewhat like it started in 1861. One of the first acts of a newly formed regiment was the election of officers to lead them to war.

The vote was taken. Ten decided the war was over for them. They started home. Approximately 590 would fight.

What Echols said of Duke that his service was "beyond praise"[16] could have been said of almost every man in the department.

This was the last official act to occur in the Department of Southwest Virginia and East Tennessee. The department faded into history shortly before the infant Confederacy died.

Also on the 12th, one of the last skirmishes, if not the last skirmish to take place in Virginia, occurred. It took place near Radford. As Gillem from Stoneman's command moved toward Lynchburg destroying the railroad, he struck an unidentified Rebel unit at Seven Mile Tree, on the Christiansburg Road near Ingles Ferry. It was a brief skirmish. Cap. G.C. Junkin was wounded, perhaps the last wound received on Virginia's soil.

The last military sound of the department was that of the feet of the men and horses as they moved out of Hillsville over Fancy Gap.

At Charlotte the command from Southwest Virginia linked up with Jefferson Davis. The entire department was less than the strength of one brigade at the beginning of the war. They were back under their old commander, now Secretary of War, Gen. Breckinridge. Gen. McCausland was also there. Gen. Dibrell, who fought at the battle of Saltville in October 1864, was there. He was in charge of the Confederate Archives.

At Abbeville, South Carolina, the generals from Southwest Virginia were at the last council of war. They urged President Davis to capitulate, but he refused. He was the "cause" and it must continue. The generals remained silent in respect for their president, but they knew there was no use in fighting further.

Duke was the last treasurer of the Confederacy. His men were placed in charge of the $50,000 in gold on May 3rd. Along with Davis, they moved south looking for a spot of safety. There was none left in the South.

On the 8th of May, Breckinridge summoned the men from the Department of Southwest Virginia and East Tennessee together. He told them, "You have done all that can be done." Duke recorded, "...for us, the long agony was over."[17]

On that day the Department of Southwest Virginia and East Tennessee ceased to exist.

On the 10th, President Davis and the $50,000 gold treasury of the South was captured.

On June 26, Kirby Smith surrendered the Department of the Trans-Mississippi.

On May 10, Maj. Gen. Samuel Jones, former Commander of the Department of Southwest Virginia, surrendered. There were no major organized Confederate armies left. The "cause" was dead. The infant Confederate States of America breathed her last. The most devastating war in the history of North America was over!

Chapter VIII

Post Log

This is a brief look at Southwest Virginia after the war, but before the harsh boot of the conqueror was fully felt in the land.

Those boys of 1861 who survived were the men of 1865. They were coming home. Most surrendered with Lee and Johnston, but some groups never formally surrendered. After hearing of Lee's demise, they simply disbanded. In order that their battle flag and company colors wouldn't fall into enemy hands, they usually cut it in small pieces, and gave each man a piece. The flag symbolized the "cause" for which they and their comrades had lived, died, and fought. That piece of cloth was all that remained. It became precious to most veterans.

One flag that didn't get torn to pieces was that of Co. G. 22nd Virginia. The company was organized from Tazewell County. It reappeared in public one last time; borne by a member of that company, Robert L. Andreth. It was draped over his casket.[1]

After the war each side looked for their dead and missing. Some were never found. Relatives came from East Tennessee looking for a Union soldier lost in Southwest Virginia. They stopped at Snavely's Store. He showed them the papers he had taken from a Federal he had buried beside the road. It was a miracle that they found their missing loved one. Shortly afterwards a wagon came, the body was exumed and moved home to Tennessee.

The loved and hated Gen. Morgan had been buried in Abingdon and Richmond, now, after the war, he made one more trip. He went back "...to his beloved bluegrass"[2] country, to Lexington, Kentucky.

Many soldiers north and south never made it home. On a hill near Emory and Henry College (Hospital) is a Confederate cemetery. Approximately 180 who died for the cause remained unclaimed there. They represent most states of the Confederacy - Alabama, Florida, Georgia, Kentucky, Mississippi, North Carolina, South Carolina, Tennessee, Texas, and Virginia. What state 23 of them were from is not known. Two of that numbers identities and state's are known only to God.

Champ Ferguson who was never charged in the massacre at Saltville, and who was released from jail at Wytheville as the Confederacy crumbled, was caught by the Yanks. He was never charged with killing Negro troops. He was hung by the

Federals October 20, 1865 for other alleged war crimes. As a token gesture, members of the 5th U.S. Colored Cavalry watched him die.

Ferguson was only one of many Confederates to die on the conqueror's gallows, or be shackled in some Federal dungeon after make-believe trials.

Many high ranking officers fled the country. Gen. Breckinridge went to Canada where he remained until he knew it was safe to return. He, like most officers, returned to the land of their birth, where they remained foreigners until they died. Many refused to pledge allegiance to the United States of America; some were not even given the option.

The Confederate States of America's major goal in foreign affairs was to be officially recognized by a foreign power. Only after her death did the South receive that recognition, and it came from her mortal enemy, the United States of America. The United States, in fact, recognized the autonomy of the Confederacy and admitted it was a foreign aggressor when it claimed the spoils of war. The U.S. confiscated all properties of the government of the Confederacy, and repudiated all debts incurred by that government.

Because he had done such a splendid job of destroying the western and central part of the state, Stoneman was appointed military governor of the state of Virginia; reconstruction had begun. Reconstruction was just a code word for continued war without bullets. The South had to be punished of her sin of leaving the Union. All those who had been instrumental in dissolving the Union must be reduced to such a low state that they could never be a threat to the Union again. (But reconstruction is another story).

Like a plague the speculators and industrialists (the South called them carpet-baggers) descended on the South. Plantations that had been in one family for over a hundred years became property of the conqueror. In Southwest Virginia the three major objectives of Union aggression (the lead mines, railroad, and saltworks) moved into Northern hands. The management and skilled labor (high paying jobs) went to Northerners, while Southerners supplied unskilled and semi-skilled labor.

The South found herself, in effect, a colony of the Union. Most people couldn't vote. They were governed by a military authority. They supplied raw materials and cheap labor to the industrial North, and were forced, because of high tarriffs, to consume the Union products.

Many Southern institutions, particularly education, suffered badly for the next one hundred years. No wonder the Republican Party, the party of the conqueror, was so roundly hated. When the people of the South could vote, they were solidly Democratic for a hundred years.

Many commentaries on the war often close with the moot question, "What if the South had won the war?" The more I study the subject, the more I am amazed that the Union didn't crush Southern Independence sooner than it did. To para-phrase Winston Churchill, "How could so few with so little, fight so many with so much, so long?"

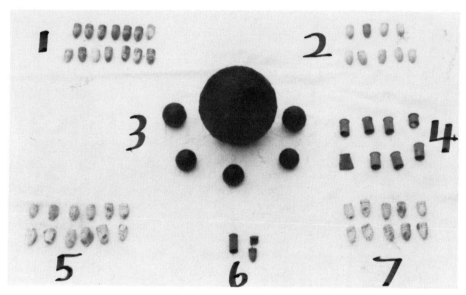

Over 120 years later, Mother Earth has not forgotten. These are from the Pat Trout collection, and all were discovered in Southwest Virginia.

1. 58 Cal. minie balls (never fired)
2. 52 cal. star carbine
3. 12 pound cannon ball surrounded by grape shot
4. 52 cal. Spencer Repeating Rifle cartridges

5. 58 cal. minie balls (after firing)
6. 44 cal. Ballard Carbine
7. Spencer (after firing)

FOOTNOTES

Foreword
1 *America Goes to War* by Bruce Catton
Chapter 1 - BEFORE THE WAR
1 *History of Wythe County* Ed. Jouet McGavock Boyd
2 *The War that Never Ended* by Robert Cruden
3 *The Population of the United States* by Donald J. Bogue
4 *A History of the Southern Confederacy* by Clement Eaton
5 op. cit. *Population*-Bogue
6 "
7 op cit. *Confederacy*-Eaton
8 Wythe County Courthouse-records
9 *History of Tazewell County and Southwest Virginia, 1748-1920* by *William C. Pendleton*
10 "
11 op. cit. *Confederacy*-Eaton
12 *A Small Boy's Recollection of the Civil War* by George Robertson
13 *Walker, Ben to Carl* by Gary Walker

Chapter 2 - COMPONENTS AND STRATEGY

1 *The Civil War* by Shelby Foote
2 *Russell County, A Confederate Bread Basket* by Theodosia W. Barrett
3 op. cit. *Confederacy*-Eaton
4 *A History of Saltville* by William B. Kent
5 op. cit. *War Never Ended*-Cruden
6 "
7 "
8 op. ct. *Confederacy*-Eaton
9 op. cit. *War Never Ended*-Cruden
10 Dixie Gun Works, Inc.-advertisement
11 *Elements of Military Art and Science* by Henry Wager Halleck
12 "
13 "
14 "
15 op. cit. *America Goes to War*-Catton
16 op cit. *Russell Co.*-Barrett

Chapter - 1861

1 *Camp Chase Gazette*-"postmaster Reagan's Lost Cause" by George Mick

Chapter - 1862

1 "The War in Southwest Virginia" by Lelia F. Huddle
2 op. cit. *Boy's Recollections*-Robertson
3 National Archives
4 "
5 *A History of the Middle New River Settlements and Contiguous Territory* by David Emmons Johnston

6 op. cit. "War"-Huddle
7 op. cit. *Boy's Recollection*-Robertson

Chapter - 1863

1 op. cit. *Confederacy*-Eaton
2 Wythe County Courthouse-records
3 *War of the Rebellion: Official Records of the Union and Confederate Armies* ed. War Department
4 "
5 "
6 "
7 letter, courtesy of the Dillon Collection
8 *The American Conflict* by Horce Greeley
9 op. cit. *Records*-War Dept.
10 "
11 "
12 op. cit. *Tazewell Co.*-Pendleton
13 "
14 op. cit. *Records* War Dept.
15 op. cit. *Tazewell Co.* Pendleton
16 *Sketches of Early Burkes Gardens* by Ida R. Greever
17 "
18 "
19 op. cit. *Records*-War Dept.
20 op. cit. *Burkes Garden*-Greever
21 op. cit. *Records*-War Dept.
22 "
23 "
24 "
25 "
26 op. cit. *Wythe Co.*-Boyd
27 op. cit. *Records* War Dept.
28 "
29 "
30 "
31 "
32 *Tazewell County* by Louise Leslie
33 op. cit. *Records*-War Dept.
34 "
35 op. cit. *Tazewell Co.*-Pendleton
36 op. cit. *Records*-War Dept.
37 "
38 "
39 "
40 "
41 "
42 "
43 "
44 op. cit. *Records*-War Dept.
45 "
46 *History of Bland County(Va.)* by Bland County Centennial Commission
47 "
48 op. cit. *Records*-War Dept.
49 "
50 "
51 "
52 "

[53] op. cit. *Tazewell Co.*-Pendleton
[54] "
[55] op. cit. *Wythe Co.*-Boyd
[56] op. cit. *Records* War Dept.
[57] National Archives
[58] "
[59] op. cit. *Records*-War Dept.
[60] "
[61] op. cit. *War Never Ended*-Cruden
[62] *Pictorial History of the War for the Union* by Mrs. Ann Stephens
[63] *Jefferson Davis-Expresident of the Confederate States of America* by Wife Varina Howell Davis
[64] op. cit. *New River Settlements*-Johnson
[65] op. cit. *Davis*-Davis
[66] "
[67] "
[68] op. cit. *Records*-War Dept.
[69] *Smyth County History and Traditions* by Goodridge Wilson
[70] op. cit. *Tazewell Co.*-Leslie
[71] op. cit. *Records*-War Dept.
[72] *The Civil War and Reconstruction* by J.G. Randall and David Donald
[73] *History of Southwest Virginia-1746-1786-Washington County 1777-1870* by Lewis Preston Summers
[74] *Recollections of the War Between the States 1861-65* by James Orr
[75] *Generals in Blue* by Ezar J. Warner
[76] op. cit. *War Never Ended*-Cruden
[77] *Civil War Times Illustrated* "The Manners of a Prince" by M. Foster Farley

Chapter - 1864

[1] op. cit. *Recollections*-Orr
[2] op. cit. *New River Settlements*-Johnston
[3] op. cit. *Recollections*-Orr
[4] op. cit. *Washington Co.*-Summers
[5] "
[6] "
[7] op. cit. *Records*-War Dept.
[8] op. cit. *Confederacy*-Eaton
[9] op. cit. *Records*-War Dept.
[10] "
[11] "
[12] "
[13] "
[14] op. cit. *Tazewell Co.*-Pendleton
[15] op. cit. *Tazewell Co.*-Leslie
[16] op. cit. *Civil War*-Foote
[17] op. cit. *Records*-War Dept.
[18] "
[19] "
[20] *Civil War Times Illustrated* "The Battle of Cloyds Mountain" by Howard McMannus
[21] op. cit. "War"-Huddle
[22] op. cit. *Records*-War Dept.
[23] "
[24] op. cit. "Cloyds Mountain"-McMannus
[25] "
[26] "
[27] "
[28] "
[29] "
[30] "
[31] "
[32] op. cit. *Records*-War Dept.
[33] "
[34] op. cit. "Cloyds Mountain"-McMannus
[35] "
[36] op. cit. *Civil War*-Foote
[37] op. cit. "War"-Huddle
[38] "
[39] op. cit. *Civil War*-Foote
[40] *The Land that is Pulaski County* by Conway Howard Smith
[41] "
[42] "
[43] op. cit. *Records*-War Dept.
[44] "
[45] op. cit. *Civil War*-Foote
[46] *Presidential Anecdotes* by Paul Boller, Jr.
[47] op. cit. *Records*-War Dept.
[48] Joe Compton
[49] *Foot Prints* by Gary Walker
[50] *Morgan and His Raiders* by Cecil Fletcher Holland
[51] op. cit. *Records*-War Dept.
[52] op. cit. *Tazewell Co.*-Pendleton
[53] op. cit. *Records*-War Dept.
[54] op. cit. *Civil War*-Foote
[55] "
[56] "
[57] op. cit. *Records*-War Dept.
[58] op. cit. *Tazewell Co.*-Pendleton
[59] op. cit. *Morgan*-Holland
[60] "History of Crocketts Cove"
[61] op. cit. *Pictorial History*-Stephens
[62] op. cit. *Records* War Dept.
[63] "
[64] "
[65] "
[66] "
[67] "
[68] "
[69] op. cit. *Pulaski Co.*-Smith
[70] op. cit. *Boy's Recollection*-Robertson
[71] Wythe County Courthouse-records
[72] "
[73] newspaper clip, courtesy Dillon collection
[74] "
[75] "
[76] "
[77] *Generals in Gray* by Ezra J. Warner
[78] op. cit. Dillon Collection
[79] "
[80] "
[81] "
[82] *Civil War Times Illustrated* "Basil Duke Managing Man" by Lowell Harrison

83 op. cit. *Records*-War Dept.
84 "
85 "
86 "
87 Letter from Private J.M. Butts, courtesy of Huddle collection
88 *Civil War Times Illustrated* "Massacre at Saltville" by William C. Davis
89 "
90 op. cit. *Records*-War Dept.
91 op. cit. "Massacre"-Davis
92 op. cit. *Washington Co.*-Summers
93 op. cit. "Massacre"-Davis
94 "
95 op. cit. *Tazewell Co.*-Leslie
96 op. cit. *Records*-War Dept.
97 op. cit. "Massacre"-Davis
98 op. cit. Huddle collection
99 op. cit. "Massacre"-Davis
100 op. cit. *Saltville*-Kent
101 op. cit. "Massacre"-Davis
102 "
103 op. cit. Huddle collection
104 op. cit. *Washington Co.*-Summers
105 op. cit. "Massacre"-Davis
106 "
107 op. cit. *Saltville*-Kent
108 op. cit. Huddle collection
109 op. cit. *Washington Co.*-Summers
110 op. cit. "Massacre"-Davis
111 op. cit. *Records*-War Dept.
112 op. cit. "Massacre"-Davis
113 op. cit. Huddle Collection
114 op. cit. "Massacre"-Davis
115 "
116 "
117 op. cit. *Washington Co.*-Summers
118 op. cit. "Massacre"-Davis
119 "
120 *Smyth County Families and History* ed. by James Presgraves
121 op. cit. "Massacre"-Davis
122 "
123 op. cit. *Saltville*-Kent
124 "
125 "
126 op. cit. *Records*-War Dept.
127 "
128 "
129 op. cit. "Massacre"-Davis
130 "
131 op. cit. *Records*-War Dept.
132 "
133 op. cit. *Washington Co.*-Summers
134 op. cit. *Tazewell Co.*-Pendleton
135 op. cit. *Records*-War Dept.
136 op. cit. *Tazewell Co.*-Pendleton
137 "
138 op-cit. *Wythe Co.*-Boyd
139 op. cit. *Records*-War Dept.
140 "
141 The (Petersburg, Va.) Daily Register (newspaper) 3-22-64

142 op. cit. *Records*-War Dept.
143 op. cit. *Civil War*-Foote
144 op. cit. *War Never Ended*-Cruden
145 *The Confederate States of America 1861-65* by E. Merton Coulter
146 op. cit. *Records*-War Dept.
147 "
148 "
149 op. cit. *Records*-War Dept.
150 "
151 "
152 *Civil War Times Illustrated* "Good bye to the Single Musket" by Eugene Sloan
153 op. cit. *Records*-War Dept.
154 "
155 "
156 "
157 "
158 *The Raid* by Thomas R. Ramsey, Jr.
159 op. cit. *Records*-War Dept.
160 op. cit. *Raid*-Ramsey
161 "
162 op. cit. *Pictorial History*-Stephens
163 op. cit. *Raid*-Ramsey
164 op. cit. *Records*-War Dept.
165 op. cit. *Raid*-Ramsey
166 op. cit. *Records*-War Dept.
167 op. cit. *Pictorial History*-Stephens
168 op. cit. *Records*-War Dept.
169 op. cit. *Washington Co.*-Summers
170 "
171 "
172 op. cit. *raid*-Ramsey
173 "
174 op. cit. *Records*-War Dept.
175 op. cit. *Raid*-Ramsey
176 op. cit. *Smyth Co.*-Wilson
177 op. cit. *Records*-War Dept.
178 op. cit. *Pictorial History*-Stephens
179 op. cit. *Raid*-Ramsey
180 op. cit. *Records*-War Dept.
181 "
182 "
183 "
184 "
185 "
186 "
187 "
188 "
189 "
190 "
191 "
192 "
193 op. cit. Huddle collection
194 op. cit. *Records*-War Dept.
195 op. cit. *Raid*-Ramsey
196 *Southwest Virginia Enterprise* "Destruction of the Lead Mines of Wythe County, Va." by John M. Johnson
197 "
198 op. cit. *Symth Co.*-Wilson
199 "

[200] *Civil War Times Illustrated* "The Northern Spencer Goes South" by Wayne Austerman
[201] op. cit. "Spencer"-Austerman
[202] op. cit. *Raid*-Ramsey
[203] op. cit. *Records*-War Dept.
[204]   "
[205] op. cit. "Duke"-Harrison
[206]   "
[207] op. cit. *Records*-War Dept.
[208] op. cit. "Duke"-Harrison
[209] op. cit. *Smyth Co.*-Wilson
[210] op. cit. *Records*-War Dept.
[211] op. cit. *Pictorial History*-Stephens
[212] op. cit. *Records*-War Dept.
[213] op. cit. *Smyth Co.*-Wilson
[214]   "
[215]   "
[216] op. cit. *Records*-War Dept.
[217]   "
[218] op. cit. Huddle collection
[219] op. cit. *Raid*-Ramsey
[220] op. cit. Huddle collection
[221] op. cit. *Records*-War Dept.
[222] op. cit. *Raid*-Ramsey
[223] op. cit. *Records*-War Dept.
[224]   "
[225]   "
[226]   "
[227]   "
[228] op. cit. *Records*-War Dept.

Chapter - 1865

[1] op. cit. *Washington Co.*-Summers
[2] op. cit. *Russell Co.*-Barrett
[3] op. cit. *Washington Co.*-Summers
[4] op. cit. *New River Settlements*-Johnston
[5] op. cit. *War Never Ended*-Cruden
[6] op. cit. "Duke"-Harrison
[7] op. cit. *Smyth Co.*-Wilson
[8]   "
[9] op. cit. *Records*-War Dept.
[10]   "
[11]   "
[12] op. cit. *Wythe Co.*-Boyd
[13] op. cit. *Records*-War Dept.
[14]   "
[15] op. cit. "Duke"-Harrison
[16]   "
[17]   "

Chapter - POST LOG

[1] op. cit. *Wythe Co.*-Boyd
[2] op. cit. *Morgan*-Holland

Other sources not directly quoted include: "Vital Roles Played by Southwest Virginia Women of the Confederacy" by Lucile M. Kincer; *Wythe Chapters* by James S. Presgrave; *Early Settlers of Lee County Va.* by Anne Laminghan; *Double Destiny* (History of Bristol Va.-Tenn.) by Robert S. Loving; *Hardesty's Historial and Geographical Encyclopeatic* by R.A. Brock; *Southwest Virginia Enterprise* "Centennial Edition"; Records from Tazewell County Courthouse; *Battles and Leaders of the Civil War* ed. by Robert Dykstra; *The Blue and the Graved*, by Henry Steele Commander *The Civil War Dictionary* by Mark Mayo Boatner III; *A Guide to Virginia Military Organization 1861-65* by Lee A. Wallace, Jr.; "Economic and Social Aspects of Negro Slavery in Wythe County, Va. 1790-1861" by Carl Wilson Musser; *History of the War for the Union* by F.A. Duyckinck; *The American Civil War* by John Formby; *Increase in Excellence* (History of Emory and Henry College) by George Stevenson; *Camp Chase Gazette* "Shanks Mare" by Isaac Brewer; *The Photographic History of the Civil War* group contributors; *The Photographic History of the Union and Confederate Cavalry in the Civil War 1861-65* ed. Theo. F. Rodenbough; *The American Heritage Picture History of the Civil War* editor-in-chief Richard M. Ketchum; *The American Heritage Century Collection of Civil War Art* Ed. Stephen W. Sears; *They Who Fought Here* - Text by Bell Irvin Wiley-Illustrated by Hirst D. Hollen; article by Thomas May on Montgomery White Sulphur Springs Hospital; "Points For The Right to Secede" by William M. Brooks

Index

About The Author

Gary Chitwood Walker was born on May 24, 1946 in Wytheville, which is located in Southwest Virginia. He is the sixth and last child of Carl and Mary Walker.

Gary attended Spiller Elementary School and graduated from George Wythe High School at Wytheville in 1964.

In the fall of '64, Gary entered the Wytheville branch of Virginia Polytechnic Institute. In 1968 he graduated on the main campus at Blacksburg with a B.S. in Business Administration. He had almost enough hours in history and political science to minor. His education can be seen when he deals with subjects from a political, economic, as well as a historical point of view.

Shortly after graduation Gary married his long time sweetheart, Sue Adams. She originates from Max Meadows, a town also located in Southwest Virginia. Together they have two fine sons, Christopher Ewell, and Kevin Forrest.

After graduation Gary continued his education studying, among other things, creative writing and photography.

Gary got his "feet wet" with his first book, *Walker, Ben to Carl,* a history of the Walker family. It was while working on his second book, *Footprints,* a history of the Adams family, that Gary saw the need to write a history of the War Between the States in Southwest Virginia. One of the characters in the book was involved in a battle. Gary was shocked to discover there was nothing reliable in print on that battle and many others in the area. At that point in the seventies he began researching the subject.

In 1981 Gary accepted employment that necessitated relocating his family from Roanoke to Wytheville. While in Wytheville tragedy struck the family. During this period Gary spent every possible hour researching and writing to help endure during this time of crisis.

Spurred by crisis and the burning desire for truth, Gary wrote the first history of the Civil War in Southwest Virginia. He used over 100 sources as he tried to re-create the vain struggle to create a new independent nation. To better understand the era and its events, Gary walked the river valleys, woods, and mountains, where the armies marched and fought.

For 120 years the vital role Southwest Virginia played in the war from its beginning to its bitter end, has been overlooked by national commentators. The major reason the nationally known authors have overlooked the area is because they had no source to pull from. Now one more candle has been lit which will provide a more accurate, more complete picture of America's most glorious, most devastating war.